MW00576645

LA CALLE

LA CALLE

Spatial Conflicts and Urban Renewal in a Southwest City

LYDIA R. OTERO

The University of Arizona Press   Tucson

The University of Arizona Press
© 2010 The Arizona Board of Regents
All rights reserved

www.uapress.arizona.edu

Library of Congress Cataloging-in-Publication Data

Otero, Lydia R.
  La calle : spatial conflicts and urban renewal in a southwest
city / Lydia R. Otero.
     p. cm.
  Includes bibliographical references and index.
  ISBN 978-0-8165-2888-2 (hard cover : alk. paper)
  1. Urban renewal—Arizona—Tucson. 2. City planning—
Arizona—Tucson. 3. Mexican Americans—Arizona—Tucson—
History. 4. Tucson (Ariz.)—Social conditions. I. Title.
  HT177.T77O84 2010
  307.3'41609791776—dc22
                                            2010021414

Publication of this book is made possible in part by a grant from
the Provost's Author Support Fund of the University of Arizona.

15   14   13   12   11   10   6   5   4   3   2   1

To the descendants of Rita Corrales and José Luis Robles

Contents

Illustrations

Preface

Both my parents were born in Tucson, Arizona, one of the oldest Mexican American settlements in the United States, in *la calle*, the area near downtown that is the focus of this book. My father's family can trace its roots in what is now Southern Arizona as far back as 1769. The Oteros dispersed throughout the Southwest, and a few, like Sabino Otero, later became influential business and civic leaders in Arizona.

My mother's family also has deep roots in Southern Arizona. During the late nineteenth century, my maternal grandmother and grandfather transcended Seri and Apache tribal animosities to produce thirteen children. Thus, like many Southern Arizonans, I represent the convergence of various ethnic ancestries. The schools I attended in the 1960s and 1970s never taught me about the contributions of families like my own who had for generations lived in Southern Arizona. Fortunately, I grew up surrounded by resourceful individuals who inspired my interest in history. My grandmother Rita Corrales, who lived to be ninety-two, told me about her many relatives in stories that required all my attention to follow. The women of my mother's family often reminisced while playing cards, at birthday parties (which seemed to take place almost weekly), after funerals, and while visiting each other's homes. On our way to family outings, I remember peering out the car window as my mother, uncles, aunts, and other family members pointed at buildings and commented on those who lived there, or used to live there. Even when my grandmother got older and outings of any kind became taxing for her, she still managed to climb into a car whenever she was offered the chance of an excursion to her old neighborhood.

Like many in Tucson, my family still remembers the area close to downtown that urban renewal destroyed in the late 1960s. I, too, remember going to la calle with my parents to buy our groceries and clothing. I remember entering the Del Monte Market, owned by Henry Gee, and immediately being greeted by either Henry, a member of his family, or Estella, an older Mexican American woman who worked in checkout.

I remember waiting impatiently for my parents, who always stopped to chat at length with old friends in la calle's stores and on its crowded sidewalks. Since I was so young and it was so long ago, however, these memories often seem unreal to me.

Since my first graduate colloquium in 1998, I have been helped by many generous mentors and friends. I will always be thankful to Karen Anderson for her steadfast support during the rough times in graduate school and for her guidance in my present scholarship, and to Sarah (Sally) Deutsch for continuing to feed my intellectual development from afar. I am privileged to have Raquel Rubio-Goldsmith as both a mentor and a colleague. Our conversations have helped clarify my thinking and have served to constantly reenergize my passion for history and the Chicana/o experience. I am grateful to Carole Srole and Francisco Balderrama, who first encouraged me to pursue graduate studies; to Vicki Ruiz, who has in so many ways helped advance my academic career; and to W. Fitzhugh Brundage, Antonia Castañeda, María Montoya, and Yolanda Chávez Leyva, who read earlier versions of my manuscript and offered invaluable suggestions. My thanks also to John R. Chávez, Gabriela F. Arredondo, María Teresa Vélez, Reeve Huston, Lorena Oropeza, Josie Méndez-Negrete, Juan R. Garía, Katherine G. Morrissey, Emma M. Pérez, and Deena Gonzales for their encouragement and support through the years.

Chair Antonio Estrada of the University of Arizona's Mexican American and Raza Studies Department has enthusiastically supported my scholarship, and colleagues Yolanda Broyles-González and Julio Cammarota read portions of the manuscript and suggested many worthwhile improvements. Their support has proved invaluable. I also need to thank valued staff members Tom Gelsinon, Veronica Peralta, Kimberly Young, Julieta Gonzales, and Adela Sanders, all of whom made my life easier and provided timely assistance during various deadline crises.

I am grateful to the undergraduate and graduate students who helped me complete this book, in particular Yvonne Montoya, Onofre Escobar, Monique Becerril, Wendy Vogt, Bryan Turo, Julia Cowen, Fawn-Amber Montoya, Annamarie Schaecher, Shiras Mannings, Grace Gámez, Kristen Valencia, and Fernando Chávez. Kim Frontz, Jill McCleary, and Kate Reeve at the Arizona Historical Society in Tucson provided invaluable assistance in locating photographs and research materials. Chrystal Carpenter, Elizabeth Perumala, and Scott Cossel in the University of

Arizona Special Collections also deserve mention for their help in completing this book project. I also wish to recognize Adam Schwartz, Sean Arce, and Jim Turner for engaging in probing and prolonged discussions with me as this manuscript progressed.

I thank Kristen Buckles and Patti Hartmann of the University of Arizona Press for approaching my book with enthusiasm, and the anonymous readers for their valuable comments and suggestions. I consider myself fortunate to have worked with freelance editor Jeffrey Lockridge, whose meticulous attention to detail and energetic support for the project made the editing process a rewarding experience.

I am especially beholden to all those who agreed to sit with me and share their lifetimes of experience and their perspectives on Tucson's history and its people. My conversations with Alva B. Torres and Guadalupe Castillo have caused me to think differently about geography and about who "makes" history. Henry "Hank" Oyama and Adalberto Guerrero have become my friends, and their recollections are historical gems that I hope one day will grace the pages of another book.

I am indebted to my sisters Rita O. Acevedo and Anita A. Grantland for patiently answering my unrelenting questions about the past. I also wish to extend my appreciation to my family of friends in California for their decades of support. Veronica M. Flores, Shirl D. Buss, Irene Martinez, and Laura Duran have kept me connected to a life that I once had that was far from Arizona and academia but one that I consider equally important. Last but far from least, I thank Maureen Campesino for her tireless patience and grounding energy.

LA CALLE

Introduction

In April 1967, Alva Torres unexpectedly became a historic preservationist in her hometown of Tucson. In the course of her daily rounds with her three children, which often took them downtown, Torres ran into the elderly Rodolfo Soto. Related by marriage, their families had known each other for generations. Soto, from one of the city's founding families who had lived in the Spanish presidio in the late eighteenth century, had a keen sense of history. Both Torres and Soto called themselves *tucsonenses*—a self-identifier dating back to the nineteenth century that expresses a distinct cultural and historical connection to the city and the region around it.[1] Noticing his distress, Torres approached Soto with concern. "Ay, Alvita," he lamented, "como estoy triste de lo que estan haciendo aquí" (Ah, Alvita, I am saddened by what is taking place here). "¿Por qué, señor?" (Why, Mr. Soto?), Torres asked. "Porque se les va a olvidar donde empezó el pueblo. Están tumbando todo y no se van a acordar de nosotros, y a nadie le va importar y no se van a acordar de nosotros y a nadie le va importar" (Because they are going to forget the people [who built the city]. They are tearing down everything, and nobody's going to remember us, and nobody's going to care).[2] Caught off-guard but feeling compassion for her lifelong friend, Torres comforted Soto as best she could. This chance encounter at the start of urban renewal would inspire Alva Torres to challenge the cultural elitism and politics that drove the destruction of downtown. She would mobilize resistance to the ongoing urban renewal and to future redevelopment projects that threatened to destroy historical structures vital to tucsonenses' sense of history and collective memory.[3]

Rodolfo Soto had made explicit the connection between the destruction of place and history. If older structures connected with the city's origins were torn down, who would remember that his people had built Tucson? Soto's impassioned lament serves to highlight two themes central to this book: (1) the importance of individual and collective memory and of recovering voices from the margins, for themselves and for the historical record; and (2) the power of historical narratives to ensure—or resist—social, cultural, and economic dominance.

On March 1, 1966, the voters of Tucson approved the Pueblo Center Redevelopment Project, which targeted the most densely populated 80 acres in Arizona. Although Mexican Americans dominated the renewal area demographically, most of the city's Asian and African Americans also lived there. The state's first major urban renewal project included plans to build several government buildings, a modern retail complex, and as its showpiece, a new performance arena and community-conference facility, the Tucson Community Center (TCC).[4] To make way for the new structures, city officials proceeded to remove all the people who lived in the area and to demolish their neighborhoods.[5]

The 1971 opening of the TCC symbolized progress for many throughout the city. For many others, however, it symbolized loss, representing the destruction of entire blocks of attached adobe Sonoran-style row houses, many dating back to the nineteenth century, and of sites where tucsonenses gathered to celebrate their culture.[6] Indeed, the urban renewal project that gave rise to the TCC profoundly changed not only the physical but also the social, economic, and cultural character of Tucson's downtown.

Clay potsherds found at the base of the city's most visible mountain, Sentinel Peak ("A" Mountain), close to the current downtown area, date Tucson's initial settlement to more than 4,000 years ago, adding credence to claims that the city may be the "oldest continuously inhabited place in the United States."[7] By the time the Spanish arrived in the late seventeenth century, the Tohono O'odham had already set up permanent villages, complete with irrigation systems that made possible a flourishing life for some two thousand farmers.[8]

In 1848, under the Treaty of Guadalupe Hidalgo, the United States acquired most of Arizona but not the southern and most densely populated quarter, which remained part of Mexico's northern state of Sonora. Five years later, the United States annexed this area, inhabited by Indians and tucsonenses, under the terms of the Gadsden Purchase, or Tratado de la Mesilla as it was known in Mexico. Although December 30, 1853, marked the official transfer of national sovereignty, Mexican troops remained in Tucson until 1856.[9] No other U.S. city remained under Mexican control longer than Tucson, where Anglo Americans represented only a small minority of settlers.[10] In fact, Mexican people outnumbered Anglos

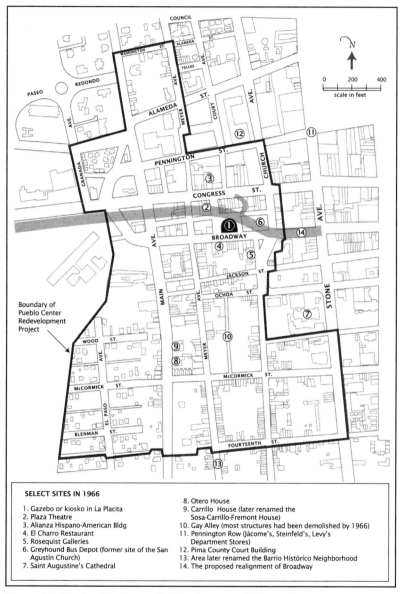

Figure I.1. The Pueblo Center Redevelopment Project, circa 1965.
(Map by Paul Mirocha)

SELECT SITES IN 1966

1. Gazebo or kiosko in La Placita
2. Plaza Theatre
3. Alianza Hispano-American Bldg
4. El Charro Restaurant
5. Rosequist Galleries
6. Greyhound Bus Depot (former site of the San Agustín Church)
7. Saint Augustine's Cathedral

8. Otero House
9. Carrillo House (later renamed the Sosa-Carrillo-Fremont House)
10. Gay Alley (most structures had been demolished by 1966)
11. Pennington Row (Jácome's, Steinfeld's, Levy's Department Stores)
12. Pima County Court Building
13. Area later renamed the Barrio Histórico Neighborhood
14. The proposed realignment of Broadway

Figure I.2. The outline of the Pueblo Center Redevelopment Project on the city's landscape, circa 1965. (Image by Paul Mirocha)

throughout the nineteenth century and up to 1920, when Anglos became the majority.[11]

Despite their minority status, the Anglo American settlers immediately asserted their dominance in Tucson, as in other regions throughout the West, spearheaded by merchants who arrived in the nineteenth century with wagonloads of new merchandise and new ways of doing business.[12] The shift in power became evident in all political and economic transactions and on the physical landscape as Anglo Americans took possession of the areas they found most desirable and most economically advantageous. In response, tucsonenses moved and carved out their own spaces in neighborhoods to the south, away from the new arrivals, creating their own "spatial reality" in and around the city's main public square in an area that most called "la calle" or the "tucsonense downtown."[13] Here, openly living and celebrating their Mexican American culture, they patronized small retail and service shops, restaurants, and entertainment venues, which they had established to serve their particular needs.

Figure I.3. A closer view of the area south of downtown, circa 1945. (Arizona Historical Society, Tucson, MS 1079, f. 1965 [C])

Starting with Albert Camarillo's classic, *Chicanos in a Changing Society: From Mexican Pueblos to American Barrios in Santa Barbara and Southern California, 1848–1930*, most Mexican American histories have concentrated on the emergence of barrios in the United States.[14] In sharp contrast, this book chronicles a period of shifting urban idealizations in the twentieth century that resulted in the destruction of a large Mexican American community in downtown Tucson. It recognizes 1938 as the landmark year when civic leaders formally adopted a planning and zoning agenda to remedy what they perceived as a decline in Tucson's urban core, which housed a large ethnic, predominantly Mexican American population.[15]

This book employs space as an analytical tool to explore the conflicts over a downtown landscape as these expressed themselves in boundaries, whether those of Mexican American space within a larger, predominantly Anglo American city, of a central business district, or of imagined landscapes. Thus, driven by an unrelenting desire for order,[16] Tucson's civic leaders wielded their power to delineate boundaries—to assign and (re)locate people to specific places—not to serve an inclusive vision of their city as a whole but to maintain and strengthen the dominant culture. "Places are made through power relations which construct the rules that define boundaries," argues feminist geographer Linda McDowell. "These boundaries [in turn] define who belongs to a place and who may be excluded, as well as the location or site of the experience."[17]

The conflicts that led to the destruction of a large Mexican American community through urban renewal in the late 1960s were fueled by the idealization of modernity, a local economy increasingly dependent on tourism, and the evolution of federal housing policies. To understand how they resulted in the spatial reconfiguration of downtown, I have drawn on scholarship from a wide range of disciplines: Chicana/o, ethnic, and cultural studies; urban history, sociology, anthropology, and planning; and cultural and feminist geography.[18]

Most scholarly studies of urban renewal in the United States in the decades after World War II assume that its displacement of large numbers of people occurred almost entirely in the Northeast. Most also surmise, with political scientist John H. Mollenkopf, that "because development took place on a clean slate [in Southwest cities], the massive clearance and redistribution of the central-city land did not need to take place."[19] Tucson's urban renewal stands as a clear exception to this line of thinking.[20] While touching on the events that made the Pueblo Center Redevelopment Project a reality, I focus on the underlying cultural values, politics, and social relations that drove the displacement of a large Mexican American community from Tucson's urban core and redrew the boundaries of that core.

To understand the city, and la calle in particular, as a "site of everyday practices,"[21] I have integrated a variety of voices, from the marginalized to the powerful. I have paid greatest attention to the conflicts over urban space and to the meanings assigned to the buildings, places, and people of la calle and its surrounding barrios. I have examined, from the perspective of those who lived in, experienced, or remembered this contested area, how la calle's Mexican Americans created, organized, and named their spaces, and how they celebrated and maintained their culture.[22] Although those displaced by urban renewal did not come together in large numbers to protest, many opposed their removal in ways that remain undocumented. They are therefore absent from the archives, which have, historian Michel-Rolph Trouillot tells us, "the power to define what is and what is not a serious object of research and therefore mention." Their absence represents the first step in creating what Trouillot calls the "silences" of history.[23] In this book, I describe how the urban renewal agenda sought to silence a people and culture, how individual and collective memory resisted that silencing, and how they do so to this day.[24]

The downtown area, and la calle in particular, meant different things to different groups of people. Early planning documents indicate civic leaders' awareness of the central business district's importance in furthering representations of Tucson's "character" and "the general well-being of the community."[25] Thus the Pueblo Center Redevelopment Project promised far more than the physical rejuvenation of Tucson's urban landscape. It promised to replace "old" residents and spaces with "new" ones. A prominent urban renewal advocate enticed supporters by reminding them of the demographic and cultural benefits the changes would bestow upon the area. Where Mexican people and culture once dominated, he promised a place "where singers, athletes, Boy Scouts, square dance people and others can come."[26] The racialized nature of the Pueblo Redevelopment Center Project, which targeted the most densely populated nonwhite area in the city, is unmistakable. This book demonstrates the inextricable linkages among race, class, and politics that allowed urban renewal proponents and planners to pursue their racialized development agendas without having to use racist language.

The development lobby was composed of the local elite, who controlled the economy and who were also the strongest planning and zoning advocates. Powerful retailers, realtors, architects, newspaper editors, bankers, and utility company executives sat on the city's most influential citizens' committees. Foremost among these, the Committee on Municipal Blight (COMB), spearheaded urban renewal.[27] The civic leaders who promoted planning and tourism continually claimed that they were acting in the city's best interests, even as they single-mindedly advanced their own and a political agenda that allowed them to delineate and control space. "Whites embraced the market imperative defense for exclusion because it was built into the materials"—real estate manuals, economics textbooks, federal guidelines, enabling acts, and court rulings—"that they used, every day, to exclude," historian David M. P. Freund explains. "Paradoxically, this sanitized narrative simultaneously encouraged whites to ignore the fact that they benefited from racist institutions and lived in race culture."[28]

City leaders and promoters thus promised that urban renewal would mean "a shot in the arm" for the downtown area without disclosing that they were also seeking to keep the area free from "undesirables."[29] As Freund points out, by the 1950s they did not need to use discriminatory language to enforce racial disparities; these had become institutionalized: "Zoning law and zoning science provided a useful language with which a mobile, increasingly affluent, and fast-growing white middle class could explain its desires for certain kinds of exclusion without invoking the ideologically loaded language of race."[30] In Tucson, as in most cities throughout the United States, a variety of zoning and other municipal ordinances had empowered city officials to treat different groups and classes of people differently and yet claim that they had not discriminated.

Those in the forefront for more restrictive zoning ordinances had targeted la calle since the late 1930s. In 1938, interested "in seeing that Tucson not only became a *larger* city, but a *better* city," a group of influential developers and tourism promoters formed the Tucson Regional Plan (TRP).[31] Passage and enforcement of the new zoning ordinances, thanks in no small part to lobbying by the TRP, gave city officials the power to designate certain nonwhite areas as "slums" and to characterize the people who lived in them as obstacles to progress.

La calle's adobe structures and its ethnically diverse residents openly challenged the spatial and cultural assumptions of postwar modernity and suburbia. According to historian Lizabeth Cohen, although fewer than one of every five Americans lived in suburbia in 1953, as the nation's principal consumers, suburbanites exercised an influence as immense as their purchasing power.[32] To attract those who no longer made the downtown their major shopping destination, Tucson's city planners set about modernizing the urban core in the image of the emerging suburban ideal.[33] Unlike most tucsonenses, who walked to la calle when they wanted to shop, run errands, or go to a show, suburbanites would have to drive downtown. The renewal planners therefore made automobile access to the downtown area and to ample parking near its new retail and entertainment sites a top priority, often at the expense of older sites that held tremendous cultural and historical value for tucsonenses. City officials also ignored the economic significance of la calle's smaller retailers and saw no future in maintaining established shopping patterns there even though tucsonenses' patronage greatly contributed to the downtown economy.

In this Southwestern city urban renewal represented the convergence of a variety of interests that have not been linked in previous urban studies. Increasingly after World War II, driven by the desire to lure tourists from across the nation, Tucson's image makers organized cultural events and carefully crafted a local history that accentuated the city's Anglo and western past. The tourist materials produced and distributed by the Chamber of Commerce and the Sunshine Club, an organization exclusively devoted to promoting tourism, shed considerable light on Tucson's local imaginings. Most of these revolved around Anglo cowboys and the Indians they were said to have subdued, and on civic boosters' efforts to generate and sustain a civic identity grounded in what I call the "Anglo fantasy heritage."[34] At the core of this and other such myths throughout the West, historian Richard White has found the desire to bring order out of chaos and the notion that the United States has a distinct and special destiny different from and superior to that of other nations. The power of these myths lies in their weaving together "national imaginings" and "local imaginings."[35] As geographer David Lowenthal reminds us:

> The past is always altered for motivations that reflect our present needs. We shape our heritage to make it attractive in modern terms; we seek to make it part of ourselves, and ourselves part of it; we conform it to our self-images and aspirations. Rendered grand or homely, magnified or tarnished, history is continually altered in our private interest or on behalf of our community or country.[36]

On the one hand, the boosters' version of the city's history imposed distinct disconnections between the Mexican people who first settled and had lived in Tucson for generations and their actual heritage. On the other, to promote their vision of a modern Anglo American future for Tucson, the boosters' tourist materials played on deeply ingrained national and regional stereotypes that associated Mexico and Mexican people with a bygone era.[37] This book argues that the city's promotion of tourism and its urban renewal agenda, though distinct undertakings, reinforced each other and shows how both reflected a persistent campaign to whiten by removing Mexican American residents, history, and architecture from the coveted downtown landscape.

In Tucson, those who had the power to dictate space and the future took the opportunity to reinterpret the past and institutionalize specific historical memories. As bulldozers leveled sections of downtown, some took this as an opportunity to construct new historical narratives to reinforce claims of Anglo dominance and exceptionalism. Mexican Americans, who never relinquished their connections to place, also organized to preserve their past and resist their historical erasure. Resisting displacement through a variety of means, including collective memory, adds another dimension to what Raúl Homero Villa describes as "the experience of being displaced in multiple ways from a perceived homeland . . . an essential element of Chicanos' social identity in their country."[38] The historic preservation efforts highlighted here also expand the historical literature by documenting a period when Mexican Americans mobilized around, not pursuing labor or immigration issues, but preserving place as a process of cultural affirmation. Under the leadership of Alva Torres, tucsonenses rallied to defend and preserve La Placita, a site with a long history and to which they had a strong attachment. In doing so, they publicly articulated their claims to history and place.

Even before the La Placita Committee held its first meeting, another preservationist group, the Tucson Heritage Foundation, had already organized to ensure the commemoration of an Anglo American hero John C. Frémont in the Pueblo Center Redevelopment Project area. In examining these competing historic preservation efforts, this book explores the role of power and voice in Tucsonans' conflicts over place and history to establish that the past, present, and future all occupied the same terrain.

Women led both efforts, which reflected emergent ideologies in larger national movements.[39] The La Placita Committee acted as an unrecognized component of the unfolding Chicana/o movement, which insisted on self-determination for Mexican Americans and affirmed their cultural identity.[40] The Tucson Heritage Foundation, for its part, represented a local version of larger impulses that historian Lisa McGirr describes as converging to promote a conservative Anglo version of the American heritage.[41] As bulldozers destroyed the downtown area, it became a battlefield for those striving to institutionalize historical narratives that would determine how future generations remembered their city's history.

A Chapter Summary

Chapter 1 touches on Tucson's Mexican American history, settlement patterns, and the character of tucsonense community life, focusing on la calle, which, until the late 1960s, had been interwoven into the central business district and the local government headquarters, as well providing a home for people from a range of nonwhite ethnicities. Chapter 2 discusses the dramatic shifts in power and population initiated by the arrival of the railroad in the nineteenth century and reflected in the growing spatial separation of Anglo and Mexican American residents after World War II. Chapter 3 analyzes how city boosters worked to refine and project images associated with the Anglo fantasy heritage to attract tourists and investors—and to keep tucsonenses out of their sight. Chapter 4 establishes the linkages between tourism and power and confirms that tourist dollars served to reinforce the economic and political dominance of local retailers. It shows how these retailers formed a crucial part of the booster coalition that aggressively campaigned to maintain the social, political, and economic status quo while "improving" the city's physical landscape; it uncovers statutes, ordinances, and covenants that enforced ethnic and class differences by, for example, permitting only owners of real property to vote in bond elections. Chapter 5 traces the collaborative efforts of city officials and growth machine leaders to remake downtown Tucson by enacting various urban renewal renditions and by officially labeling la calle a slum in the 1960s. Chapter 6 chronicles the emergence and evolution of the La Placita Committee members who championed formal and institutional recognition of their Mexican American history and who, as the voice of tucsonenses, both articulated and fostered a historical consciousness that eventually found expression in local ordinances designed to preserve noteworthy historic structures. Finally, chapter 7 examines the cultural and political forces that framed the conflicts over historic preservation and representation, in particular, over the history and naming of what would eventually be called the Sosa-Carrillo-Frémont House.

La Calle, the Tucsonense Downtown

> You talk to people from the South Side, to a señora or señor in
> their sixties or seventies and they'll say, "Oh, yeah, I used to live
> over there. I lived right there on McCormick or on Ochoa." Or,
> "Oh, yeah, I lived on Meyer or I lived on Convent." At one time
> everybody lived in this area.
>
> —Pedro Gonzales, November 2007[1]

In 1856, when Mexican troops finally withdrew from Tucson, most of
its people lived in Court Plaza, the area delineated by the original presidio, built in the late eighteenth century. Early maps indicate that spatial
and social apartness occurred almost immediately after Tucson became
incorporated into the United States. As Anglos arrived, they appropriated the most commercially desirable, developed, and established sections that had evolved during the Spanish and Mexican periods. By 1862,
"Anglos owned twenty-one (64 percent) of the thirty-three residences
within the crumbling walls of the presidio."[2]

In this dynamic of displacement, tucsonenses moved south from the
presidio to create new spaces, establishing their own public square, religious institutions, mutual aid societies, newspapers, and service and
retail businesses. Described by city planners as "marginal," these spaces,
where tucsonenses' daily social and commercial exchanges took place,
formed collective sites of cultural resistance, or "thirdspace," described
by Edward W. Soja as holding the potential for "new spaces of opportunity and action."[3] Anglo Americans had the power to assign spaces, but
tucsonenses infused the spaces with their own collective cultural meanings. Here they not only practiced and celebrated their Mexican culture,
they also ensured its survival in a time of rapid social and economic
transformation.

One chapter cannot come close to relating the history of the Mexican
Americans who carved out their own spaces in Tucson.[4] A brief look at

early settlement patterns is necessary, however, to understand the community that would be targeted and destroyed a hundred years after its creation. Although urban renewal documents often refer to this area as a single barrio, namely Barrio Libre, the eighty acres that were bulldozed encompassed a complicated geographical amalgam of several barrios and la calle, which tucsonenses claimed as their downtown.

Understanding the area destroyed by urban renewal is central to understanding Tucson's character and the web of its interconnected social networks. Many civic leaders failed to appreciate what la calle and its nearby barrios meant to tucsonenses. As a prominent urban renewal advocate once stated off the record, "If you lived in a barrio, you wouldn't try to save it." Tucsonenses' shared connection to place and history fueled the historic preservation efforts of the La Placita Committee (covered in greater detail in chapter 6). The committee called for preserving the city's Plaza de la Mesilla and the buildings that surrounded it, some of which dated back more than a century, as a tangible reminder of the key role Mexican Americans had played in building the city. To the members of the La Placita Committee, and to many other tucsonenses, the places their ancestors had created through their labor and patronage mattered. History mattered.

The Move South

After the United States acquired the territory that would become Southern Arizona through the Gadsden Purchase of 1853, Anglo Americans imposed new social hierarchies and new economic and political structures on Tucson. Anglo newcomers had access to national networks that allowed them both to create and to manipulate a new local regime, which the larger U.S. legal system legitimized and supported.[5] In 1860, Anglos constituted less than 20 percent of Tucson's population but controlled 87 percent of the wealth. As Thomas Sheridan observes, "Less than a decade after the Gadsden Purchase, Anglo capital had firmly entrenched itself in Tucson. Once in control, it never let go."[6] Despite their demographic domination throughout the nineteenth century, tucsonenses' collective civic, economic, and social stature declined in the new Anglo American system.

Increasingly, and as early as 1862, tucsonenses started to spread to outlying areas, breaching the spatial barrier that the presidio walls had

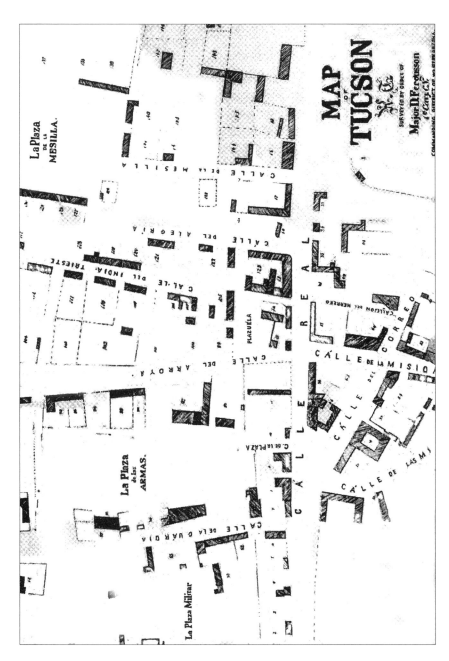

Figure 1.1. The 1862 map of Tucson by David Fergusson. (Courtesy Arizona Historical Society, Tucson)

provided. The David Fergusson map, produced that year, confirms an early southward settlement pattern (see fig. 1.1). Two main thoroughfares had evolved: Main Street, Tucson's El Camino Real, or "Royal Road," which led south to Mexico along the Santa Cruz River; and Mission Street, which led residents west to the fields, Sentinel Peak, and El Convento, a Catholic outpost established on the riverbank. The significance of Main Street's orientation indicates the importance of this route as a connector to the rest of Southern Arizona, as well as Sonora and Mexico as a whole. At this time, as indicated on the Fergusson map, Tucson's streets still had Spanish-language names. Calle de la India Triste (Street of the Sad Indian Woman) branched off Congress Street and Stone Avenue and the area eventually became known as "the wedge."[7] Calle de la Alegría (Happiness Street) became Congress Street. The Fergusson map also indicates the location of La Plaza de las Armas, the site of the original presidio. In 1862 the irregular lots and streets were far from geometrically aligned. Geographers studying this period have concluded: "There is little evidence in the street pattern to suggest that Tucson was anything but a rural Mexican village in spite of the early influx of Anglos."[8]

This generally southward movement reflected a displacement dynamic wherein recent Anglo arrivals displaced tucsonenses from the presidio area. Those from the lower classes were the first to relocate. Geographer Jonathan Harris confirms this dynamic: "Pushed out of the old core area were the poorer residents of the community. The map of occupations shows that most were farmers or laborers, a few aged and widowed. . . . The majority of Mexicans moved south and resettled around the Plaza de la Mesilla."[9] The plaza area, which tucsonenses began to refer to simply as La Placita, thus became the focal point of the displaced Mexican American community.

As "Tucson's new grid, based on the American traditions of William Penn," became more evident,[10] the shift in economic power became imprinted on the landscape, all the more so when Tucson was formally incorporated as a federal survey township in 1871. Creating a township called for reordering the infrastructure to reflect reorganized land-use patterns and served to expedite the processes of speculation and expansion.[11] Anglo Americans cast aside older Spanish and Mexican models, which organized streets around a plaza.[12] The Anglo American imprint became evident in the rigid 90° angles and straight lines that formed the definitive "orthogonal grid of north-south avenues and east-west streets."[13] Before urban renewal, a glance at a map would reveal the differences in the street patterns that evolved as Mexican Americans moved south and Anglo Americans moved north and east (see fig. 1.2).

Tucson's incorporation strengthened the Anglos' grip on the economic life of the city. Architect Abigail A. Van Slyck outlines the dramatic changes that took place in landownership:

> Since little of the land outside the presidio walls had been covered by Spanish or Mexican land grants, few [tucsonenses] were able to establish the continuous chain of title required to acquire property under the terms of the Gadsden Purchase. Once the town was incorporated, the federal government would donate the ungranted lands to municipal officials, who in turn could grant individuals a mortgageable interest in land that they had taken up and improved. That Tucsonans were aware of the potential economic impact of incorporation is evident from the makeup of the men who petitioned for the change—P. R. Tully, Estevan Ochoa, S. R. Delong, Samuel Hughes, Solomon Warner, W. L. Zeckendorf, Isaac Goldberg, and others . . . merchants who shared an interest in promoting Tucson's commercial base.[14]

Although still the overwhelming majority demographically, less than a handful of tucsonenses joined the movement to incorporate, a movement dominated by Anglos and "relative newcomers."[15]

By 1880 settlement patterns of ethnic separation had become more pronounced as "Anglos were firmly in control of the central business district."[16] Most of the businesses in the district were located between the old presidio and the Plaza de la Mesilla. South Meyer Avenue could boast of having the greatest number of commercial establishments, followed by Congress and Main streets, Calle de la Mesilla, and Pennington Street. As tucsonenses moved south and later west, Anglos moved north and east, drawn to the commercial enterprises, restaurants, and lodging houses linked to the new railroad development and the University of Arizona, established in 1885, northeast of downtown.[17] Sheridan observed that, by the turn of the century, the same "patterns which began in the 1850's—geographic segregation, political and economic subordination—shaped and limited the lives of most Mexicans in Tucson."[18]

This southward settlement pattern reflects the complicated ethnic, social, and economic negotiations that took place during a time of tremendous change. Historian Albert Camarillo calls the interplay of legal, political, economic, and ideological forces that resulted in segregated

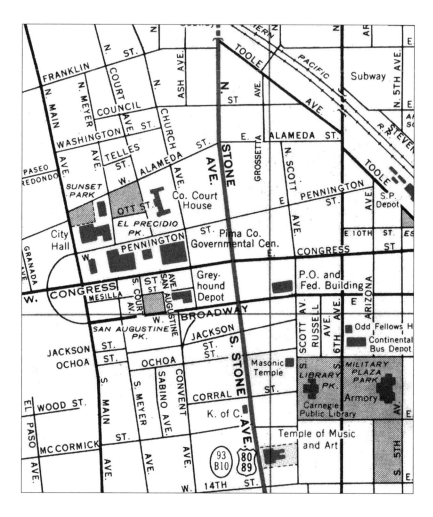

Figure 1.2. The 1965 map above shows a number of streets in the lower left quadrant that disappeared with the implementation of the Pueblo Center Redevelopment Project. The 1969 map, above right, shows the projected Tucson Community Center, new police and fire departments, and the Frémont House. Note the realignment of Broadway and Main Avenue. Both maps refer to La Placita as San Augustine Park. (Maps by H. M. Goshua; reproduced with permission from Rand McNally, R.L. 099-S-102)

communities "barrioization."[19] He explains that top-down, institutionalized directives based on both class and racial differences encouraged the creation of ethnic enclaves—and ultimately defined them. Anglo

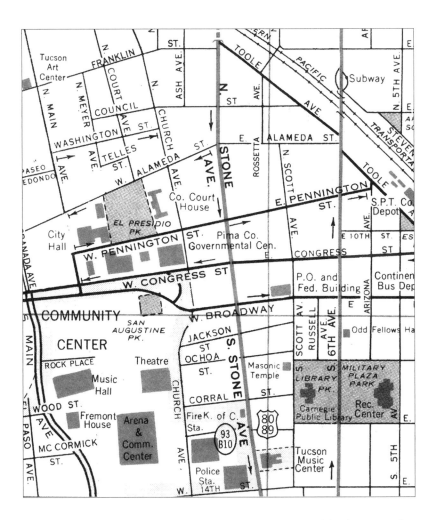

Americans came to control those spaces most suitable for capitalist development and assigned tucsonenses marginal ones.

Tucsonenses reacted to barrioization by transforming their assigned spaces, indeed by creating their own places. This collective act of forming a community away from the dominant culture's judgment and surveillance is historically and culturally significant. To enhance their sense of belonging, tucsonenses turned to familiar Mexican forms and structures, re-creating a cultural ambience based on memory and tradition.

The resultant architectural forms and street layouts that radiated southward indicate a quest to reaffirm and maintain tucsonenses' older cultural priorities in their new spaces. Not only did they choose to live with others like themselves; they also created a landscape that looked and felt like their homes in Sonora or in Tucson before the arrival of Anglos. This conscious preference for sites of cultural affirmation under a new national regime gave rise to la calle and the nearby barrios. Smaller service and commercial businesses established themselves in la calle on Congress, Broadway, and Meyer to cater to the needs of the large population of Mexican Americans. Indeed, since the late nineteenth century, South Meyer Avenue served as "the commercial axis around which the southern barrios turned."[20]

This settlement pattern never resulted in complete segregation, however. There is no evidence of an effort to deny tucsonenses access to public space and commercial services in the older sections of town. Their pronounced demographic presence made their purchasing power a potent force in the local economy despite the constant influx of new Anglo Americans. Between 1900 and 1920, the population of Mexican Americans in Tucson nearly doubled, to just under 7,500. During those same two decades, however, Anglo arrivals outnumbered tucsonenses as Tucson's total population nearly tripled to more than 20,300. "Mexicans had finally become a minority in the community they had founded, roughly 37 percent of Tucson's rapidly growing population."[21]

At one time, early in the twentieth century, a few wealthier Anglo and Mexican Americans had built their homes on South Main or South Meyer (between Broadway and McCormick). Increasingly, however, elite Anglos moved northwest to bigger and more luxurious residences in a neighborhood outsiders called Snob Hollow. They set the trend for Anglos moving to the northeast, on the other side of the Southern Pacific Railroad tracks.[22] In his prosperous later years, Roy P. Drachman recalled the racial differences that had made him feel "out of place" as a boy:

My brothers and I lived on the wrong side of the tracks during the early part of our lives spent in the old adobe family house at 233 South Main Street with its high ceilings, thick walls and screen porch. The neighborhood on South Main Street was at one time one of the better residential districts, with many of the more affluent families living in that part of town. However, by the time I was growing up all but three of the Anglo American families had moved to other neighborhoods.[23]

"We All Used to Live Over There"

In 1965, as planners targeted the downtown landscape, fewer than 300,000 people lived in the city. By then, most of those born in Tucson, regardless of their ethnic background, could trace at least one branch of their family tree to the area targeted for destruction. The few Anglo families who had once lived in the area, however, had moved away at least two generations before. Their attachment and sentimental links to the area remained distant in time and memory. In contrast, as this chapter's epigraph indicates, most tucsonenses throughout the city could claim that either they or their parents "used to live over there." The area destroyed by urban renewal marked the point of entry for the vast majority of Mexican Americans, who could trace both their paternal and maternal ancestors to the downtown region. Clearly, tucsonenses had a long history in Tucson. By the 1960s, most had descended from families who had arrived in Tucson before or immediately after the Gadsden Purchase. Only a minority, around 18 percent, had been born in Mexico.[24]

When the City of Tucson opened its urban renewal office in 1958, most Mexican Americans lived in barrios that radiated south and west from the central business district (CBD). There were no maps of these barrios, however. Tucsonenses' intimate knowledge of the city's landscape had eluded both academics and archivists. When anthropologist James E. Officer sought to identify and tally the number who resided in these spaces, he needed help to complete his research project. Thus he relied on interviews with local informants for insight into barrio names and borders.[25] Officer then had to interpret and distill what he had learned in order to construct a map. Although Officer's map provides some insight into barrio boundaries, these were much more complicated than it suggests.

Here we need to keep in mind that all inhabited spaces, even those proclaimed "empty," have encoded cultural and political meanings; none is neutral or passive. Such spaces hold different meanings for different people and cultural groups. Latina cultural critic Mary Pat Brady argues that understanding the linkages between space and identity remains vital to understanding how individuals perceive themselves and those who live in different spaces, and how spaces serve to differentiate neighborhoods and people. Brady argues that "hidden or visible [spaces] have an enormous effect on subject formations—on the choices people can make and how they conceptualize themselves, each other, and the world.

Interactions with space are not merely schematic but also highly affec-
tive; places are felt and experienced, and the processes producing space
therefore also shape feelings and experiences."[26]

Tucsonenses' knowledge of the cultural and physical landscape came
from their lived experiences—from walking, shopping, and working
there and from the socializing that their extended family networks provided.[27] Likewise, outsiders also based their "feelings" about Mexican
American spaces on their own lived experiences. In various spaces scat-
tered throughout the city, tucsonenses created and socially reproduced
their own mental and emotional maps wherein they recognized the distinctiveness of these spaces as they delineated boundaries and gave them
names. This collective dynamic is evident in some of the names assigned
to barrios. Barrio Tiburón, for example, got its name from the convergence of two washes that formed what residents saw as the outline of a
shark. Other names were more incidental: a barrio might be named after
membrillos, or quince trees, that flourished there, the *hoyo*, or hollow, or
the Carrillo Elementary School nearby.[28]

Born and raised only blocks away from the area targeted for demolition, Guadalupe Castillo confirms the importance of shared geographical
knowledge by stating, "When I was growing up I never called any place
other than by its specific name. For example, El Hoyo or El Membrillo."
Nevertheless, even though each barrio gained a reputation for its distinctive character, barrio boundaries sometimes overlapped.

Barrio Libre

The name of the area destroyed by urban renewal was contested at the
time and remains contested to this day. Most public and archival documents refer to the area as Barrio Libre. Guadalupe Castillo and other
tucsonenses disagree, however. "I never heard [the urban renewal area]
called Barrio Libre," she told me in February 2008. "I never heard it
called Barrio Viejo. I never heard anyone in my family call it any of those
names. They referred to specific places: Suey's [Market], Del Monte
Market, and La Calle Meyer or La Calle Convento. Each place had its
own specific name."[29]

Literally translated, "Barrio Libre" means free or liberated neighborhood. Repeatedly, Anglo American sources describe this as a place to
which Mexican Americans "fled" in order to avoid law enforcement and

freely engaged in "decadence, vice, and corruption." A passage from G. W. Barter's *Directory of the City of Tucson for the Year 1881* sheds light both on how some Anglo Americans understood the barrio's name and on what they thought of the place and those who lived or gathered there:

> This designation was given by the Mexican residents to that quarter of the city lying along Meyer and adjacent streets, southward of the business portion of the city, occupied by the Americans. It means Free Zone, and in earlier times was allowed to remain without legal restraints or the presence of policemen. Here, the Mescalian could imbibe his fill, and either male or female could, in peaceful intoxication, sleep on the sidewalk or in the middle of the streets with all their ancient rights respected. *Fandangoes, monte,* chicken fights, broils, and all amusements of the lower class of Mexicans were, in this quarter, indulged without restraint; and to this day much of the old-time regime prevails, although the encroachments of the American element indicate the ultimate doom of the customs in Barrio Libre. It must be understood that these remarks apply only to the lower class of Mexicans, and not to the cultured Mexican residents of the city, who, for intelligence and enterprise, are foremost among our people.[30]

Two years later, a similar narrative characterized the barrio as an "inferior" space, populated by "deviants": "In Tucson's younger days the Barrio Libre was a quarter of town, in the southern part, where the lower class of Mexicans and the Papago [Tohono O'odham] and Yaqui Indians held high or low carnival without being interrupted by officers of the law."[31] The authors of these narratives intentionally highlight what they consider the immoral and disagreeable aspects of this barrio. Although the first excerpt also suggests that only the most decadent Anglo Americans crossed the boundaries of respectability to mix with "bad Mexicans," the second confirms the area's history as a multicultural place where Mexican Americans, Tohono O'odham, and Yaqui joined in each other's collective celebrations.

Reflecting a widely shared attitude among Anglo Americans of the time, the city directory elevates the few Mexican people in Tucson from the higher classes by calling them "cultured," although it is more than likely that Barter was referring to those who openly embraced not their own Mexican culture but the dominant Anglo American one. The directory exemplifies the propensity among many Anglo Americans, then as now, to essentialize and generalize about an area inhabited predominantly by Mexican people.[32]

The city directory confirms that, as early as the 1880s, the lower classes and the most marginalized of Tucson's Mexican Americans were the first to seek refuge from the influx of Anglo Americans as these new arrivals acquired land and increasingly asserted their power. But how far south did the southern boundary of Barrio Libre lie? It is clear that Mexican culture or the "old-time regime" dominated the area, but did the economic penetration of the "American element" change the character and therefore also the boundaries of the barrio? The observation that in the city's "younger days the Barrio Libre was a quarter of town" raises important questions. Did the barrio later disappear? The 1881 directory situates Barrio Libre directly south of the "business portion of town." By 1940, the same area came to be known as La Calle Convento or La Calle Meyer and Barrio Libre had moved farther south.[33] In 1960, however, James Officer relocated the barrio's boundary northward to Broadway, in the midst of the central business district.[34] In 1986, Thomas Sheridan alerted readers to the subjective nature of locating Barrio Libre: "Despite the high visibility in the press . . . the exact location of Barrio Libre is difficult to pinpoint." He described it as a "wandering barrio . . . something of a moveable feast, steadily moving southward as Tucson grew."[35] To complicate matters further, Sheridan's map of local barrios placed Barrio Libre much farther south, away from downtown on the other side of 22d Street, a placement that reflects the tendency of many locals today to refer to an area in the City of South Tucson as Barrio Libre (see fig. 1.3).[36]

Urban renewal destroyed the neighborhood on the north side of 14th Street but spared the one on its south side, which was "far enough away to guarantee its exclusion from high density business and commercial development."[37] This neighborhood, now called Barrio Histórico, remains an architectural and cultural extension of the area destroyed and stands as testimony to what that area would have looked like had it survived.[38] Indeed, according to an architectural report, it stands as "the sole reminder of a Tucson that existed a century ago."[39]

By the 1970s, the loss of a densely populated, 80-acre core area had aroused the city's collective preservationist consciousness. Most Tucsonans came to appreciate the heavy price they had paid for urban renewal and the irrecoverable loss it had inflicted on their city. Historically minded Anglo Americans and speculators who moved into the barrio

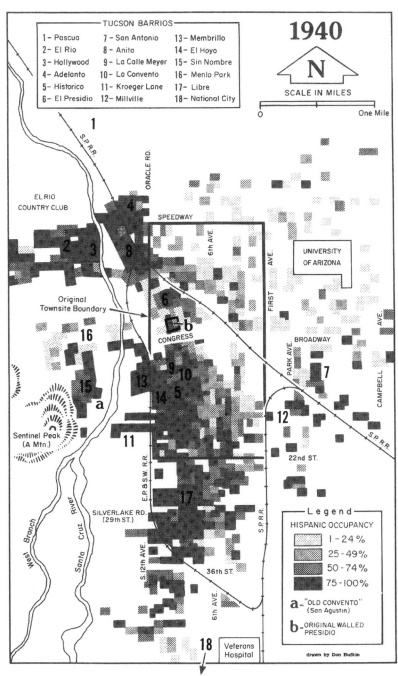

Figure 1.3. This shows the Mexican American barrios and settlement patterns as they were in 1940. (Map by Don Bufkin; Sheridan, *Los Tucsonenses*, 238)

that survived changed the area's power dynamic. They joined forces to have the area designated a historic district and to protect their newly acquired adobe houses. Their presence ensured the neighborhood's survival. In 1971, when the city planners proposed a freeway corridor that threatened to eliminate more of the few remaining buildings dating back to the Mexican era, a coalition of new property owners and tucsonenses rallied to save the older neighborhood, described as consisting "primarily of continuous, flush-fronted adobe structures."[40] As they attempted to transform their barrio into a prime commercial, professional, and residential neighborhood, the vocal new residents embraced previous historical descriptions of Barrio Libre, promoting a narrative in which "Barrio Histórico," so named in the 1970s, and "Barrio Libre" became interchangeable. Appropriating the imagery and history of Barrio Libre also strengthened the residents' public claims to the past in a language most Tucsonans could understand.

The varying descriptions of Barrio Libre speak to regional complexity and the subjective factors that influence spatial perceptions. City documents produced to promote and explain urban renewal marked the targeted 80 acres as a "slum" and a "blighted area." Planners and developers never bothered to get to know or to research the area destroyed. In fact, city officials consistently hired outside companies and agencies to draft their designs.

Like most other cities throughout the West, Tucson did not need laws or law enforcement officers to force Mexican Americans into designated areas. Most willingly located in communities with others of the same culture and ethnic origin. The historian Richard Griswold del Castillo argues that Mexican American spaces in themselves represented a vital resource for their residents. He confirms that barrios provided an escape and that the "creation of the barrio was a positive accomplishment. . . . The barrio gave a geographical identity, a feeling of being at home, to the dispossessed and poor. It was a place that offered security in the midst of the city's social and economic turmoil."[41] Moreover, these spaces served as a site of resistance to the social changes and prevailing racial attitudes of the late nineteenth century. As tucsonenses of different classes faced downward mobility, they looked to each other for support and situated themselves in places where they could share a life with others like them for strength, safety, and survival.

The fact that many from the Mexican American elite—families like the Carrillos, Sosas, Oteros, and Samaniegos—also moved south of downtown and stayed there indicates that there were advantages linked to living among those with a similar culture. They did not consider themselves as living on "the wrong side of the tracks." Elite tucsonenses presumably had more choices available to them, yet many also felt the sting of economic displacement and tried to avoid the hostility and discrimination of Anglo Americans by increasing their physical distance from them. To many of its residents of all classes, Barrio Libre meant freedom from Anglo American laws, and their ways of doing business. The sentiments expressed by those who assembled the *Tucson and Tombstone General and Business Directory for 1883 and 1884* indicate an early tucsonense reluctance to being included in Anglo American records: "In the present case a considerable portion of the population is composed of Mexicans and Spanish speaking people, many of whom are ignorant of the objects or utility of such a publication, and in many instances show great unwillingness to furnish their names, or other requisite information, appearing to fear that the unfortunate compiler is either a Deputy Sheriff, a City Marshal or other limb of the law."[42]

That tucsonenses preferred anonymity and feared the consequences of inclusion in various institutional records and programs provides insight into their complicated and antagonistic historical experiences with Anglo Americans. Record collectors declared them "ignorant," but some tucsonenses actively and consciously sought to keep a physical distance from tax and law enforcement agents. Their steady southward movement served to ensure a safe physical and social distance from Anglo Americans. This movement also accounts for the shifting boundaries of Barrio Libre.

"La Calle"

In order to appreciate the nuances of particular places, and this is certainly true in studying Tucson's urban renewal area, geographer Daniel D. Arreola suggests we must "begin to understand human association with place and how localities become defined by varied interests."[43] Although, as a group tucsonenses lost the power to define Tucson as a city after the influx of Anglo Americans, they retained the power to define and refine their immediate landscapes. Tucsonenses' differing perceptions of urban renewal resist essentialist characterizations. Many who possessed intimate knowledge of their landscapes—Guadalupe Castillo, Pedro

Gonzales, and my family included—did not rely on Anglo American assessments to name and recognize them. Most tucsonenses understood that the area destroyed by urban renewal comprised parts of several barrios, El Hoyo, Membrillo, and, depending on their perspective, Barrio Libre. Most agreed that that urban renewal destroyed a highly commercial area, the tucsonense downtown, which they called "la calle," where they or their families had once lived, and which they continued to patronize after they had moved away. According to Castillo, "'Vamos a la calle' meant 'We are going downtown.'"[44] As tucsonenses understood and used it, "la calle" meant not just downtown but the city's commercial heart, whose boundaries were both generous and flexible.

Unlike city dwellers throughout most of the Spanish-speaking world, who referred and still refer to their city's downtown as "el centro," tucsonenses and Mexican Americans in a few other southwestern cities often did not.[45] The use of "la calle" came from those who lived in the city's downtown area or descended from families who had. In their everyday language, it made no sense for them to refer to the downtown as "el centro" because their residences (or those of their families) stood in the center of town. On the other hand, differences between private and public places did make sense. This led tucsonenses to use an expression that best described the public spaces they collectively and intimately inhabited for a century or more.

"La calle" literally means "the street." Residents stepped out of their homes and found themselves in the midst of retail activity, of high pedestrian and, in recent years, automobile traffic. In *My Life and Music*, distinguished singer, composer, and tucsonense Lalo Guerrero recalls: "Meyer Street was the main thoroughfare where everything happened. . . . As soon as I stepped out through the front door, I was in the middle of the action."[46]

Enrique García described la calle as he had experienced it: "People were walking; the sidewalks were full of people. Not only in the daytime but at nighttime, too. People were living; you could feel it, you could see it. You could smell it. Now we're all spread around."[47] As García astutely noted, urban renewal dispersed the highly concentrated Mexican American population to other parts of the city.

By 1960, most tucsonenses were intimately familiar with la calle. They patronized the wide variety of businesses along its congested thoroughfares, from services such as García Cleaners and shoe repair shops, clothing and furniture stores, and restaurants to *panaderias* (bakeries), grocery stores owned mostly by Chinese Americans, tortilla factories, and meat markets. They bought tamales, vegetables, *cimarronas* (snow cones), and other foods from the street vendors on its corners.

Tucsonenses continued to patronize the businesses of la calle even as urban planners of the 1960s classified the businesses as "outdated" and "marginal." Business people forced out by urban renewal recognized all too well the importance and value of being located in la calle. In their recollections, they do not speak of leaving an obsolete commercial area. Far from it. They had relied on la calle's established business patterns and high pedestrian traffic, on its commercial vitality, for the success of their businesses. African American dentist Floyd Thompson, whose office was located on Main Street for twenty years, recalled that "I did not want to be far from town [la calle] because I wanted to retain clients. Many were poor and had no cars." "I kept 75 percent of my old customers," reported Robert García (of García Cleaners), "because I didn't move too far away." Indeed, when El Poblano Café did relocate "too far away," business fell off drastically: "Few customers come from the old place. They don't have cars."[48]

Driven by the need to map and control spaces through zoning, city planners designated fixed "official" boundaries for the central business district. These rigid boundaries stood in stark contrast to the more flexible borders many tucsonenses had internalized when it came to la calle. Spaces on streets like Jackson, Ochoa, Convent, Meyer, and Broadway in particular served a variety of functions. Multi-unit residences and retail, service, and financial businesses coexisted in la calle. In keeping with older traditions, many barber shops and grocery stores, as well as leather repair and jewelry shops, operated out of Mexican and Chinese American homes, which served as both residential and commercial spaces. This mixed use flew in the face of long-established Anglo American notions of home and business as distinct opposites.[49] These shops and stores formed an integral part of what tucsonenses considered their shopping and financial districts. The large number of small commercial establishments, bakeries, grocery stores, and restaurants located on these streets depended on Mexican American patronage, a commercial tradition that dated back to the nineteenth century. Moreover, business development in the downtown area correlated with the southward movement of people. In typical urban fashion, services and shops emerged to serve the expanding market. This dynamic increased the number of people on downtown streets and decreased the need for automobiles.

La Placita

After the Tratado de la Mesilla in 1853, better known as the Gadsden Purchase, La Plaza de la Mesilla became the social hub of the tucsonenses. The exact date of its origin remains uncertain, but it appeared as a rectangular open space surrounded by a few residences, all tucsonense, in the first map of Tucson, commissioned by Major David Fergusson of the Union Army in 1862, six years after the final withdrawal of Mexican troops.[50] It was also a terminus of the wagon trail route that connected Tucson to the territorial capital in Mesilla, New Mexico. Typically, people were drawn to the plaza to greet passengers or see them off, hear the latest news, gossip, and speculate why each new arrival had come to their desert town.[51] In the early days, the plaza's shade trees were "surrounded by a fence and had an outside trough for watering the animals."[52]

Most plazas in Mexico and other Latin American countries trace their origins back to Spanish rule and the Laws of the Indies, which determined how colonial settlements were to be laid out, although some had been established before then by indigenous populations. Surrounded by churches and government buildings, they served as central sites and main marketplaces for towns. Abigail A. Van Slyck notes that "colonial-era plazas reiterated the institutional links between church and crown, and reinforced their mutually supportive roles in Spain's colonizing enterprise," but "in contrast, Tucson's church plaza—like many plazas in the southwestern United States—was a product of the American Era; it was established seventy-five years after the settlement's founding and developed independently of Spain's legislative guidelines." Instead, "the Plaza de la Mesilla seems to have been a product of a set of shared assumptions."[53] Van Slyck confirms the powerful role of collective ideals that emerged from shared memories as tucsonenses reestablished older cultural forms in a new place, and in a new nation. They constructed landscapes strongly connected to Mexico and Mexican culture and architectural forms that made their imaginary a lived reality. La Placita and the neighborhoods near la calle expressed an ethnic sense of place.[54] Around 1863, desiring to attend further to their cultural needs, the tucsonense community built a Catholic church in their newly established neighborhood.[55] They chose to locate their church on La Plaza de la Mesilla, on present-day Church Street and Broadway. Firmly committed to the project, wealthier tucsonenses provided the funds for construction materials, but the faithful of all classes provided the labor needed to build

Figure 1.4. La Placita, circa 1894. Note the San Agustín Church in the background. (Courtesy Arizona Historical Society, Tucson)

the new church. "After each morning's religious services the community made the adobes," Ana María Comadurán Coenen remembers. "The entire church was built by the people of the parish." "The men made the adobes," Atanacia Santa Cruz adds, "and the women carried water in ollas on their heads for the mixing of the adobe mud. The finished adobes were also carried by women, who fashioned a ring of cloth and placing it on their heads, placed the adobes on it and carried it to the men building the walls."[56] By 1868, they had completed San Agustín Church, named after Tucson's patron saint, along with an adjacent school.[57] The open courtyard in front of the church became known as La Plaza de San Agustín (see fig. 1.4). In time, tucsonenses began to refer to this location simply as La Placita.[58]

For a hundred years La Placita represented a unique place, created by tucsonenses and based on their memories or "shared assumptions," where they could socialize and celebrate their Sonoran traditions. Indeed, La Placita became the site of most of Tucson's major celebrations. The yearly celebrations of San Agustín lasted for more than two weeks. Anthropologist Thomas Sheridan describes this festival as beginning with Mass at the church, "followed by a procession around the church plaza, the old Plaza de la Mesilla. . . . It was Tucson's celebration of its Catholic heritage, its rural heritage, and above all, its Mexican heritage." When the San Agustín festivals came to an end in the early twentieth century, according to Sheridan, "a part of Tucson's Sonoran soul died."[59] Familiiy networks, memory, and the strength of the oral tradition kept Tucsonenses attached to Sonora, however.[60] Subsequent generations continued to remember the San Agustín festivals and the old church itself. Indeed, preserving the commercial, social, and religious elements that marked the site's uniqueness became the main motivating factor that inspired and fueled the La Placita Committee's historic preservation efforts in 1967.[61]

La Plaza Theatre

Urban renewal demolished the only movie theater that featured Spanish-speaking films, located around the corner from La Placita on the south side of Congress. Obviously, the original owners recognized the significance and advantages associated with naming the theater La Plaza: it served to enhance the movie house's connection with its principal customers, the tucsonense community. Upon opening their doors in the early 1930s, the theater management recognized the needs of their bilingual audience, many of whom had never set foot in Mexico, by delivering programs and films in both English and Spanish (see fig. 1.5).

As a child who lived in la calle in the late 1940s, Ruben Moreno collected and sold bottles so that he could spend "all day Saturday at the movies." "They used to show two serials—one cowboy movie, Roy Rogers or Gene Autry or Tom McCoy, and one Spanish movie," he explained. La Plaza also had various live performances, such as "the stage show, which were amateurs. Lalo Guerrero was there with his group, the Carlistas."[62] Mary Angel Pérez remembered La Plaza as "our special place." watching films from Mexico and other Latin American countries, she said, "was a very wonderful experience because I was able to learn my Spanish even better. And then be able to appreciate the Hispanic culture. . . . This is my home. There's nothing like the United States. But when I go to Mexico, I feel at home, too, because I can speak the language, love the music, and enjoy the Hispanic culture."[63] The African American Howard Simms, who loved the westerns and cartoons shown there, declared that La Plaza Theatre was his "favorite place." He also noted that it "wasn't segregated

Figure 1.5. La Plaza Theatre, circa 1950. (Photograph by John Gabusi; courtesy Arizona Historical Society, Tucson, AHS photo no. 62643)

mainly because no one went there but blacks and Mexicans. You seldom found a Caucasian in the Plaza Theatre."[64]

As the rest of Tucson debated urban renewal and the destruction of downtown, La Plaza Theatre continued to fill its seats through programming tailored to tucsonense tastes until it closed its doors in 1969. Popular Mexican recording artist Luis Pérez Meza performed several engagements at La Plaza Theatre in 1952. He also spent much of his time in the Itules Home Furniture Store at 160 West Congress, where fans got to meet him and have their photographs and records autographed. Since most mainstream outlets did not carry music from Mexico and other Latin American countries, la calle stores like Itules (which later became the Imperial Furniture Store) provided an important commercial and cultural service (see fig. 1.6). Joseph and George Itule claimed their furniture and record shop "had some 500 Latin singers and musicians visit them since they opened."[65]

La Plaza Theatre also connected Mexican Americans to the larger Latin American community by bringing an assortment of renowned

Figure 1.6. An aerial view of La Placita taken from the corner of West Congress Street and South Meyer Avenue. (Special Collections, University of Arizona Library; Jack Schaefer Collection)

artists to Tucson. Mexican comedian German Valdez, known as "Tin-Tan," and his sidekick, Marcelo, brought their urban humor to Tucson in 1963.[66] Libertad Lamarque, a native of Argentina who had received various entertainment awards as a singer and film artist, appeared with her Artistic Caravan in 1965 for two shows at La Plaza. Tucsonenses, like most people throughout Mexico, appreciated her musical renditions and her intricate tango dancing.[67]

Radio host Jacinto Orozco played an important role in letting tucsonenses know who would be performing at La Plaza and when, and in keeping them connected to their Mexican culture. Don Jacinto's three-hour morning radio program *La Hora Mexicana* blared from most tucsonense radios from 1938 to about 1965. One listener remembered: "He made us feel like a community within a town." Don Jacinto, who was likened to Arthur Godfrey, often personally connected with his audience—and thus kept them connected with each other—by broadcasting calls of concern to their homes when he heard of an illness or death and by delivering personal birthday wishes.[68]

The Alianza Building

On January 14, 1894, fifty-six tucsonense men, sensing their decline in social and economic stature, met to "organize a constructive fraternal force to withstand the gathering clouds of prejudice and hate." "In the spirit of fraternalism," they formed the Alianza Hispano-Americana, with Carlos Velasco as their president, to "break down man-made barriers" and to offer "new hope, new courage, new expression, new faith to the people."[69] Incorporated under the laws of Arizona Territory as a fraternal society in 1897, with Tucson as its first lodge and headquarters and a membership of 17,000 at its peak, the Alianza eventually established chapters throughout Arizona, New Mexico, California, Colorado, Texas, Wyoming, and Mexico.[70]

Upon its completion in 1916, the Alianza's impressive two-story headquarters building at 129 West Congress became the "center of Mexican American culture and society" in Tucson.[71] During World War II and the Korean War, many Mexican American military personnel stationed in nearby Davis-Monthan Air Force Base gravitated to events held at the Alianza Building. Downstairs, its nightclub atmosphere provided a critical meeting place for tucsonenses. Alicia Rodríguez García remembered dancing there: "[The dance floor] was downstairs. They used to call it La Selva [The Jungle]."[72] The site also housed celebrations, in particular the crowning of the Mexican Independence Queen.[73] Many of the local Mexican American social clubs held their events at La Selva. Club Cienna held its "Cherry Pink and Apple Blossom White Dance" there in the 1950s and Club Azalea held its "Leap Year Dance" there in 1960. In 1966, fifty years after its christening, the Alianza Hispano-Americana Building was demolished to make way for a new Pima County government complex.[74]

Diversity in La Calle

Since its inception, la calle welcomed, served, and sometimes housed the city's marginalized citizens. The following description from the 1930s attests to la calle's cultural diversity:

> Residents of Mexican extraction comprise around 45 per cent of the Old Pueblo population. Most of them live in Old Town, called

El Barrio Libre (Free Neighborhood) in Spanish. Old Town is centered around South Meyer [Avenue] near the city's main business
area, is also peopled by Chinese and Negroes . . . for this is the exclusive Mexican shopping district. . . . In most of the bars around Meyer
Street, Negro chefs are busy concocting hot chili sauce to pour over
barbecued short ribs.[75]

The tucsonense downtown welcomed newcomers, and a sizable number
of African and Chinese Americans, who often spoke Spanish for social
and economic reasons, also called it home. Howard Simms, who shined
shoes as a child, recalls that blacks and Mexicans could work on Meyer
Avenue and the south side of Congress but were not welcomed north of
the corner of Stone and Congress because police would "arrest us and run
us back down to the lower [southern] part of town."[76] The Fox Theatre,
Floyd Thompson recounted, forced African Americans to sit in the bal-
cony.[77] According to Margaret Jean Simms Price, most of the soda fountains also refused to serve African Americans except for Tito's Drugstore
on Congress and Meyer, owned by Tito Flores.[78] The racial discrimination so apparent on the northern side of downtown faded away on the
southern side.

Small commercial establishments run by Jewish, Lebanese, and Syrian
merchants joined the Chinese grocery stores, Mexican bakeries and restaurants, and Japanese barbershops in la calle. Faris Ganem, of Syrian
descent and known to tucsonenses as Don Felix, ran the Yellow Front
Clothing Store on Meyer Avenue for nearly thirty-eight years.[79] As a child,
Henry García "heard all languages" in his downtown neighborhood.[80]

As mentioned above, during and after World War II Mexican
Americans from Davis-Monthan Air Force Base and African Americans
stationed at Fort Huachuca found that businesses in la calle tended not
to discriminate. Many African Americans decided to stay after the war,
leading to an increase in black-owned businesses, which added to la calle's
diversity. "The blacks started all kinds of little businesses there," García
recalled, "and so I got acquainted and learned a lot about their culture
and became very good friends with them, you know. The most famous
one was Jimmy's Chicken Shack. They specialized in fried chicken and
used to bring black floor shows from Los Angeles and Chicago."[81]

The Chinese arrived in Tucson in the late nineteenth century. Anna
Don remembered that her father often visited friends in Tucson's
Chinatown, a vibrant residential and commercial community that

included a Chinese Community Center. "What was then Chinatown," she recalled, "is in the middle of the [Tucson Convention] Center today."[82] "Meyer Street used to be the Speedway of Tucson," Suey Gee recalled, "and all [Chinese American markets] were doing good business."[83] Located close to where their customers lived, family-run grocery stores and restaurants often offered small rewards for customer loyalty. Joe Yee remembered the long-established "older [Chinese American] practice of giving customers some candy or fruit free of charge in appreciation of their business."[84]

Tucson's Downtown: La Calle versus the Central Business District

City governments and planners in the United States generally define central business districts by their financial institutions and commercial activity. Typically, skyscrapers and high urban density outline the central business district or downtown of a U.S. city. By the 1960s, accommodating automobiles by providing parking and efficient access, and protecting pedestrians in light of the increased traffic, had become major urban concerns. In Tucson, as in other cities, business leaders also worried about decentralization caused by suburban development and the attendant economic decline of downtown properties. A research study published in 1960 concluded, however, that "although Tucson is undergoing typical suburban expansion found throughout the United States, the Tucson Central Business District (CBD) remains strong and viable. In fact, certain circumstances of the location, character, and growth of the community have provided centripetal pull at a time when other American CBD's are experiencing destructive centrifugal forces." The study also found that retail sales had "kept pace with the population growth."[85]

To be sure, the construction in 1961 of Tucson's first shopping center, El Con, a few miles east of downtown, provided shoppers an alternative to the shops downtown. However, as Anna Don contends, "From the 1940s to the 1960s, downtown was still viable. We still went downtown to do our shopping—clothing, there were jewelry stores, there were five-and-dimes, there were dress shops. . . . Everything was concentrated downtown."[86]

Tucsonenses defied negative portrayals of their spaces and heeded their own mental maps by refusing to accept the dominant culture's economic and social boundaries, which defined downtown as a space separate from their own. Lydia Carranza Waer remembers that she "used to go over [to] the Plaza Theatre, and just [take] the whole day off for it. And we went to lunch. So it was really a day of enjoying for us housewives. I used to hit the stores. It wasn't hard because I used to enjoy doing it."[87]

In 1963, as the drive for urban renewal gained momentum, the *Tucson Daily Citizen* decided to sample citizen sentiment about the city's downtown. Its reporters interviewed six individuals. None lived in the neighborhoods near downtown, and none were Mexican Americans. The newspaper asked, "What could downtown merchants do that would lead you to make more trips?" J. S. Palmer replied that he would "rather not come downtown; the outlying shopping centers are simply closer to home." Dorothy Dilliner agreed: "I wouldn't mind shopping downtown if it weren't so far." So did C. Robertson: "I just hate to drive downtown." Indeed, with the solitary exception of Henrietta Robinson, all of the interviewees preferred to stay away from the downtown area.[88]

These responses disturbed local tourist promoters and encouraged urban renewal advocates, who recognized that Anglo American Tucsonans had found shopping alternatives they preferred to the downtown area. In addition, when tourists arrived in the desert city, they inevitably observed the large number of tucsonenses in the downtown area, contrary to what the contrived promotional materials had led them to expect. A 1956 study by Robert E. Waugh of the University of Arizona's Bureau of Business Research substantiates the strong tucsonense presence. Situated in "certain designated points," Waugh's research team relied on "visual observation to distinguish Mexican Americans from all others." Using manual mechanical counters, one group recorded a click each time they spotted a member of the target population, and another counted everyone in the area. Interestingly, determining the boundaries that delineated the downtown area posed a fundamental problem for this research endeavor. Waugh wrote that his team "found little or no agreement as to what precisely constitutes the downtown Tucson shopping area geographically."[89] The team had clearly encountered the "flexible" borders of la calle so familiar to tucsonenses.

The research team decided to conduct their survey on "any block in which a retail outlet was located."[90] They set up seventeen stations in an area that extended beyond the urban renewal boundaries drawn up almost ten years later.[91] They also selected stations that tucsonenses infrequently patronized, stating: "Certain stores within the downtown area appear to get more trade from [Mexican Americans] than others."[92] The high-end department stores Jácome's and Steinfeld's on the north side of Congress were comparable to Macy's and Gimbels in Manhattan,[93] and most working-class families, mine included, usually did not shop in them or in Tucson's other high-end department store, Levy's. The Waugh team steered clear of analyzing tucsonenses' relationship to retail sites north of Congress, which included most financial institutions and title companies. This must be taken into consideration because, with the exception of one Friday evening, the team conducted its week-long research during the daytime hours, when many employees of the banks and financial offices nearby made up a large part of a transient nine-to-five population. It is likely that most of those surveyed also lived in the outlying suburbs. Cumulatively, the survey's selection of high-end retail establishments, inclusion of employees from the developing suburbs, limited hours of data collection, and reliance on phenotypic identifiers served to significantly underestimate the tucsonense presence.

After taking all these factors into consideration, Waugh's team found "a preference among Mexican Americans for shopping in the downtown area." It determined that, in 1956, tucsonenses made up between 14 and 17 percent of the city's population, yet at times they constituted some 42 percent of the pedestrians on the downtown streets. The report attributed the high visibility of tucsonenses to the "fact that the downtown area lies between home and working locations," accounting for higher volumes of pedestrians in the morning and evening hours. And, most important, it found that tucsonenses contributed greatly to the economy of the downtown shopping district.[94]

A 1958 study of women shoppers in downtown, which did not attempt to make ethnic distinctions, indirectly confirmed the importance of tucsonenses for the downtown economy. "Newer inhabitants," it noted, "made a much lower fraction of their purchases in the downtown area than did longer-term inhabitants," and those who had lived in Tucson for more than twenty years did most of their shopping downtown. "This," the survey suggested, "may be a result of store loyalty on the part of the longer-term residents."[95] In a city where newcomers arrived daily, it can be assumed that tucsonenses made up many of the "longer-term inhabitants." The report also surmised that those from the lower classes did more of their shopping downtown because "in general, the lower income groups may be located closer to the downtown area. They may be less mobile as far as outlying shopping areas are concerned. In that respect, they may constitute part of the bus riders who concentrated their purchases heavily in the downtown area."[96]

These and other studies confirm the importance of Mexican American patronage of the downtown area. Because city officials had already opened their urban renewal office in 1958, these reports should have served as a warning for business and city leaders who purportedly based policy decisions solely on economic factors. As mentioned earlier in this chapter, a 1960 report had also assured concerned business leaders that, despite "typical suburban expansion," Tucson's downtown area still remained "strong and viable."[97]

Of particular interest to the merchants, these studies highlighted the patronage that fostered the economic well-being of downtown. "Relocating residents to other parts of the community," the 1960 report warned, "may substantially interfere with the well-established shopping pattern in the downtown area."[98] Mainstream city officials and urban renewal advocates ignored such reports and instead actively engaged in an urban renewal plan that deliberately sought to curtail the patronage of Mexican Americans.

Claiming that "the CBD has lost its dominance as *the* retail center," urban renewal proponents predicted only doom for the city's economy unless the dramatic changes they proposed were implemented. They did not seek to revitalize the area or to improve its retail potential. Instead, they wanted a "cleansed" downtown with a new purpose. City leaders wanted tourists and a "new" breed of people to take pleasure in the new downtown they promised and eventually developed. They sought to "further reinforce the administrative function of the CBD." Even more important, the Pueblo Center Redevelopment Project was intended "to re-orient the resident population and tourists to the CBD through its provisions for major entertainment and cultural land use."[99] Reorientation takes on added significance because it underscores urban renewal's goal of creating a new space at the expense of existing ones. Notably, urban renewal proponents never deviated from their public claims that economics framed the need for the Pueblo Center Redevelopment Project and that they were acting in the city's best interest and well-being even as they led the charge to destroy its commercial and cultural core.

2

Asserting Economic and Spatial Dominance

> If we could only go back to Jackson [Street]. We were happy there,
> even though the roof leaked and the wallpaper was falling off.
> There wasn't so much vandalism there, and I didn't have to worry
> about a car to get around. But most of all I miss my old friends.
> None of them moved here, and I only see them once in a while.
>
> —Sara Valencia, December 1970[1]

In time, advances in transportation, first the railroad and later automobiles and airlines, would bring a million people to Tucson. Spatial alterations and ethnic realignments began immediately as newcomers assessed their new surroundings and insisted on re-creating their former social and physical environments. Transplanted ethnocentric ideas eventually transformed the physical landscape in ways that expressed the newcomers' desire to expunge Tucson's "foreign" characteristics—its Mexican past and people. The quest for uncomplicated, homogeneous white environments ignored the structural issues that had given rise to the city's uneven development, particularly in Mexican American spaces.

The process of inscribing political, economic, and cultural dominance onto the local landscape has an extensive history dating back to the nineteenth century. The dedicated effort to transform Tucson into an "American" and more modern city had dire implications for ethnic neighborhoods, however. Urban promoters looked on these neighborhoods not only as eyesores; they saw them as threats to the city's future and modern development.

Increasingly after World War II, Anglo middle-class suburban ideals came to define "proper" standards of living in Tucson. The urban renewal campaign depicted tucsonenses and the poor who lived in the neighborhoods downtown as obstacles to progress who were excluded from planners' visions for the future Tucson, because their designs prioritized making the downtown area inviting to suburbanites and tourists.

Ethnic Realignments in a Changing Economy

The first Anglo American men, assumed to be trappers, passed through Southern Arizona as early as 1826,[2] but most of those who stayed in the area arrived after the California Gold Rush in 1849. Conscious of their minority status in an isolated Mexican community, these Anglo men initially adapted to local customs, although they never veered from their entrepreneurial ambitions. They quickly became the city's leading merchants and acquired the most desirable property in the business hub, inside or close to the former presidio. They understood that being on cordial and even intimate terms with the majority population was the key to the smooth transfer of power and the acquisition of property. Southwest historian C. L. Sonnichsen noted that early Anglo arrivals formed amicable relations with the surrounding people in order to survive and thrive: "Mexican food and Mexican ideas became part of their lives. Mexican women became their wives, and the Mexican heritage shaped the lives of their children."[3] Before the arrival of large numbers of Anglo women, intermarriage helped Anglo men to gain knowledge of and become part of the established familial networks. These intimate bonds temporarily suspended ethnic social distances and diminished negative racial thinking.[4]

Tucson's economic transformation greatly affected its Mexican people. The 1870 census indicates that even the most elite tucsonenses' fortunes were only a fraction of those amassed by their Anglo counterparts. Merchant Leopoldo Carrillo ranked first with a net worth of $75,000, and Estevan Ochoa, also a merchant, ranked second at $30,000. By contrast, Anglo merchant William Zeckendorf's wealth totaled $124,000, and Hugh L. Hinds, a beef contractor and freighter who had secured lucrative government contracts to provision outlying military encampments, had a net worth of $200,000, almost three times that of the wealthiest tucsonense.[5]

A similar shift in fortunes took place in most former Mexican territories during the nineteenth century. Historian Deena J. González credits merchant capitalism not only for "opening up new markets" but also for the sweeping economic changes that resulted in Anglo dominance throughout the Southwest. She argues that this financial pattern "undermined older, established systems of interdependence; injecting new products into a depressed economy; and encouraged local people . . . to begin working for wages."[6] González's observations highlight the shrinking entrepreneurial opportunities and variable economic alternatives encountered by Mexican Americans throughout the Southwest, which led to their eventual loss of land and social stature. The arrival of the railroad in 1880, for example, undermined economic patterns that had provided goods and food to Southern Arizona through commercial linkages with Sonora.[7]

Estevan Ochoa stands as a classic example of the downward mobility that awaited the vast majority of tucsonenses in the new economic environment. Born into wealth and influence in Chihuahua, Ochoa put his family's resources and networks to work and became one of Tucson's leading entrepreneurs. His economic success allowed him to "cross an invisible boundary" and to gain both acceptability and high esteem within the ranks of elite Anglos.[8] Indeed, the town elected Ochoa mayor in 1875, and he remains the only tucsonense so elected since the Gadsden Purchase. Ochoa also used his political power to spearhead the establishment of the territory's public school system and served in the territorial legislature for three years. Along with his business partner, Pinckney Tully, this well-connected tucsonense established a diversified conglomerate that combined long-distance freighting, mining, cattle ranching, and merchandizing. The arrival of the railroad, however, lowered the cost of transporting goods and served to undermine the integrity of Tully, Ochoa and Company. Thomas Sheridan sums up Ochoa's economic decline: "In November 1880 a Southern Pacific locomotive ploughed into two of Tully, Ochoa and Company's freight wagons, smashing the vehicles and killing the mules. That accident symbolized the end of an era." Ochoa died destitute in 1888.[9]

Interethnic business partnerships like Tully, Ochoa and Company virtually disappeared and the social space between Mexican and Anglo Americans widened as the nineteenth century drew to an end. Most of the tucsonense elite spiraled downward into the lower classes, as did their offspring. Historian David Montejano outlines the dynamic of dispossession that swept throughout the West when the Mexican American elites were "not replaced [on the economic ladder] by their descendants or by other Mexicans. Thus, market development for the Mexican community signified a collapsing of the internal class structure. With few exceptions, the propertied classes of the Mexican settlements did not reproduce themselves."[10] Although the diminishing numbers of the tucsonense elite deprived the entire community of visible role models of Mexican American success, a few did manage to achieve entrepenuerial success in the new economic environment. In 1880, they owned 12 of the 139 businesses in town.[11]

By the turn of the century, the issue of class became central to racial formations.[12] Indeed, class and race became inextricably bound. Upper-class tucsonenses such as Carlos Jácome and Federico Ronstadt stand as exceptions who, unlike Estevan Ochoa, retained and expanded their economic base. Their wealth allowed them to transcend class and racial barriers and to gain acceptance into the elite Anglo circles. Thus the descendants of elite tucsonense families had fiscal advantages that allowed them to negotiate and participate in the evolving economic system.[13] Their privileged social standing also shielded these families from anti-Mexican sentiments. In time, many of their descendants intermarried with Anglos, and despite individual and selective claims to a tucsonense ethnicity, they often embraced Anglo culture, and just as often, Tucson's larger Anglo society accepted them as "white." Nevertheless, this handful of families shared little in common with the majority of tucsonenses, who remained outside the boundaries of whiteness and who were thus deprived of the privileges that accompanied this advantaged racial marker.[14]

On the East Coast, in a racial environment that insisted on clear racial boundaries, European Americans of Jewish, Irish, Welsh, German, Polish, or Italian descent (to list the most notable examples) encountered strict racial boundaries and were considered racial "Others"— outside the parameters of "whiteness."[15] But racial protocol in the West, particularly in Tucson, greatly expanded the boundaries of whiteness. That Mexicans and Indians outnumbered Anglo Americans in Southern Arizona accelerated the process by which European ethnic groups were, in the words of Matthew Frye Jacobson, "'whitened' by the presence of nonwhite Others."[16]

Newly immigrated Europeans were far more likely than Mexicans to be welcomed into "American" society in Tucson. Jewish merchants Philip and Samuel Drachman escaped rampant anti-Semitism in Europe in 1852 to achieve immediate financial success in Tucson.[17] Fellow Jew Jacob Mansfield, who arrived from Germany in 1870, would come to wield tremendous local political power, as would his descendants. Similarly, German-born William Zeckendorf encountered few problems in his quest to become a powerful Tucson merchant. Samuel Hughes, a Welsh immigrant, thrived as a butcher and the owner of a hardware shop that supplied military needs, in addition to being a money lender. These are only a few examples of European immigrants with limited English-speaking skills and perceptible foreign accents who were allowed inside the walls of whiteness and who formed the core of Tucson's elite entrepreneurial classes.[18] As such, they also became powerful political and community leaders. In stark contrast to the vast majority of tucsonenses, who rarely escaped negative associations and who remained outside the boundaries that surrounded their "fellow Americans," the national origins of these immigrants never impeded their access to capital and an opportunity to rise in the new system. To put it plainly, whatever their language skills or accents when they arrived in Tucson, European immigrants did not *look* Jewish or German or Welsh.

The Battle for Statehood and the Issue of "Too Many Mexicans"

When both Arizona and New Mexico attained statehood in 1912, President William Howard Taft commented, "Well, it is all over. I am glad to give you life." In addition to full integration and membership in the nation, many in Arizona hoped that their new state would become a magnet for new capital. Commercially minded individuals hoped that eastern industrialists would no longer consider Arizona a "remote, dangerous, and unruly territory," as described by journalist J. Ross Browne, and would instead decide to invest there. According to historian Howard R. Lamar, "A large number of citizens in the Southwest had come to believe sincerely that territorial status was a terrible stigma, an insufferable mark of inferiority." Obstacles to statehood included local, regional, and national partisan rivalries, and the belief that corruption stemmed from the enormous power that the Southern Pacific Railroad and the large mining corporations wielded in the territory. But national antagonisms and prejudices directed at the large Mexican American populations of both Arizona and New Mexico also proved a major impediment to statehood.[19]

Senator Albert J. Beveridge stood as the principal opponent to statehood for Arizona and New Mexico. As chairman of the Senate Committee on Territories, Beveridge had blocked Arizona's statehood drive for more than ten years. Along with other powerful men of that period, like Theodore Roosevelt and Henry Cabot Lodge, he viewed the West as "not quite as civilized as the more settled east," in part because of the area's large Mexican American population. He also shared their belief that Mexican people were mentally and culturally inferior, "second-class citizens—passive, pliant, and uneducated."[20] Mexican Americans' ethnic ties and resistance to assimilation provided Beveridge with rhetorical weapons to denounce them as undeserving of first-class citizenship or membership in the nation. Lamar argues that, to men like Beveridge, "the refusal to learn English was tantamount to a mild form of treason."[21] Beveridge insisted that the populations in the territory "must be on equality with the remainder of the people in the Nation in all that constitutes effective citizenship" in order to qualify for statehood.[22] In 1902, on a visit to the territories, he looked for justifications to block Arizona and New Mexico from achieving statehood. He asked whether Mexican Americans "spoke American" and even ordered that photographs be taken of "Mexican 'loafers' in the Barrio Libre" to support his racist sentiments regarding Mexican American unsuitability for citizenship.[23]

The statehood debate informed economic and civic leaders in Arizona that Mexican people could indeed serve as an obstacle to progress. Ascribing foreignness to tucsonenses justified Mexican American marginalization and exclusion. Ethnocentric perceptions of tucsonenses as not Americans and therefore not citizens also served to justify denying them equal rights and entitlement to social services.[24] Situating groups outside the boundaries of citizenship was not simply a matter of prejudice, however. Historian Matthew F. Jacobson argues that "racial stereotypes like inborn 'laziness,' as applied to Mexicans or Indians, were economic assessments that had economic consequences" which typically came in the form of disposession. "Moreover," he notes, "race had been central to American conceptions of property . . . central to republican notions of self-possession and the 'stake in society' necessary for democratic participation."[25]

The Arizona statehood debate reflects racialized ideas of what ethnic groups constituted appropriate and "fit" citizens and who qualified as "American"—ideas that endure, albeit to a lesser degree, to this day. Albert Beveridge was expressing national sentiments when he declared in 1902: "'Americans' are made up from every nationality except Mexicans. Germans, Italians, French and all nationalities are called 'Americans.'"[26]

Asserting Spatial Dominance

Architects Anne M. Nequette and R. Brooks Jeffery attest that "as Tucson was searching for an image appropriate for its identity as a prosperous mining, ranching, agricultural, and commercial center, architecture was used as a vehicle to express the town's new, American identity." Anglo Americans intentionally began to build their structures in styles and with materials that marked them as distinctive. These new forms also served to assert Anglos' spatial and social dominance. Brick replaced adobe as Tucson moved "well on its way toward developing the appearance of an American town."[27]

In his analysis of the changes ushered in by the railroad, C. L. Sonnichsen observes: "What was respectable or at least tolerable to the first comers [Anglos] is insupportable to those who arrive later." Drawing on local newspapers from the early 1880s, Sonnichsen concluded, "With the growing Anglo influence came a change in building styles. Brick and lumber were in; adobe was out. Newcomers preferred to freeze in winter and stew in summer rather than to live in one of those 'ugly mud houses.' The idea of stepping out of one's front door into the street was equally repugnant." The homes Anglo Americans built for themselves included "decent-sized" front yards, unlike the Sonoran-style row houses that many tucsonenses preferred; despite the desert environment and limited water supply, "the new residents imported the green lawn."[28]

In 1883, practically every building in Tucson was made of adobe, and it remained the primary construction material for Mexican Americans well into the first half of the twentieth century. Adobe became an identifiable ethnic marker, synonymous with Mexican people. By 1914 "the greatest number of Spanish surnames were located south of Broadway in the long narrow area between Main and Stone"—the area of greatest concentration of adobe houses.[29]

Thus adobe became associated with Mexican Americans and "the wrong side of the tracks" as "new" construction styles became the visual marker of a new era of Anglo dominance. Anglo Americans, historian Bradford Luckingham tells us, looked to start anew in the Southwest: they "wanted [their] towns to look 'American' like those they had left behind . . . distinctly 'American' in design." Achieving this goal "became a source of pride to local Anglos."[30] In describing the structural changes Anglos preferred, urban geographers Thomas Saarinen, John Crawford, and Karen Thomas note that "instead of building houses right up to the

Figure 2.1. The Del Monte Market at 116 South Meyer Avenue, circa 1950. (Courtesy Arizona Historical Society, Tucson, PC 193 f. 18 [B])

street line [a trait that prevailed in la calle], homes were set back. Small front yards appeared instead of private interior patios as had previously been the fashion. . . . Pitched roofs began to replace flat ones."[31]

Throughout la calle and areas south of downtown, functional differentiation did not apply. Structures looked alike and were often built in continuous rows, although they served a variety of mixed residential and commercial functions, as "small neighborhood commercial uses so typical of the Mexican village areas."[32] In la calle, owners who lived in the back of their shops could tend to their children, and their gardens, between selling groceries, mending shoes, and the like (see fig. 2.1).

Privacy did not prevail in this settlement pattern. Many row houses had an overhang that provided much-needed shade,[33] and sitting on the front step and socializing with neighbors served to strengthen a sense of community. "The people all lived close together," Henry García explained. "There was no such thing as wide-open spaces, you know, because there was no parking. . . . So all the people used to be tightly packed. All the houses were right next to the other one. In fact, the walls were right next to the other, so people used to interact because they lived so close together, you see. We knew everybody and knew what everybody was doing."[34]

According to architect Robert C. Giebner, Sonoran-style row houses testified to the "inventiveness" of tucsonenses, who made practical decisions

Figure 2.2. Sonoran-influenced architecture in the area now called Barrio Histórico. (Photograph by the author)

regarding their desert environment. Although he was referring to the barrio south of 14th Street that survived urban renewal, the same types of architectural styles dominated in la calle and the surrounding, later-razed barrios (see fig. 2.2):

> [Barrio Histórico] exists today as the only extant example of the Southwestern 19th century urban environment, based upon the Spanish/Mexican tradition found in Arizona's major cities. Man's resourcefulness in solving the problems of survival in the hostile climates of the Southwest are evidenced in structures such as those found here. The major significance is found in the barrio's unified urban form rather than its individual structures. . . . The buildings were uncompromising in their simplicity and were based upon tradition and the available materials and technology.[35]

Indeed, urban renewal destroyed many of the oldest, most historically significant and architecturally noteworthy structures in the city. As they walked southward, however, most people encountered Gay Alley, and some, including most urban promoters, could never get beyond their first impressions of it.

First Impressions: Gay Alley

"There was not a saloon or church in the town" in 1862, recalled Fred D. Hughes.[36] In 1877, eleven years after the departure of Mexican troops, Tucson had ten saloons, along with two breweries, two hotels, two flour mills, a county courthouse, and a branch United States depository, according to geographer Donald H. Bufkin. The growing number of saloons corresponded to the growing number of Anglo Americans, especially single males, who worked as miners, soldiers, and ranch hands. Bufkin saw in the new buildings and "urban activities" "the clearly implied change from the characteristics of a Mexican frontier village to a bustling Anglo American supply center for mining, ranching, transcontinental travel, and the Army, which was conducting the Indian wars."[37]

By 1893, Tucson's population had reached 5,000 and the number of saloons had more than quadrupled to 42.[38] Most of these establishments located themselves in "the wedge," a narrow strip of land south of the former presidio between Calle de la Alegría (Congress Street) and Calle de la India Triste (later renamed "Maiden Lane"). In 1862, residences dominated this area; three decades later, dramatic demographic changes had transformed it into the "salon district," which "fulfilled a requirement of the frontier. This district served the demands of a population which had a great preponderance of males."[39]

In 1891, as the nation moved toward moral reform, Tucson also sought respectability, and city officials addressed the problem of the hyper-masculinized red-light district, which they considered too close to their developing downtown. Indeed, civic leaders felt so strongly about the matter they donated their own funds to raze the area.[40] They did not outlaw the illicit behaviors, however, at least not at this time. Instead, they looked the other way as the red-light district relocated southward to Gay Alley in la calle—farther south and away from respectable establishments in the developing downtown north of Congress.[41]

Their decision had severe consequences for tucsonenses. Many outsiders and civic leaders quickly came to associate "immoral" activity with Mexican Americans and their neighborhoods. Increasingly, civic leaders represented Mexican American spaces as places of disorder and crime, whose residents did not and could not properly regulate sexuality or alcohol consumption. Ignoring their own role in manipulating this spatial outcome, they pointed the finger of blame at the indigenous population as the source of moral degeneracy—and at Gay Alley (sometimes called Sabino Alley) and the tucsonense downtown as the embodiment of the city's vice and corruption.

Moving Out of La Calle

Despite a shortage of physical space, lack of privacy, limited front and back yards, and for some, inadequate indoor plumbing, many residents did not want to leave their old neighborhoods in or near la calle. As the tucsonense population grew, however, those who aspired to home ownership often moved to other areas. After World War II, the increasing population density and diversity in the neighborhoods close to downtown caused many residents to move away. In this instance, the ideological motivations of creating spatial and social distance from people of color did not apply. Most did not move east but rather south and west to newer barrios that housed predominantly Mexican Americans.

Like many other tucsonenses, my parents relocated to another barrio. During World War II, while my father served overseas, along with most of the men "from the barrios," my mother was living with her two young daughters on South Meyer Avenue in la calle. She used the money the family had saved to purchase vacant land about one and a half miles away from downtown. She and her sisters made enough adobes in the backyard to build a small one-room house in Barrio Kroger Lane. After the war, they added five more rooms and an indoor bathroom.

Tucsonense Alicia F. Cruz also left the downtown area in 1937 and moved to the West Side when "there was nothing. Just farmland and St. Mary's Hospital. These farms were being broken up, and these lots were sold for $150 each." Working-class families who moved to areas best described as Tucson's outskirts looked for affordable properties or "good deals." Once they owned land, they could invest their labor in building their homes. They turned to traditional building styles and materials to keep construction costs low by depending on the labor that family and friends provided, especially in making the primary building material, adobe bricks. Alicia Cruz described the emergent West Side barrio: "All these houses looked the same. They were small. Someone would do what we did—build two rooms and then after a few years put another room here and another there. There were no sewer lines. For a long time, the bathrooms were outside in the back."[42]

My mother often said she would have preferred to stay near her other family members and stores. Moving away from la calle posed an understandable inconvenience since she never learned to drive. In their quest to become home owners, my parents found properties downtown more expensive than lots that they could develop to the south. Their southward resettlement in Barrio Kroger Lane followed an outward movement that had been in play for the past hundred years, a movement that also explains why so many people who remained behind were renters by the time the Pueblo Center Redevelopment Project relocated them in the 1960s.

Of course, not all tucsonenses built their own homes. Some moved to the newer developments. Those with larger disposable incomes moved west of the city's main river (the Santa Cruz) to neighborhoods such as Menlo Park. Although this area "was the most prosperous Mexican neighborhood," it did not come close to matching the northeastern Anglo neighborhoods in "either income or educational attainment."[43] Despite this outward movement, my family and most tucsonense families continued to patronize retail, banking, and leisure establishments in la calle.[44]

Ensuring Racial Separation

When a 1938 headline in the *Arizona Daily Star* read, "No Color Line Found in City: Lack of Restriction for Colored Residents Is Indicated," it is not surprising that white Tucsonans looked to local government to "protect" their neighborhoods. Couching their racism in the language of market imperatives, concerned Anglo home owners appealed to the city council to provide "protection from the erection of homes for Negroes in their neighborhoods. . . . It was not a matter of race prejudice but rather the facing of the inevitable lowering in their property values which always follows the occupation of a district by Negroes." The city council responded by informing them that, under both the U.S. Constitution and the Arizona Constitution, "the city had no power to place restrictions on property ownership and residence for race or color." Deputy Real Estate Commissioner William F. Kimball proposed a workable alternative, however: "the subdivider of [a neighborhood], or later, . . . all the property owners acting together" could enter into "a form of contractive restriction agreement"—or covenant—which, if "properly drawn" would achieve the same end, namely, racially homogeneous white neighborhoods.[45] The purpose of restrictive covenants, explains historian David M. P. Freund, was to "effectively define the rights of specific properties and, thus, the responsibilities of property holders to uphold those supposedly intrinsic rights," most notably, for whites, the right to racially exclude.[46]

Research confirms efforts to confine Mexican Americans and other people of color to certain areas of Tucson. In his 1942 study, sociologist John Kestner Goodman found that Tucson realtors refused to sell homes to Mexican Americans, particularly in newer, middle-class, Anglo American areas. He also discovered that certain apartment houses also intentionally excluded Mexican people "because they feel if Mexicans were admitted their Anglo tenants would move out." Mexican Americans, he said, were, "in almost every case, relegated to buying old homes in declining residential districts, and paying high prices for them."[47]

In 1946, early in the suburban movement, Harry T. Getty identified eighty-three locations under restrictive covenant throughout the city. Clearly, Tucsonans had followed Kimball's advice. All these covenants included specific racial exclusions, such as "restricted to whites," "restricted against other than whites," or "restricted against 'persons of African, Mongolian, or Mexican descent,'" designed to establish racial boundaries in Tucson and to keep them intact.[48]

By 1960, restrictions had become less stringent. James Officer observed that there were at "least a few Mexican Americans residing in all parts of Tucson, including the most exclusive subdivisions within the city limits." Nevertheless, his study "conclusively" determined that "Mexicans in Tucson in 1959–60 were still generally separated, in terms of residence, from Anglos."[49]

Suburbs and Shopping Centers

In the 1960s, throughout the United States, suburbia represented the ideal place to live: downtown areas were no longer expected to house people.[50] Suburbanization, writes historian Eric Avila, is "a mode of urbanization in which cities extend outward rather than upward to accommodate the spatial appetites of home owners, retailers, and industrialists. [This process] reached a pinnacle in the years between 1945 and 1975,"[51] fueled by consumer culture and the media. Although tucsonenses had radios, they still were not fully integrated into the mainstream consumer culture. Panoramic photographs of la calle and its adjacent neighborhoods taken in the 1960s indicate that most residents did not have access to the two main material items that lay at the core of the U.S. consumer-driven culture: automobiles and televisions.[52]

The idealization of suburbia as a symbol of prosperity also reflected Anglo middle- and working-class families' aspirations to maintain their own separate spaces away from people of color. In general, after World War II "white flighters" collectively considered poor and ethnic neighborhoods as "dangerous" spaces that needed to be "contained" in order to preserve the public good. Suburbanites also freely relinquished ethnic and kinship ties to older neighborhoods in exchange for a life surrounded by strangers in their idealized neighborhoods. Of particular importance to this study of urban renewal, postwar Americans coveted new things, particularly new consumer goods, houses, and neighborhood developments, all of which represented their newfound prosperity.[53]

Thomas J. Sugrue and Kenneth T. Jackson, authorities in the evolution of housing policies, have implicated the federal government's housing policies for encouraging ethnic separateness. Exclusionary polices became institutionalized in various housing programs that helped Anglo Americans move away from cities and create new lives as home owners in the suburbs. Both historians argue that after World War II the Federal Housing Administration and the Veterans Administration mortgage policies provided Anglo Americans access to the "good life" even as they restricted communities of color to deteriorating urban environments.[54] David Freund further argues that such policies "promoted restrictive zoning and created a flush new market for housing that required racial segregation, yet encouraged whites to believe that it was the free market, not racial prejudice or government policy, that set the rules of competition: that the exclusion of minorities was not about race per se but about the principles of real estate economics and home owners' rights to control their communities."[55]

The reality of a growing population that preferred suburban lifestyles led a group of downtown merchants who "saw that Tucson could be overwhelmed by mass 'suburbia' if a little preventive medicine wasn't justifiably administered" to form the Tucson Trade Bureau in 1954.[56] Two years later the bureau initiated the Ride and Shop Plan to encourage Tucsonans from the outlying areas, "especially housewives to shop downtown even though the family car had gone to work with [their] husband." The plan provided shoppers a free bus ride home from downtown upon obtaining the appropriate retail stamp on their tickets.[57]

"It's National Downtown Week," declared the *Tucson Daily Citizen* in October 1958. As for Tucson's downtown, the paper boasted, "Look out! It's moving! Growing, expanding and improving." Six large buildings had been built in that year alone. The J. C. Penney's, Walgreen's, and Woolworth's chains had also established new stores. A number of banks and land title buildings headquartered in the central business district. Cele Peterson had set up her fashion shop for upscale women, and Jácome's Department Store had acquired room to expand.[58] Among these upbeat announcements were early warnings that downtown needed to make itself attractive to a new breed of shoppers. In appealing to this new breed, promotional articles and advertisements simply ignored established customers and patterns of commerce. "We hope you'll enjoy this new look of your hometown," the *Tucson Daily Citizen* told newcomers in October 1958, "and when you're finished, maybe you'll want to mail it to a friend elsewhere."[59]

As noted in chapter 1, retail sales were an important activity in Tucson's downtown before urban renewal. The larger downtown department stores were located a few blocks north of Congress on "retail row" near Pennington and Stone.[60] Unlike the businesses in la calle, all escaped urban renewal. Being so close to each other may have heightened competition, but all benefited from having the same customers. In fact, J. C. Penney's and Jácome's had contracted for long-term leases from Harold Steinfeld, who owned their properties. With the exception of J. C. Penney's, these department stores had evolved from more modest beginnings. Steinfeld's Department Store, which opened its doors in 1906, was one of the first businesses to draw commerce to the north side of downtown.[61] The Jácome family had operated their downtown department store, which started out as La Bonanza, for decades.[62] Jacob Levy, who operated a store in nearby Douglas, had established a Tucson branch in 1946.[63] Not coincidentally, these local enterprises, with which many Tucsonans deeply identified, supported and promoted the urban renewal agenda.

In 1961, El Con Mall became Tucson's first indoor, air-conditioned shopping mall, located some three miles away from downtown.[64] In 1965, the national chain Sears, Roebuck and Company set the decentralization trend for Tucson when it moved from its downtown store, established in 1928, to what then constituted the extreme eastern edge of the city on Broadway just west of Wilmot.[65] The area incorporated abundant parking and became known as Sears Park.[66] Speaking in general terms, architectural historian Richard Longstreth describes the shopping center as "more than a place of convenience; it served as a destination and as a focus of activity in the fast-growing suburban landscape. These new complexes were also distinctive in their physical presence, highly individualistic in character, possessing memorable imagery and configurations that set them apart from most commercial development in city centers and outlying districts alike."[67]

Large merchants and city planners reacted to suburbanization not by enhancing the unique urban experience that downtown offered but by making every effort to imitate suburban malls.[68] Cognizant of the advantages that covered, indoor malls provided, especially during the hot summer months, in 1958 the *Tucson Daily Citizen* reported on plans for a geodesic dome to cover areas of downtown. The paper predicted that "'Let me off at the geodesic dome,' rather than 'Let me off downtown,'" would enhance the downtown experience for future shoppers.[69] "Presently downtown has the biggest shopping center in the entire Southwest," declared Harold Steinfeld in 1960, "comprising . . . five large department stores, a dozen or more fine specialty shops, and all the prominent chains, variety and drug stores—all within one block's walking distance in any one direction."[70] In promoting downtown as a huge shopping center, Steinfeld emphasized the area north of Congress and excluded la calle's smaller retailers and ethnic specialty shops.

As it did for cities that turned to urban renewal throughout the United States, the suburban shopping center became the "literal model" for rebuilding Tucson's downtown. As Jeff Hardick has observed, "Take the elements that give 'going downtown' its magnetic attraction—the lights, the variety, color, and even the crowds; at the same time eliminate the noise, dirt and chaos, replacing them with art, landscaping, attractively paved streets, and you have America's newest institution, the suburban shopping center."[71] The goal of recasting Tucson's downtown area into a suburban mall took priority over appreciating and promoting the commercial energies and vigor that sustained it and gave it life.

In 1958, Tucson had already outlined, and the federal government had approved, an urban renewal plan that promised to "return a huge square of land in the downtown area to full, active use" and to rebuild it to "maximum use and value." The plan encompassed 360 acres, and City Manager Porter Homer called it one of the largest plans in the country.[72]

It aimed to close Congress to traffic and, through landscaping, to make the street "gay and cheerful." The plan included two sidewalk cafes, a play area for children, and a pedestrian mall to give downtown a "suburban look." Congress Street would be transformed into a pedestrian park with continuous canopies in front of stores, fountains, and floodlights for evening business. "This is the Tucson of the future. It will come sooner than you think," predicted architect Russell Hastings. "You wouldn't know the place."[73]

The same ideological goals that sustained and encouraged suburbanization also sanctioned urban renewal. Eric Avila makes a distinct connection between the cultural ideals of urban planners and promoters and those of their suburban counterparts: "Their efforts in implementing homogeneous, uniform spaces within the parameters of downtown and . . . obliterat[ing] the existing spaces of complexity and diversity reflected the same principles that informed the design and construction of [suburban] communities [and] the cultural institutions that sustained their quality of life: shopping malls, theme parks, and freeways."[74] Although never adopted due to its overly ambitious goals and the lack of support among the city's voters for the public housing it required, the 1958 plan provides insight into the evolving ideology and goals of urban renewal in Tucson.

At the helm of the campaign to persuade voters to approve the Pueblo Center Redevelopment Project stood prominent realtor, shopping center developer, and tourism promoter Roy P. Drachman, who was completing work on Campbell Plaza in 1960, the city's largest shopping complex at the time. The new sixteen-acre landscaped center offered air-conditioned sidewalks and promised an "open feeling . . . [and] unified design . . . as well as a more comfortable atmosphere and inducement to leisurely shopping."[75] By then, Drachman and his partner, Del E. Webb, who owned a construction company, had become well known for building shopping malls in the suburbs.

With the campaign's electoral success in March 1966, the urban renewal tide in Tucson would never ebb. But it had to rise more than once before the city could claim renewal had brought "art and culture" and dealt with the downtown "slums." Dismissing social and cultural environments that did not match the idealized images of suburbia, civic leaders and planners paid little or no heed to the emotional attachment that some tucsonenses felt to their old ways, homes, and neighborhoods. Indeed, mainstream society in Tucson looked with suspicion upon those who did not actively seek or desire life in the suburbs but preferred instead to live in ethnic enclaves. Which is not to say that Anglos encouraged people of color to move into their suburban neighborhoods. Far from it. Restrictive covenants and federal government mortgage policies served to keep Mexican Americans on "their side of tracks." Urban renewal provided a means for a few Anglo Americans to control the urban core's social and physical environment. Starting with the Ride and Shop, downtown revitalization strove to convert suburbanites into loyal downtown patrons. Urban renewal planners, absorbed as they were with designing an idealized place for tourists and fictitious shoppers, simply ignored the dynamics that had brought life and commercial success to the downtown area.

Selling Tucson: Rewriting History and Recasting Place

> It [la calle] would have made a fantastic place. Tourists would
> have flocked there like flies because they knew it wasn't phony,
> you know. It was the real thing.
> —Henry García, June 1987[1]

The statehood debates had informed Arizonans that race mattered.
Major cities throughout the state reacted to national perceptions of ethnic Otherness that might discourage visitors and investors.[2] An examination of literature scripted and distributed by official booster groups
in Tucson reveals efforts to diminish, cloak, or distort the presence of
Mexican people and the Mexican past in order to attract tourists, investors, and new residents to the city.[3] Cumulatively, the public celebrations,
writings, speeches, images, fundraising goals, and narratives featured in
the promotional materials of these groups provide insight into the cultural paradigms that framed the boosters' pursuit of economic goals and
urban development.[4] (Tucson's tourist economy is discussed in greater
detail in chapter 4.)

This chapter surveys an imaginary space crafted for tourists. It explores
the mythical landscapes and accompanying narratives of the Anglo fantasy heritage—those calibrated and intentionally distorted or exagger-
ated to advance perceptions of Tucson as an Anglo place and to market
a civic identity based on modernity and whiteness. Promoting the Anglo
fantasy heritage situates some historical contributions front and center
while marginalizing or excluding others.[5] In Tucson, booster organizations responded by manufacturing myths about Tucson's past and present that tourists and other outsiders found alluring. But, in time, these
invented representations morphed into "truth" narratives. They became
powerful forces with dire consequences for the city's people, its economy,
and the neighborhoods downtown when booster organizations acted to
make the imagined a reality. When they did, those who held the power

to manipulate images also held the power to advance their perceptions of space and race (see fig. 3.1).

The boosters' pictorial representations and textual narratives reveal subtle, complicated ways of reenvisioning Tucson as a tourist destination. The absence of tucsonenses in these materials—and of narratives that speak to their historical contributions—implied that they did not exist in the actual landscape. But, as discussed in the previous chapter, even though their economic power and social stature had declined, tucsonenses remained highly visible.

Ethnic Denigration

In 1864, journalist J. Ross Browne described Tucson as "a city of mud-boxes, dingy and dilapidated, cracked and baked into a composite of dust and filth . . . baked and dried Mexicans, sore-backed burros, coyote dogs and terra-cotta children." Indeed, he declared, the town was "infested with the refuse population of Sonora—the most faithless and abandoned race, perhaps, on the face of the earth."[6] Typical of travel journalists, Browne embellished his observations to satisfy eastern audiences, who craved stories that centered on the taming of the exotic and dangerous West. Some of the "features" Browne so unflinchingly exposed would reemerge in the statehood debates in pronouncements that Mexican people were simply incapable of becoming "worthy citizens and Americans."

Such scathing assessments cast an enduring shadow on the town that was home to the largest and most visible Mexican American population in Arizona. In 1881, writing on behalf of an early real estate consortium in Tucson, C.M.K. Paulison protested the "excessive ignorance" of citizens in the "older" states who remained ignorant of Arizona's resources and capabilities and who had seen "only the dark side of the picture."[7] Citing federal censuses of the territory, he proclaimed that the "progressive American element" had increased 1,000 percent between 1870 and 1880 and its powerful presence now "entitled" Arizona to admission into the United States.[8]

According to historian Michael F. Logan, "Tucson's Mexican character as well as its geographical location [too close to Mexico] became issues in the political debate over placement of the territorial capital."[9] In 1864, that honor went to relatively small Anglo populated and dominated Prescott, although three years later political maneuvering would

Tucson in Civil War Days was comprised of a few adobe buildings standing between the cacti. There were no pavements, only a few wooden sidewalks. The same area, viewed from "A" Mountain today reveals a modern city, with monumental buildings, elegant homes and good landscaping.

Figure 3.1. This Chamber of Commerce production compared the "Mexican Village" set at Old Tucson, a movie studio near Tucson, to a "modern city with monumental buildings, elegant homes and good landscaping." Versions of the past that portrayed isolated remnants of Tucson's past as "a few adobe buildings standing between the cacti" also implied that the people who once inhabited the area had disappeared. (Tucson Chamber of Commerce, *Welcome Visitor* [1950–51], 2)

convince lawmakers to move the capital to Tucson, the only town of any economic and demographic significance in Arizona Territory.[10]

In contrast to Tucson, Phoenix did not emerge from a Mexican or Spanish past and thus never had to "rehabilitate" its image. Indeed, in the words of historian Bradford Luckingham, Phoenix "was run by Anglos for Anglos" ever since its founding in 1868.[11] Incorporated as a city in 1881, it became the territorial capital in 1889 and the state capital upon Arizona's admission to the Union in 1912, surpassing Tucson in both population and industry by 1920. It came to represent the boomtown model of growth, industry, and modernity in Arizona.

Many factors led to Phoenix overtaking Tucson, although the path was by no means direct.[12] Tucson had many early economic advantages. The Southern Pacific Railroad had connected Tucson to the West and East Coast in the 1880s while a major railroad would not connect Phoenix to the rest of the nation until 1926.[13] As early as 1891, however, Phoenix declared itself a modern American town, claiming the coveted mantle associated with Anglo settlement: "Here are none of the sleepy, semi-Mexican features of the more ancient towns of the Southwest."[14]

Meanwhile, ambitious local promoters in Tucson understood the "civilizing" influences associated with a large population of Anglo American residents. They recognized the promise of positive recognition that such a population would bring their city in the "expanding nation."[15] As soon as the aesthetics and "social attractions" of the older states became available to Tucsonans, C.M.K. Paulison predicted the arrival of "a permanent population of a class of people who would greatly accelerate its growth in all the elements of a refined Christian civilization."[16] With this growth dynamic in mind, on February 24, 1896, local businessmen formed the Chamber of Commerce.[17] This marked the appearance of the first organization in the city that focused on selling Tucson to outsiders. In its promotional materials, the chamber would construct various alluring representations of Tucson in the years to come. Once tourists visited, it reasoned, the city's climate, economy, and social atmosphere would persuade them to relocate there.

The Sunshine Club

As far back as the late nineteenth century, local boosters had succeeded in selling the city as an ideal place to battle tuberculosis.[18] A Chamber of

Commerce brochure proclaimed Tucson a "clean" city—free of "contamination."[19] In the early 1920s, however, local tourism promoters sought to broaden Tucson's appeal and "shed Tucson's popular image as a place for sick people to recuperate and instead promoted the city as a healthy place for people, sick or well, to live."[20]

When the Tucson Chamber of Commerce members learned that Phoenix's population had surpassed Tucson's by nearly half in 1920, they did not take the news lightly.[21] No longer could the business community refer to Tucson as "the metropolis of Arizona."[22] The Chamber of Commerce and civic boosters "were determined that Tucson should again become the premier city in Arizona. But how?"[23] Tourism became the solution. In 1922, business elites formed a new organization, separate from the Chamber of Commerce and dedicated solely to attracting tourists: the Tucson Sunshine-Climate Club.[24] Coincidentally, an important marketing strategy emerged at this time in U.S. history. According to Michael Kammen, "shrewd Western entrepreneurs recognized commercial potential in a Waning-of-the-West Syndrome. . . . The West began to promote the Wild West when it recognized that the real thing was just about gone."[25]

Realtors, mining and banking executives, physicians, owners of construction companies and construction materials sales agents, as well as the managers and owners of larger department and drugstores made up the Sunshine Club's officers and board of directors in the 1920s.[26] From the club's inception and in decades to come, the same prominent business and civic leaders would be members of both the Sunshine Club and the Chamber of Commerce. But where the Chamber of Commerce also tried to bring industry and commerce to Tucson, the Sunshine Club concentrated solely on tourism.

By 1930, the Sunshine Club was boasting that it had attracted countless tourists, at least 7,000 of whom had decided to make Tucson their permanent home.[27] National advertising agendas concentrated on reaching audiences who subscribed to *National Geographic*, *Outlook*, and the *Ladies Home Journal*. City government and businesses that benefited from tourism paid for advertisements designed to persuade people in the "older states" to make Tucson their tourist destination.[28] Although the Chamber of Commerce and Sunshine Club promotional magazines and booklets shared many of the same photographs and narratives, the formation of the Sunshine Club marked a significant turning point in Tucson's history: now the city's leaders would favor tourism at the expense of more diverse industries.

Erasing the Mexican Past

Most of promotional materials produced by the two principal booster organizations simply ignored Tucson's Mexican past, asking readers instead "to think of those days when Indian and Spaniard were against each other for supremacy . . . and how later the Indian, Spaniard and Anglo Saxon formed a triangle of opposing forces."[29] Nor did the Mexican people and the Mexican era receive much, if any, attention in Arizona history books, which celebrated Anglo accomplishments and either portrayed Mexican people as antagonists or ignored them altogether.[30] These narratives were rarely contested in the historical record as evidenced in 1972 when, seeking to "find new ways to preserve and develop our history and culture," the University of Arizona compiled the *Twenty-First Arizona Town Hall on Arizona's Heritage—Today and Tomorrow*. That ninety-seven influential lawyers, business and civic leaders, teachers, and history professionals from throughout the state came together to approve the final 175 pages of text makes this collaborative effort notable. The two paragraphs describing "Mexican Arizona" highlight "political chaos" and "economic stagnation" as well as a lack of direction and "progress" in the region. Within these paragraphs, Anglo American trappers receive the most attention, with trappers James O. Pattie and Ewing Young being the only individuals mentioned by name. The remainder of the text focuses on "great" Anglo American men and early historic preservation efforts.[31] Indeed, well into the 1980s historical works would accentuate the same "triangle" of Indians, Spanish, and Anglos in their accounts of Tucson's history.

Contrary to most representations of Tucson in the Mexican period, which portray it as stagnant, frozen in time, and awaiting the arrival of Anglo Americans, the town had a social, political, and economic vitality all its own under Mexican rule. Tucsonenses elected their first mayor, José de León, in 1824 and thanks to their resourcefulness, the town's presidio, strategically located on Mexico's northern frontier, persevered despite decreased support in provisions and military equipment from the newly established Mexican government. The settlement linked Alta California to Sonora, establishing crucial trade networks that Anglo

Americans would exploit to such great effect.[32] Tucson also served as a rest and resupply stop for both Mexican and U.S. travelers in this isolated region.[33] The many battles this greatly outnumbered community fought against the Apaches mark the Mexican period as the most perilous in the city's history. The military campaigns launched by tucsonense commanders and the alliances they forged with nearby Indian communities would play a vital role in making future Anglo settlement possible.[34]

Instead of identifying it as a transition from the Spanish to the American period, many historians view the Mexican period as an interlude or hiatus between the two.[35] Such an approach ignores the powerful influence of Mexican Independence and the rise of the new republic, which gave tucsonenses a sense of national and ethnic identity. In the shared and preferred version of history, Tucson finally "awakens" with the arrival of the Southern Pacific Railroad, undergoing a "metamorphosis" when "energetic businessmen saw the golden opportunities presented by this new western city."[36]

The escapades of Anglo mountain men, trappers, miners, and various westward expeditions dominated the historiography of early Arizona. These portrayals left "Mexico and Mexicans, to whom the stage still belonged, to serve as the backdrop," writes historian David J. Weber. "Lost between the Spanish and American periods," he goes on to say, "the Mexican interlude has become something of a dark age in the historiography of the Southwest, even though it represented a turning point for both the United States and Mexico."[37]

Attempting to dispel historical "lies" and "myths" about the region in his 1989 book *Hispanic Arizona, 1536–1856*, James E. Officer traces many of these to Hubert Howe Bancroft's 1889 history of the region, which served to promote Anglo achievements and dominance.[38] Subsequent historians continued to use Bancroft's work as the authoritative standard instead of referring to relevant Spanish and Mexican documents. According to Officer, historians preferred to portray Mexican people as "passive bystanders in the development of the frontier, as rustic immigrants, or as treacherous *bandidos* and, later, as potentially dangerous revolutionaries."[39]

The history presented in the 1965 official city report on the Pueblo Center Redevelopment Project testifies to the pervasiveness and power of these exclusionary narratives:

The area is the oldest continually inhabited community in the United States. Its original inhabitants lived in Indian Pueblos. In the late 1600s, Spanish Missions were established along the Santa Cruz River. In the late 1800s, white settlers arrived in the area and a military garrison was established during the Civil War. After the arrival of the railroad, in 1880, the community grew as the headquarters for ranching activities in Southern Arizona, and as a gateway to Northern Mexico.[40]

The report, commissioned and approved by local government, goes on to mention links with the Confederacy but has not a single word to say about Tucson's Mexican past, between 1823 and 1856.

The Spanish Fantasy Heritage

A 1906 Chamber of Commerce pamphlet described the tucsonense community as "the older section of town, where the Mexicans and Spanish inhabitants still retain the romantic customs of their native lands, showing a glimpse of medieval Spain in the heart of a busy, throbbing American city."[41] Here, as in other local promotional materials, are threads of what Carey McWilliams has called the "Spanish fantasy heritage" so popular in Southern California at the turn of the century.[42] The Spanish missions, historian Phoebe Kropp argues, represented the first outposts of civilization to Anglos, who "imagined the missions as an endorsement of American conquest, linking California past and present to the nation through a common celebration of progress. They imagined the padres not just as heroes but as patriots."[43]

The fantasy heritage found expression in the Spanish colonial revival architecture that typifies the Pima County Courthouse—built in 1928 and designed by Roy W. Place upon his arrival from San Diego—and in the various Spanish mission styles of other structures, such as the Arizona Inn, built in 1930. In the late 1920s, the new suburbs of El Encanto Estates and Colonia Solano emerged on the east side of town, giving upper-class residents the opportunity, by living in "civilized," commodious Spanish-mission-style houses, to place themselves on a continuum with the early padres.[44]

Chamber of Commerce and Sunshine Club publications sometimes expressed a longing for the bygone Spanish colonial period. The fantasy of the "old Spanish influence of the sixteenth century," complete with "brave and intrepid padres . . . carrying the cross of Christianity wherever adventure or ambition led their followers," appealed to Anglos who liked to think of themselves as contemporary conquistadors.[45] It is no accident that in a local contest to name one of the first major hotels, "El Conquistador" won out.

Pressing this narrative of the distant Spanish colonial past provided tourist promoters a means to avoid representations that linked Tucson to its more recent Mexican one. The rare references to the city's Mexican people, most appearing after World War II, portrayed them as quaint, colorful, and invested in fiestas that visitors could take part in (see fig. 3.2). By referring to Tucson's Mexican American barrios and people as "Spanish," boosters attempted to whiten the city's tucsonenses for outside consumption and to deflect attention from the city's Mexican influences. Indeed, Phoebe Kropp argues, such references were clearly grounded "in conceptions of race." They represented "a celebration of Anglo and American conquest. The historical narrative it implied applauded not only previous territorial triumphs but also confirmed Anglos' regional supremacy in the present and made Mexican and Indian people only of the past."[46]

On the other hand, Tucsonans themselves had little practical enthusiasm in the 1920s for Tucson's Spanish colonial past. Thus, in 1922, when Charles Lummis from Los Angeles, the main framer and promoter of the Spanish fantasy heritage, urged locals to preserve missions and other structures that embodied the "romantic" Spanish past, no one heeded his advice. The old Convento fell into ruins, and the nearby San Xavier Mission into serious disrepair. Nor did their enthusiasm for preserving that past grow by much in the coming decades. In 1960 the Arizona Historical Society's journal reported that Lummis's "plea was then premature" but that now, nearly forty years later, its time had come. The society's statewide Committee for the Preservation and Restoration of Historical Sites was ready to heed Lummis's advice.[47] It did so on its own terms, however. The committee moved to restore Fort Lowell, a monument to Anglo American occupation, "headquarters of the Army during the Apache wars and the social hub of old Tucson."[48] Whatever the appeal of the Spanish fantasy heritage as a promotional device to attract tourists or to sell upscale houses, the drive to showcase a distinctive Anglo American civic identity definitively trumped any desire to preserve physical signs of Tucson's more distant Spanish past.

FIESTAS AND SIESTAS

Mexican Fiestas are held each Fall and Spring at La Placita in downtown Tucson. They include music, dancing and booths for the purchase of Mexican delicacies.

Figure 3.2. A rare photograph of Mexican Americans featured in Chamber of Commerce promotional materials. (Tucson Chamber of Commerce, *Welcome Visitor* [1955–56], 27)

The Old Pueblo

In the latter half of the nineteenth century, boosters increasingly referred to Tucson as the Old Pueblo in their promotional materials, a term tucsonenses and other Spanish speakers understood to mean simply "old town." As used by boosters, however, "Old Pueblo" served to market the city in the "older states" by reminding tourists of Tucson's long history—without also reminding them of its Spanish or Mexican past.

When historian Michael F. Logan writes that, as "promoters of tourism began marketing the local Hispanic culture, Tucson became 'The Old Pueblo,'"[49] he misses the larger implications of this marketing strategy. Local tourist promoters recognized that "Old Pueblo" conjured up different—*non*-Hispanic—meanings outside the U.S. Southwest. By mid-century, "pueblo" had evolved to mean an Indian village in the United States.[50] As discussed later in this chapter, promoting Tucson as an old *Indian* village enhanced the imagery associated with the Anglo fantasy heritage, with its uncomplicated versions of cowboys and Indians in an archetypical Wild West setting. As the Sunshine Club pointedly explained, "Tucson . . . wears with pride and distinction its sobriquet the 'the Old Pueblo'. It was an ancient Indian village long before the Pilgrims arrived in Plymouth Rock."[51]

Appropriating this nickname also tapped into the desire of national audiences to see Native Americans and old Indian ruins. In 1958, Robert E. Waugh found that tourists sought to engage with, see, and simply find Indians present in their western experiences. To uncover vacationers' motivations for visiting certain sites, Waugh conducted a series of interviews. The typical vacationer, his study concluded, "wants to see something he conceives of as *The West*. Of course, this is an over-simplification. No adman can do anything with a picture of some part of Arizona carrying such a brief and pointed copy as 'This is the West. Come on out!'" Using the archetypal and idealized two-child family as a model, Waugh determined that mothers mostly wanted to see the Grand Canyon; fathers had a "nagging interest in the prehistoric," meaning Native American archaeological ruins; and children wanted "above all else to see Indians." Young people's exposure to cowboys and Indians through movies, television, and books had sparked desires to see the "real" West (see fig. 3.3).[52]

The Gateway to Old Mexico

Historian Gilbert G. González highlights the role of writers in characterizing Mexico and Mexican people to U.S. readers from as early as 1880:

> The numerous authors' narratives read as if they came off an industrial production line, molded by a seemingly mystical template that guided them and controlled their pens. . . . Words and photographs combined to create images and draw conclusions—at best superficial and for the most part demeaning—of Mexico that the American audience would easily grasp. . . . Mexicans of the poorer classes, the vast majority of Mexico's population, were described as a rather

YOU STILL CAN SEE THIS IN ARIZONA

Figure 3.3. Luring tourists with Indians. (Tucson Chamber of Commerce, *Welcome Visitor* [1938–39], 20.

uncivilized species—dirty, unkempt, immoral, diseased, lazy and unambitious. . . . Derogatory images of Mexico and Mexicans took on a life of their own and became the conventional wisdom regarding qualities characteristic of the average Mexican.[53]

The negative perceptions disseminated by these writers, and by the various national and state debates highlighted above, became inscribed in the national consciousness and internalized as factual. In time, González argues, these perceptions were institutionalized into public policy, history, and educational institutions.[54]

Although promotional literature frequently referred to Tucson as "the gateway to Old Mexico," advertisements were careful to situate the city as unconditionally American, an Anglo place free of any Mexican influences. In their promotional materials, boosters had no problem calling Mexico the "Land of Mañana."[55] They committed themselves to the concept of a "gateway" because it clearly placed Tucson on the U.S. side of

IN THE OLD SPANISH QUARTER, NOGALES, SONORA

Tucson the Gateway to the Wonderful West Coast of Mexico

Figure 3.4. The gateway to Mexico. (Tucson Chamber of Commerce, *Welcome Visitor* [1935–36], 12)

the "gate" while also heightening the distinction between their modern city and Old Mexico (fig. 3.4).

Late in the nineteenth century, cultural productions increasingly began to use the term "Old Mexico." Image makers' investment in highlighting Tucson's modernity relied on oppositional and "Othered" representations of Mexico. To this day, many of Tucson's tourist materials invoke the imagery of Old Mexico, inviting visitors to take a sixty-mile trip to a different and foreign culture.[56] Most tourist brochures include at least one photograph of mariachis, Mexican dancers, or both. These portrayals stand, and stood, in stark contrast to actual Mexican entertainment and culture that tourists could encounter in la calle and throughout the city. The fact that the City of Tucson Planning Department often used "Old Mexico" on the maps it created and developed speaks to the pervasive efforts to highlight American modernity.

As local boosters tried to conceal cultural influences in Tucson that could be perceived as foreign, they also understood that the city's proximity to Mexico could be used to enhance the city's desirability as a tourist destination. The article "Everybody's Dudin' It" in the 1935–36 edition of *Welcome Visitor* emphasized the fun and adventure tourists could have once they crossed the border by stating, "The land along the Border will invite you to include a visit to a foreign country during your vacation."[57]

By the 1940s, however, most Anglo Americans considered Mexico not only backward but also a more violent and less civilized nation. For close to three decades, all they had read or heard about the Mexican people centered on a nation in disarray following the unrestrained calamity of the Mexican Revolution.[58] Additionally, most easterners who arrived in Tucson had never seen, much less had personal contact with, Mexican Americans. Newly arrived Anglo Americans in Tucson, reported John Kestner Goodman, felt uncomfortable even being near tucsonenses.[59]

Although Mexican Americans worked for lower wages, Anglo Americans were often reluctant to employ them. According to the Arizona State Employment Service, in the early 1940s Mexican American domestics received between five and six dollars a week, in contrast to Anglo American domestics, who earned between five and fifteen dollars, and African Americans, whose wages ranged from seven to fifteen dollars weekly.[60] Goodman notes that potential Anglo American employers held many misconceptions and stereotypes regarding Mexican American domestics:

> They do not know how to answer a telephone. They are stubborn and unwilling to learn new ways of doing household tasks, and this makes them hard to get along with. Their cooking is too "hot" for the Anglo palate; they are inclined to sloppiness in the kitchen. They often do not understand hygienic methods of food preparation, and the use of modern equipment, nor do they make any attempt to understand them. Therefore, they usually fall into the lowest paid jobs of household cleaners and manual labor as they are suited for little else.[61]

On the eve of urban renewal in 1964, James Officer found that, overall, tucsonenses "lagged behind the Anglos (and even behind other less privileged minorities) in educational attainment, enjoyed substantially lower median incomes, and mingled socially with Anglos to a remarkably limited degree."[62]

Characterizations of Mexicans as dangerous, backward, poor, and uneducated had become widely accepted as facts among many Anglo Tucsonans well before 1965. Those who promoted and sanctioned urban renewal argued that poverty and poverty-blighted areas were the principal obstacles to progress, but they assigned blame for these to the poor themselves. "To the majority of white observers," writes historian Thomas J. Sugrue, "visible poverty, overcrowding, and deteriorating houses were signs of individual and moral deficiencies, not manifestations of structural inequities."[63] John Goodman identified the root cause of this "increased amount of prejudice" as "the immigration of easterners, ignorant of Mexican people, their ways, their history, and their original ownership of Tucson."[64]

To allay any misgivings outsiders might have about their city's "Mexicans," local boosters focused on promoting Tucson as a cultured place. They promised tourists courteous service and properly prepared meals.[65] Chamber of Commerce literature highlighted Anglo American refinement and exciting adventures for Anglo cultural appetites. Boosters offered outsiders the opportunity to experience a new and Western way of life in Tucson (see fig. 3.5).[66]

The Anglo Fantasy Heritage

Dime novels in the late nineteenth century and early silent films that made heroes of G. M. "Bronco Billy" Anderson and Tom Mix had fueled popular infatuation with the West.[67] As a whole, the nation remained captivated by this type of imagery well into the 1970s. According to historian John Mack Faragher, "In the years following World War II, Westerns remained the most popular American story form. Western paperbacks flew off the racks at the rate of thirty-five million copies a year, and Western movies remained popular. From 1945 through the mid-1960s, Hollywood studios produced an average of seventy-five Western pictures each year, a quarter of all films released. Westerns also dominated television programming during the 1950s and 1960s. In 1958, for example, twenty-eight prime-time Westerns provided more than seventeen hours of gunplay each week."[68]

Popular novelist Harold Bell Wright helped promote the Western genre and ignited a specific interest in Tucson. His book *The Mine with the Iron Door*, released in 1923, attracted a large number of readers and soon found its way into film.[69] As historian Michael F. Logan observes, "Tucson's business leaders understood that the city derived great benefit from its association with popular novels and movies, and Wright's novels were central to the development of Tucson's image as a western

Figure 3.5. Promoting Tucson's "Way of Life". (Tucson Chamber of Commerce, *Tucson: A City, an Opportunity, a Way of Life*, [1958] n.p.)

locale."[70] Wright, who had moved to Tucson in 1919 and had formed a strong alliance with the local elite, dedicated his book to his friends in the "Old Pueblo."[71]

As the twentieth century progressed, local boosters promoted a picturesque and rugged Western lifestyle that prized Anglo American cultural attributes. Sunshine Club correspondence reveals a fastidious attention to minor details to ensure the success of their publications. Letters to and from their Los Angeles consultants discuss, for example, whether a girl in a promotional drawing needed to look more like an easterner upon her arrival in Tucson and whether she should wear a turbanlike headdress to accentuate her donning a cowboy hat soon thereafter.[72] The Sunshine Club also sought to disseminate images that made Tucson distinct from Florida and California resorts.[73] These promotional materials advanced versions of the past wherein Anglo Americans actively carved a place for themselves against tremendous odds. Boosters invited newcomers to experience the pride they would gain from the venturesome Western excursions that Tucson offered. Just as Anglo Americans had risked their lives at the battle of the Alamo, according to the locally scripted past, Anglos in Southern Arizona had single-handedly overpowered Indians and the environment. The campaign to highlight these heroic efforts lay at the core of the boosters' reluctance to recognize Mexican contributions to the area's development, which clearly established that the landscape Anglos first encountered was far from empty.

By mid-century, boosters were marketing a mix of winter sunshine and a mythical cowboy past. This reified vision made Tucson and the West one and indistinguishable. At dude and guest ranches, visitors "enacted" scenes of hardship and physical prowess similar to those associated with the cowboys.[74] As a testament to the power of this experience, the number of dude ranches in the Tucson area rose from two in 1923 to more than forty by 1938.[75] Celebrities and others who could afford to do so flocked to the "Dude Ranch Capital of the World."[76]

In the 1950s, however, recognizing that "the average person . . . would be content to let someone else do the bulldoggin' and ride the wild-eyed bronc' for them," boosters offered an alternative: people could enjoy the "cowboy life on a Dude Ranch without suffering too great a change from the comforts of ordinary life." At guest ranches, tourists could have it all: "cowboy" experiences as well as comfort and luxury.[77]

City boosters' single-minded concern with tourism added yet another celebratory layer to Tucson's Anglo fantasy heritage. The creation of La Fiesta de los Vaqueros, more often referred to as the Festival of Cowboys or the Tucson Rodeo, which would soon become a local tradition, stands as a powerful expression of the boosters' drive to recast Tucson as a cow town.[78] This public display of Western symbols and cowboy skills also stands as a telling example of manipulating history to serve contemporary commercial needs.[79] In 1924, the Arizona Polo Association (some of whose members also belonged to the Sunshine Club) led the drive to launch the Tucson Rodeo, brainchild of Leighton Kramer. Upon Kramer's death, La Fiesta de los Vaqueros came under the sponsorship of the Chamber of Commerce, which scheduled it for mid-February on the weekend closest to George Washington's Birthday, at the height of the tourist season.[80]

The lure of the rodeo proved to be a bonanza for the local economy. *Welcome Visitor* described Rodeo Week as a time when "cowboys, cow-girls and boss cowmen, Indians and 'Pale faces,' from everywhere gather in the 'Old Pueblo.'"[81] People from a variety of classes and from across the nation flocked to Tucson for the rodeo, which included Indian Days featuring dances performed by "real Indians." The limited availability of lodging became apparent when "motorcades filled with spectators and airplanes [full with passengers]" arrived in Tucson. Local schools, the University of Arizona, and government offices were closed on Thursday and Friday for the culmination of Rodeo Week festivities, which included a half-day parade. Local newspapers urged the local population to support this event because "what the Tournament of Roses is to Pasadena . . . the Annual Rodeo will be to Tucson, IF YOU DO YOUR BIT."[82]

The rodeo, which engaged local residents across class lines to promote and participate in a citywide experience, garnered significant support for the Anglo fantasy heritage. Rodeo Week festivities typified "growth machine" goals as "they encourage[ed] public celebrations and spectacles in which the locality name can be proudly advanced for the benefit of both locals and outsiders."[83]

Although absent from most of the representations used to sell Tucson and the rodeo, tucsonenses found many aspects of the Western heritage tremendously appealing. This is hardly a surprise in that Mexican people had shaped the cowboy way of life in the Southwest. "When the first Anglo settlers entered the region," writes Thomas Sheridan, "they ran their cattle, irrigated their crops, and extracted their ore in ways that had been refined over the course of the last two centuries by Hispanics in arid North America. Branding, roundups, cattle drives—all were aspects of the livestock industry learned by Anglos from Mexican ranchers. Even much of the western vocabulary reflected this Hispanic heritage—buckaroo (*vaquero*), lariat (*la reata*), chaps (*chaparreras*), dally (*dar la vuelta*)."[84] Indeed, the cowboy way of life had been one that many tucsonenses, and their ancestors, had experienced firsthand. Although tucsonenses would be classified as an urbanized population after 1930, many continued to wear *norteño* (northern Mexican cowboy-style) clothes, large belt buckles, and boots as a way of reaffirming their connection to their Sonoran roots.[85]

In 1939, Columbia Pictures established Old Tucson, the motion picture location and sound stage for the filming of *Arizona*. Although the company had announced its intention to "build a replica of the real Tucson of the 1860s," rather than recapturing the Sonoran architecture that prevailed south of Congress Street it designed a movie set that commemorated the Anglo fantasy heritage, incorporating one "Mexican Village" among the set's "many western streets."[86] As noted in chapter 2, the Tucson of 1870 was predominantly a Mexican village. The creators of Old Tucson, however, tapped into tourists' preferences. By 1960, the movie set had become the second largest attraction in the state, next to the Grand Canyon.[87]

Throughout the twentieth century, tourist boosters continued their campaigns to "rehabilitate" Tucson's image on the national stage by shaping and disseminating various forms of historical distortion that served to commodify the Western experience. By putting tourists first and foremost, the city's economy became almost entirely dependent on their dollars. The success of the boosters' tactics gave rise to a powerful tourist and pro-business alliance. This alliance, in turn, manufactured and marketed representations of Tucson that accentuated ethnic differences, promoted exclusion, distorted the character of the large tucsonense population downtown, and with the approval of fewer than 4 percent of the city's residents, made it all but completely disappear.

4

The Politics of Belonging and Exclusion

> It [La calle] was not declining [in 1967] but the city was sending
> out the message that they wanted to destroy it. The mayor called
> it "diseased." He said that "disease grew here." It was like they were
> calling us that!
>
> —Pedro Gonzales, November 10, 2007[1]

As we have seen, the tourist boosters actively promoted corporate illusions of Tucson as an Anglo gateway to Mexico, not a place of Mexican people and spaces. Yet, despite their persistent, elaborate, and multipronged efforts, these illusions often failed to displace reality. Lasting impressions of Tucson as a Mexican place managed to survive. James Officer recounts that, when he lived in Phoenix in 1944, "some of his friends from that community still viewed Tucson as 'mostly a Mexican' town."[2] At this time, tucsonenses made up almost a third of the city's population and were largely concentrated in the downtown area. No matter how hard boosters tried to conceal their presence in the imagined spaces of tourist pamphlets, brochures, and guides, tucsonenses remained strikingly visible on the actual streets of la calle.

Chapter 3 details the power of representations and texts to produce meanings that defined the city's spatial boundaries and civic identity. This chapter builds on that examination by analyzing the structural forces, particularly the political and economic forces, behind the ideology that drove tourist representations of the city. The powerful development coalition—realtors, bankers, architects, construction company, hotel, retail business, and restaurant owners, as well as pro-development city officials—charted an economic path for the city that relied predominantly on tourism and on perceptions of Tucson as an "attractive" place to live as well as visit.

Thus most of the key individuals and organizations that coordinated efforts to attract tourists also seized every chance to alter the city's physical landscape and to gain greater control over its spatial organization. In 1966, the Anglo fantasy heritage, which left little room for competing histories, proved a formidable ideological force: with the approval of nearly 60 percent of those voting (although less than one-fifth of all "eligible" voters), urban developers succeeded in erasing eighty acres of visible, tangible evidence of a Mexican past.[3]

The economic, political, and social system rewarded those who sought to bring "progress" to Tucson. With the major newspapers fully on board, dissenting voices had few opportunities to express their dissatisfaction with the pro-growth and anti-industry policies pursued by tourism boosters and urban developers alike. Reminiscent of early political debates, the campaign to convince voters to approve the urban renewal agenda reveals how the political system at the local, state, and federal levels defined the tucsonenses of la calle as a transient population, not "American" enough to merit equal social services and inclusion in the city's present and so far outside the developers' idealized suburban vision of Tucson as not to merit inclusion in plans for the city's future.

Racializing Space

In a time when tourism generated most of the city's revenues, la calle and its people defied imaginary tourist representations. Although the gangster story line in the 1936 film *Gay Desperado* takes place in Mexico, Hollywood filmmakers never had to leave the United States to find a realistic setting for their Mexican scenes. South Meyer Avenue in Tucson so closely resembled a Sonoran town there was no need for alteration (see fig. 4.1).[4]

Earlier, in a 1931 article, the *Tucson Daily Citizen* had described how la calle, only steps away from the central business district, struck the typical outsider:

> one experiences the same sensations that are felt when crossing the International line at Nogales. Geographically we may be still in the United States; but in every sight and sound and every varied impression we're in the heart of old Mexico. As we proceed down this bizarre old world *rialto* we realize that we have left the land of the hot dog for the land of the *chile con carne*; the land of the go-getter for the land of *mañana*. . . . And to think that America is up there, a block away on Congress Street.[5]

Figure 4.1. The filming of *Gay Desperado* on Meyer Avenue, circa 1936. (Courtesy Arizona Historical Society, Tucson, AHS photo no. 52275)

In their promotional materials, Chamber of Commerce boosters featured portrayals of "quaint" places on the southern side of the U.S.–Mexico border, but "Old Mexico" in the center of Tucson presented a marketing problem. Appearances mattered in a city heavily invested in tourism, and such stark side-by-side contrasts provoked anxiety. In time, with the success of the local rodeo, displays and spectacles of white "modernity" with an added cowboy twist had become mandatory parts of the civic identity promoted by Tucson's boosters.

Architect Edward H. Nelson, an energetic advocate of urban renewal since the late 1950s, put the matter more bluntly in his 1966 response to an unfavorable editorial: "The industrialist who visits Tucson will have a bad impression of the city if he sees slums such as these so close to the downtown businesses."[6] Nelson clearly used "slums" to evoke a range of negative associations in the minds of his readers: poverty, crime, crowded, unsanitary conditions well below contemporary living standards.[7] Nelson's "slums" stood in distinct opposition to middle-class suburban ideals and the pro-development agenda. As urban sociologist Jan

Lin explains, "For decades the nemesis of city managers, ethnic places were perceived as undesirable districts of congestion, vice, and other social pathologies. From the interwar to the postwar period, they generally faced the wrecking ball. . . . These practices of developmental modernization and urban decentralization were coupled with the design aesthetic and planning ideology of modernism, which sought to raze deteriorated ethnic places in the name of cultural assimilation and progress."[8]

Urban renewal advocates, in Tucson as in other cities across the United States, relied on an ideological consensus to advance their agendas. Those in power did not need to use loaded racial language to enforce social and ethnic boundaries. Postwar zoning laws and planning directives had already done that.

In the early 1990s, geographer John Gourley reexamined coverage of urban renewal by Tucson's two major newspapers. He concluded that urban planners and developers, with the cooperation of newspaper writers and editors, unmistakably avoided discussing race even as they rallied support for implementation of a plan that targeted a large community of people of color. Pursuit of urban renewal relied on consensual racial silence and collective cultural understandings; when the plan talked about race, it did so indirectly, through inference and innuendo:

> The text rarely mentions that the Pueblo [the area targeted for urban renewal] is mainly Mexican, whereas the rest of Tucson is mainly Anglo or that it contains a significant proportion of the city's Blacks. . . . That Mexicans and Blacks are scarcely mentioned in 15 years of reporting on the Pueblo "as a problem" is strongly indicative that within the "Anglo community" there was a "situation" about which they did not speak, suggesting that there were underlying "tensions" that did not surface in the public debate.[9]

Using various qualitative measures, John Goodman had come to a similar conclusion in his 1942 study of Tucson. "Some Anglos," he found, "are ignorant of the fact they practice [racism], while others deny that they do, even though their actions prove otherwise. The fact is that prejudice against Mexicans does exist and is ever-growing is evident throughout almost every field of Mexican life."[10]

Boosting Tourism

As early as 1937, a Sunshine Club pamphlet revealed that the club's goals went well beyond inviting outsiders to make Tucson their tourist destination. It hoped to change the city's social fabric by "'pepping' up the town and bringing in new blood."[11] The club's advertising schemes appealed in no uncertain terms to moneyed Anglo Americans to make Tucson their home. Indeed, the club clearly implied, their mere presence or decision to make Tucson their destination had a moral dimension. In a message printed compliments of the Consolidated National Bank, the Sunshine Club promised newcomers: "The moment you enter our gates you are not a stranger, you are one of us. . . . If one wants friends he may have acquaintances at once among people of his own sort, whose tastes are his own."[12] In effect, the Sunshine Club marketed ethnotourism or a whites-only experience.[13] Not only did boosters manipulate images and silences, in targeting a particular class of people, they also embraced "race [as] a kind of social currency."[14]

The ideal tourist, according to the Chamber of Commerce and Sunshine Club, had already acquired wealth and had retirement in mind. As a local public official told urban planner Roy Kenneth Fleagle, the wealthy retired "require no schools and few services. They make a steady contribution to our economy. They live off their investments. If the stock market drops, they know it but it doesn't have any effect upon their spending power in the community. When a factory closes its doors, a lot of people and the local government are financially hurt. What Tucson needs is more wealthy retired."[15] Encouraging those from the upper classes to move to Tucson gained the strong support of banks, which hoped to serve the newly relocated in need of depositing cash, moving trust funds, and managing various other investments. To doubters who questioned tourism's contributions to the local economy and its importance as a stepping-stone to selective demographic growth, one prominent booster responded, "You ask, 'What are people going to do here for a living?' The answer is: 'The same thing they've been doing here for the last fifty years.' Working to augment the income they receive from 'back home' and/or finding a service business to get into."[16]

The single-minded, consuming effort to make tourism the city's primary industry would have dire consequences, however, for its entire population, economic infrastructure, and local hierarchies of power. In any number of ways, tourism in Tucson resembles what historian Hal

K. Rothman calls a "Devil's bargain." Looked on as a "panacea for the economic ills" of cities throughout the U.S. West, tourism failed to meet expectations. Rothman outlines the larger issues: tourism transforms places; it benefits elite groups to the exclusion of most others and "triggers a contest for the soul of a place." "As places acquire the cachet of desirability," he concludes, "they draw people and money; the redistribution of wealth, power, and status follows, complicating local arrangements."[17]

Boosters who manufactured images of Tucson as a Western, modern, cultured, and white place also changed the city's actual landscapes and traditional narratives. In the process, they changed Tucson's "soul." Despite grandiose promises of wide-reaching economic benefits, tourism enriched and empowered only a small segment of Tucson's society. Indeed, in Rothman's view, "tourism is the most colonial of colonial economies. . . . Locals become mirror images of themselves as they too begin to consciously market their city and participate in the collective prioritization of visitors' needs, wants, and desires." In the end, locals "must be what visitors want them to be in order to feed and clothe themselves and their families."[18]

Booster coalitions represented the convergence of common economic interests and goals. As an active partner, the media participated in advancing perceptions of elite businessmen as civic volunteers who practiced an unselfish form of local patriotism. Accordingly, the press reported that those who engaged in efforts to sell Tucson to tourists "work[ed] without any compensation of any kind, simply for the joy of doing something well for the benefit of Tucson."[19] Urban sociologists John R. Logan and Harvey L. Molotch argue that this type of reporting highlighted the elite's civic goodwill and benevolence in order to distract from their economic motives. "All capitalist places," they contend, "are the creations of activists who push hard to alter how markets function, how prices are set, and how lives are affected." In the twentieth century, powerful local business leaders, virtually undisputed, and in fact encouraged by mayors and city councils, typified a "growth machine" in which the "growth ethic pervades virtually all aspects of local life, including the political system." Although this activity "is often portrayed as beneficial to all residents of all places [neighborhoods of assorted socioeconomic status], in reality the advantages and disadvantages of growth are unevenly distributed."[20]

Throughout Tucson's history, economic developers who focused on encouraging tourism conflated Tucson's demographic growth with the

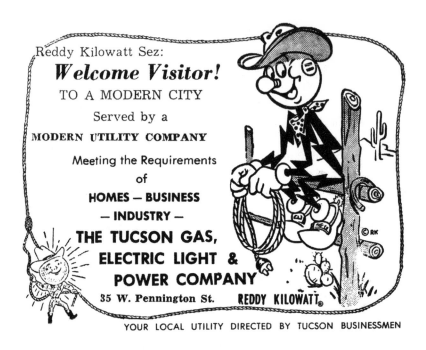

Figure 4.2. The commoditization of the "Anglo fantasy heritage." (Tucson Chamber of Commerce, *Welcome Visitor* [1955–56], 2)

public good. Driven by self-interest, the individuals and businesses that made up the Chamber of Commerce and the Sunshine Club had the most to gain from tourism. Between 1925 and 1940, a conglomerate of local banks (Valley, Southern Arizona, and others) ranked as the Sunshine Club's largest private contributor, giving the club a total of $14,954. Steinfeld's Department Store followed with $12,100, the Southern Pacific Railroad with $9,025, Tucson Gas and Electric with $8,870, the Pioneer Hotel with $5,950, the Santa Rita Hotel with $5,500, and the Mountain States Telephone Company with $3,750 (see fig. 4.2).[21] Utility companies, of course, directly benefited from population growth, as transplanted newcomers, whether renters or home owners, ordered electricity, gas, and telephone services.[22]

Although the Sunshine Club relied in part on private contributions such as these, the city funded most of the club's advertising campaigns, as it did those of the Chamber of Commerce.[23] With city officials as their active partners, these two major boosters' groups acquired what

Logan and Molotch call "systematic power." "Once organized, they stay organized. They are 'mobilized interests.'"[24]

The minutes of a May 15, 1959, Board of Directors meeting of the Tucson Regional Plan, almost all Chamber of Commerce members who had advocated the merits of planning and zoning since 1938, indicate that the directors deliberately cultivated perceptions of themselves as not representing any "special interests." Indeed, at that same meeting the board decided to invite a representative from the League of Women Voters to join them for future gatherings. Women were thought by the all-male directors to "carry weight"; their inclusion would strengthen perceptions of the Tucson Regional Plan as "being interested only in the general good of the community."[25]

Pro-Growth = Anti-Industry

Chamber of Commerce and Sunshine Club members also led all the city's civic development projects and bond drives. The City of Tucson authorized the Chamber of Commerce to devise, manage, and implement all industrial development plans. To that end, elected and salaried city officials acted as silent partners, allocating the chamber whatever funds it needed. Since the chamber also played an active role in electoral politics, few politicians rose to challenge its prominent role in economic development.

Despite the chamber's announced intentions, it made no significant effort to bring industries other than tourism to Tucson. In its 1906 promotional pamphlet *Tucson: Arizona's Playground, Home of Health and Sunshine,* the chamber proclaimed, "Prosperity and commercial progress are everywhere."[26] Nonetheless, with the exception of the mining industry, Tucson remained economically undiversified and underdeveloped as late as 1972, the final year of this study. Apart from Davis-Monthan Air Force Base and Hughes Aircraft Company, most businesses specialized in serving local needs.[27]

Contrary to portrayals of Tucson as a cowboy town, and even though cattle ranching in the outlying grassland areas of Southern Arizona made Patagonia and Arivaca major shipping hubs for cattle destined for other locations, there is scant evidence that either ranching or associated activities survived in the greater Tucson area after the late nineteenth century.[28] Importing its meat from Phoenix and Los Angeles, the city was home to only one packinghouse in 1940, and a minor one at that.[29] The U.S. Census "List of Occupations" of those who had lived in Tucson over the last hundred years confirms that none were even loosely associated with the cowboy way of life, with the possible exception of specialty souvenir and western apparel retailers.

The year 1963 marked the start of a dramatic and enduring economic recession. A growing number of voices began to insist that elected officials play a more aggressive role in the city's industrial development.[30] Ideas surfaced that would fuel the public debate over the city's growth agenda in the late 1970s.[31] Until then, however, the history of industrial development in Tucson amounted to the history of the Chamber of Commerce's "involvement" in the same.

Department store owner Harold Steinfeld stands as one of the local power brokers involved in both tourist promotion and urban planning. A member of the Chamber of Commerce and the second largest contributor to the Sunshine Club, he also chaired the Tucson Regional Plan Executive Committee in 1940. He remained active in urban development projects until his unexpected death in 1972.[32] Ownership of the Pioneer Hotel explains his interest in promoting tourism, as does his ownership of Steinfeld's Department Store and many key properties on the north side of Congress, which made him the most influential merchant and private property owner in Tucson.

In response to the economic slump in 1964, Harold Steinfeld openly declared his anti-industry stance and his preference for a local economy based on tourism: "We'll rock along at a slower pace than in the past and it'll be just fine. There's no big industry in sight for Tucson and it's just as well."[33] Tucson's commitment to an undiversified economy but a growing population brought wealthier shoppers to the city. This dynamic did not threaten either Steinfeld's investments or other established patterns of doing business in Tucson.

Adding his powerful voice for keeping Tucson's economy firmly rooted in tourism, in 1964 Roy P. Drachman explained the importance of a pro-growth and anti-industry policy: "What's going to make Tucson grow if we 'don't get industry here'? . . . Well, the answer is fairly simple to me. Good 'Ole Sol.' . . . Let's face the fact, once and for all, that Tucson in our lifetime is not going to be an industrial or manufacturing center! . . . Let's recognize this and concentrate on . . . tourism, where our long-range future lies."[34]

That same year, in the midst of the debate over the economic slump, University of Arizona Professor Andrew Wilson from the Geography and Planning Department proclaimed Tucson a "merchant-controlled" city, a "type of monopoly" that encouraged "nonaggressiveness" in attracting industry.[35] Wilson identified *Arizona Daily Star* editor William Mathews as "the dominant leader in Tucson."[36] In his 1961 study of the local power structure, James E. Officer had also named Mathews Tucson's most influential citizen, who "used his paper as a bully pulpit, setting a community agenda."[37] Indeed, in the first years after World War II, Mathews and the *Star* would determine the fate of any development project. Despite his outward displays of power, however, Wilson contended that merchant advertisers heavily influenced the newspaper editor's political opinions.[38]

As further evidence of the consolidation of power, both major newspapers decried Wilson's claims of a "merchant-controlled" city. They also condemned suggestions that the mayor and city council consider actively engaging in industrial development.[39] In January 1965, responding to pressure from influential merchants and both major newspapers, the mayor and council decided in executive session that, aside from funding the Chamber of Commerce, they would not accept responsibility for industrial development.[40]

Also in January, three months after the chamber had publicly reaffirmed its commitment to industrial development, the *Tucson Daily Citizen* commended it for "taking hold of the job with energy, imagination—and results." The paper maintained that only a "unified effort with full cooperation between public and private forces" would bring about industrial development, yet a few sentences later declared that it was "a false assumption to assert that the mayor and council have 'responsibility for the economic well-being of the community.'" Like architect Nelson and other tourism promoters, the paper highlighted the importance of industry in framing its pro-development position, noting that something as simple as improving a street "may be the hinge on which an industrial prospect swings into Tucson or away from it." "The people themselves fit into the picture, too," the editorial went on to say. "Public support for capital improvements will be tested at bond elections [for the Pueblo Center Redevelopment Project] this year. Attractiveness of the community is everyone's business, too. A visitor's frank reaction on this score was noted here yesterday—to the effect that Tucson was 'just as trashy as ever."' The *Citizen* concluded that "to argue that the city administration should take over industrial development is wrong."[41]

The Tucson Regional Plan

Most of the Chamber of Commerce and Sunshine Club leaders were also actively involved in promoting planning and zoning that ensured "orderly" municipal development. Chief among these leaders was real estate broker, tourist promoter, and civic leader Roy P. Drachman. In 1939, while director of the Tucson Chamber of Commerce, Drachman spearheaded the successful campaign for passage of a federally assisted "slum clearance program" in response to the Federal Housing Act of 1937.[42]

After the war, Drachman quit his job as the paid chairman of the Sunshine Club Board of Directors and set up his own real estate office in the downtown area north of Congress. He joined the Urban Land Institute, an association of real estate developers and a national think tank that concentrated on "the importance of building cities right." It was during this time that Drachman, who called himself "a student of urbanization," formulated an abiding axiom for his long career as developer: "Build for permanency. Build something that will last, and build something that you'll be proud of and that you're not going to be ashamed to have your name on."[43] Upon his death in 2002, the local newspapers anointed him the "Father of Tucson" for his civic contributions. Tributes to his achievements sustain claims that, among those who charted Tucson's development and growth, Drachman was the most influential. His success as realtor and land speculator would also make him one of the wealthiest men in Tucson.[44]

An analysis of the history of planning and zoning policies in Tucson indicates that they provided the business elite a powerful means to regulate, protect, and enhance the value of private property.[45] The creation of the Tucson Regional Plan, a nonprofit pro-development organization incorporated in 1938, demonstrates the city's commitment, on behalf of its "leading men," both to ensure proper planning and to promote demographic growth.[46] The businessmen who formed this organization stressed the role of citizen participation in resolving planning and zoning issues in Tucson. Business leaders from the Sunshine Club and the Chamber of Commerce hoped to "improve" the city's image because, again, appearances mattered when it came to promoting growth. That the members of

the Tucson Regional Plan acted to advance their shared economic interests in the city's urban renewal efforts is typical "growth machine" behav-
ior. As urban sociologists John Logan and Harvey Molotch explain, "by
working through a local government . . . the efforts of [a business] elite
gain the appearance of a civic campaign waged on behalf of a legal entity
and its citizens, rather than a conspiracy of vested interests."[47] In Tucson,
elected officials, ostensibly representing the people's interests and needs,
did not initiate and develop the plan that would shape visions of the
city's future. The Tucson Regional Plan did, suspending its operations
only in 1953, when the city and Pima County established a joint planning
department. Five years later, however, when Tucson established an urban
renewal office, the organization was reactivated to serve "as a broad citizen influence in obtaining newer and broader planning goals."[48]

A survey of Tucson Regional Plan documents indicates that those
most likely to benefit economically by promoting tourism collected close
to $60,000 in 1942 in order to hire and import a planner from Cincinnati,
Ladislas Segoe, and his assistant, Andre Faure, to develop a master plan
for the city. Members framed this as an act of civic generosity: "The plan
for the City of Tucson was paid for by private funds and given to the
city as a gift."[49] Harold Steinfeld, chairman of the Tucson Regional Plan
Executive Committee, provided Segoe office space, and city and county
officials provided the furnishings and office support.[50]

In 1942, Ladislas Segoe and Andre Faure offered their "gift"—a blueprint designed to remedy Tucson's urban problems and aptly named
the "Tucson Regional Plan"—to city officials. The plan determined that
"blight" first needed to be identified so that it could then be swiftly eliminated. As the planners defined it, "blight" amounted to spaces occupied by poor people of color. Their two principal criteria for "blight and
decadence" reflected both their time and their cultural background: (1)
unsanitary and inadequate housing conditions; and (2) the "intermix-
ture of racial and ethnic groups."[51]

Throughout the United States, ethnic and racial diversity ranked
among the top determinants that qualified certain areas to be labeled
as blighted. La calle, where such diversity thrived, easily met this cri-
terion. In *Origins of the Urban Crisis*, historian Thomas Sugrue documents that neighborhoods having even a handful of African American
families were assigned a "D" rating by banking and home owner associations. Their residents found themselves unable to qualify for mortgages or loans to improve their properties.[52] A local 1961 report on urban

renewal confirmed a similar dynamic in downtown Tucson by stating, "Naturally, financial institutions, in making improvement loans available are even more sensitive to the hazards of neighborhood blight and, therefore, satisfactory financing is unavailable."[53] Sugrue uncovered evidence that middle-class neighborhoods used restrictive covenants to bar multiple housing and other "undesirable uses" that some whites believed would attract people of color (such covenants were widely adopted in Tucson, as we have seen). He concluded that discrimination in the private sector was "a direct consequence of a partnership between the federal government and local bankers and real estate brokers."[54]

Segoe and Faure divided Tucson into thirty-six "Areas," designating the general vicinity of la calle "Area 22," which they described as comprising "most of the old Latin-American section," populated by "a general mixture of Negroes and Latin-Americans, with one block predominantly Chinese." They ranked it as one of the two areas that required "major redevelopment," although they were quick to note that "its narrow streets and mostly unbroken house frontages are quite picturesque in parts, are considered attractive by visitors, and some motion picture scenes have been [filmed] there." They found that this neighborhood had the lowest rents in the city, that 35 percent of its residential units were overcrowded, and that 80 percent of the homes still made use of outhouses.[55]

According to Segoe and Faure: "The City found it necessary to condemn some of the buildings in this area [before 1942], even though the Census reports less than 3 per cent of the thousand or more dwellings in need of repair."[56] The planners disputed overarching descriptions of la calle as "blighted"; they pointed out that enforcement of city building and sanitary codes and provision of city services could easily prevent conditions from arising that would indeed qualify la calle to be declared a "slum area" (as indeed it would be in the 1960s). Although they drew attention to one section "where housing conditions are among the worst in the city," they did not recommend the destruction of the entire Area 22. Instead, they called for the "judicious removal" of "certain portions," which "are so bad that nothing short of clearance and complete redevelopment will meet the problem." On the other hand, they emphasized the need for "rehabilitating the rest," noting that "some parts of this quaint and historically significant section can be and should desirably be reclaimed."[57]

Regrettably, city officials, with the complicity of private interest groups having an avowed interest in planning, disregarded the advice of these hired experts. For the next two decades, officials would fail to provide city services to la calle and would allow building and sanitary regulations to go unenforced. For their part, bankers would deny la calle's home owners and landlords access to loans to maintain, let alone improve, their properties. By the mid-1960s, "la calle" had become synonymous with "old," "dilapidated," and "dangerous."

According to the Segoe and Faure report, owner occupancy in the la calle neighborhood stood at about 20 percent in 1942, with the other 80 percent of the families as renters.[58] After the war, African Americans increasingly moved into the area, making the racial mix even more undesirable for local policy makers who valued "ethnic homogeneity." Henry García remembers that many African Americans stationed at Fort Huachuca near Sierra Vista looked forward to spending their weekends in Tucson: "They couldn't go to Congress Street, you know, where all the Anglo businesses [were located]. So they used to come to Meyer Street, . . . where all the Mexican businesses were, and they felt like they would not discriminate there. They could eat there, and I guess they stayed. They wanted to stay . . . after the war."[59]

The Politics of Exclusion

Those of Tucson's elite who benefited from tourism and demographic growth—portrayed by the media as unselfish negotiators working for the betterment of the city and all Tucsonans—implemented their visions of modernity without dissent. Selective development and systematic denial of citizen participation became institutionalized in the many chapters of Tucson's urban renewal process. This is not to say that white social and political domination was absolute; Mexican Americans always had a few insiders in the local power structure. One was tucsonense Louis J. Felix, president of the Southern Arizona Bank. Another, more visible one was department store owner Alex Jácome, who served as president of the Sunshine Club in the 1940s. A strong supporter of tourism, Jácome also supported urban renewal. On the day of the bond initiative election to approve the Pueblo Center Redevelopment Project, he and a few other prominent citizens ran a large advertisement in the *Tucson Daily Citizen* offering voters free transportation to the polls.[60] He paid for both ad and transport as a private citizen.

Historian Lisbeth Haas highlights the potent, interrelated ideas and practices used to maintain local racial hierarchies: "Notions of whiteness had to be constantly reaffirmed by the deliberate spatial ordering of society, an ordering that was tied not only to a social segregation but also to a related economy of monetary worth. The notions of 'white' and 'citizen,' essential to the construction of difference, were defining property values."[61] Building on this argument, historian Suzanne Mettler contends that New Deal federal policy introduced narrower, exclusionary constructions of citizenship. Notwithstanding ratification of the Fourteenth, Fifteenth, and Nineteenth amendments decades before, the nation as a whole recognized only white American males as "full citizens" and believed, therefore, that only white males had the right to participate in public and civic affairs. Federal lawmakers affirmed these sentiments in policies that recognized exclusively Anglo American males as "full citizens" entitled to the privileges and perquisites of being "true" Americans.[62]

As discussed extensively in the introduction and previous chapters, nonwhite places and neighborhoods in the United States had always been marked socially as "inferior" and "Other." In the postwar era, however, definitions of whiteness were refined and expanded as white Americans demanded that government at all levels, act on their behalf to protect their private property. And act it did. The Federal Housing Authority, for example, restricted its mortgages and loans to those living in "racially homogeneous" (read "segregated, white") neighborhoods.[63] Historian Thomas Sugrue claims that white Americans linked home ownership and citizenship to "service to country [which federal policy makers understood to mean service by white citizens in the armed forces] and the rights and entitlements that would be their reward."[64] White Americans expected local and federal government programs to concentrate on and fund their housing needs, often at the expense of communities of color. The extension of home owners' benefits in the GI Bill and the expansion of Federal Housing Administration programs confirmed Anglo American expectations, as the federal government moved to finance private housing for "deserving" citizens.

From the late nineteenth century on, declining income and home ownership and limited access to certain areas of the city made it difficult for tucsonenses to retain a stake in society. This marginalizing process would continue and intensify throughout the twentieth century. Carole Pateman examines this dynamic in "The Patriarchal State": "Citizens thrown into poverty lack both the means for self-respect and the means to be recognized by fellow citizens as equal in worth to themselves, a recognition basic to democracy."[65] Evidence from Tucson's urban renewal process indicates that local civic leaders and government agents affirmed social distinctions that designated some members of society as "deserving" or full citizens and others as not. For example, the vast majority of residents in la calle were not allowed to vote in the urban renewal initiative, not because they were not legal citizens, which almost all were, but because they did not own their homes.

These exclusionary constructions of citizenship based on property ownership and race had profound ramifications for residents targeted by the city's urban renewal agenda. According to federal guidelines, local voters needed to approve any urban renewal designs. In 1966, however, Arizona law specified that only "persons who are real property tax payers [property owners] and registered to vote and who have lived in the state for one year and the county six months and in their ward for 30 days" would be allowed to vote in the urban renewal bond initiative.[66] The statewide electorate had amended the Arizona Constitution in 1930 to include this stipulation, on the rationale that municipal "bonds are liens" placed on real property owners and thus only they should be allowed to decide the fate of those bonds.[67] As the Tucson Regional Plan report indicated, only 20 percent of the residents in la calle and its nearby neighborhoods owned their homes in 1942,[68] a proportion that would decline by 1965. The property ownership stipulation thus served to silence the overwhelming majority of those most directly affected by urban renewal.

As blatant as this exclusionary policy seems today, it received only limited attention in the local newspapers and never sparked a public debate. In 1966 the *Arizona Daily Star* felt the need to affirm its support for the policy: "the restriction . . . is a reasonable one and is a check and a balance in the normal processes of government."[69]

In addition to being excluded from voting on the bond initiative, those who lived in la calle and its nearby neighborhoods were also excluded from sitting on the citizens' committees required by federal guidelines for urban renewal projects. The mayor and city council defined "citizen" in keeping with established social practices and history. Thus, instead of selecting individuals with a particular expertise or knowledge of the community, they appointed "responsible" and "civic-minded" individuals from the upper strata of the local power structure to the committees. As a result, from the first Citizens' Advisory

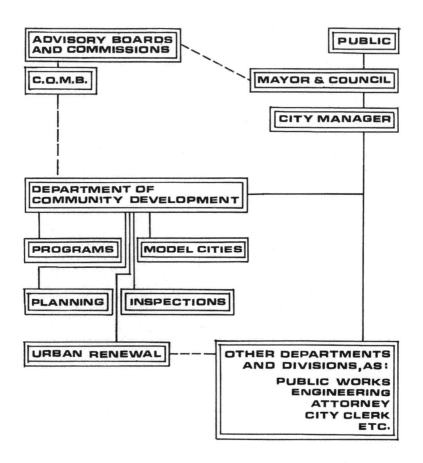

Figure 4.3. The organizational chart of the administrative network prepared by the City of Tucson to highlight public participation and the Committee on Municipal Blight's role in implementing urban renewal. (Newlon, *Pueblo Center Redevelopment Project, 1967–1969*, 15)

Committee in 1958 to the Committee on Municipal Blight (COMB) in the late 1960s, the city's top business leaders and often the most ardent urban renewal advocates—bank presidents, major realtors, resort operators, and newspaper, television, and radio executives—served as the city's "citizen" advisors (see fig. 4.3).[70]

In a 2003 interview, former Tucson chief urban renewal officer Donald Laidlaw recalled that the citizens' committees exerted tremendous influence and that city officials, like himself, relied on them for direction, information, and ideas. When asked why residents who lived in the areas targeted by urban renewal were not appointed to these committees, he replied, "That's a good question and it's a very tough question. . . . I don't think anywhere near as much cooperation and consciousness as we have now existed then. This did not occur until Model Cities, which marked a radical departure. We went out to the neighborhoods, where [residents] helped design neighborhood plans; we met in neighbors' houses and asked ourselves, what can we do to include them?"[71] The composition of COMB, for example, reinforced Anglo American authority in Tucson and highlighted the consequences of century-long cultural practices that served to minimize the Mexican American presence in the city's landscapes, whether imaginary or actual. These deeply ingrained and accepted practices allowed city officials to claim "substantial community involvement through the large citizens' committee," even as they remained oblivious to the absence on the committee of citizens most directly affected. In "The City Tells Its Story: COMB Untangles Tucson," Assistant City Manager Vincent L. Lung touted the city's "democratic process," claiming that COMB

> numbered more than 100 citizens from every walk of life. They were selected by the mayor and council. COMB operated through a steering committee and sub-committees on: planning, and land use, project marketability, housing and relocation, public information, and referendum campaign. These subcommittees met weekly for many months. The city provided staff services to them. . . . While the citizens' committees deliberated, City of Tucson staff and consultants concentrated on the technical aspects of the redevelopment project. . . . Citizen action to secure approval for the Pueblo Center Urban Renewal Project is one in a string of related successes by Tucsonans who've caught a vision of what their city can be ten years from now.[72]

Commending the aptness of the acronym in 1964, the city council announced its intention to "go over" the "slum area with a fine tooth comb to get rid of blight."[73] COMB sought to bring "order" to Tucson and to confirm the power of a select group of elite citizens to dictate policies that would then be institutionalized in the city's programs.

In a time when the suburban ideal of modernity dominated urban planning and development projects, COMB members and other civic boosters recognized that appearances mattered. "We must improve the overall appearance of our city," one urban renewal advocate asserted. "We must have a convention facility so that we can develop a more complete image as a place to visit. We must expand our cultural facilities. We must do something to clean up and clear out the unsightly near-downtown slum areas."[74] And the city, with the cooperation of county, state, and federal officials, moved to do just that.

5

Reaffirming Order

> I saw everything being leveled in la calle. I used to work down-
> town, so I had to walk through the area. Everyone was leaving,
> . . . people that we knew and that we were very close to. [City offi-
> cials] emptied out everything. It was literally a ghost town, and
> then it was leveled and they left just one huge, big empty space. . . .
> Everything that used to be ended up being totally dismantled into
> one huge empty lot.
>
> —Guadalupe Castillo, February 2008[1]

A review of key events leading up to the grand unveiling of the Tucson
Community Center (TCC) in 1971 demonstrates that the history of place
is also the history of power. The Pueblo Center Redevelopment Project,
which boosters and city officials proclaimed would transform Tucson's
downtown and reenergize the city's economy, called for the construction
of various government complexes, specialty shops, and a new community-
convention center. But, as the showpiece of Arizona's first urban renewal
project, the new center required the most space of all the proposed buildings and garnered the most attention. Indeed, city officials would level all
structures on the TCC site months before they had funds to build it.

For thirty years, the City of Tucson had devised and supported a
series of redevelopment plans in response to the concerns of a variety of
growth coalition's and citizens' committees' demands. In each instance,
however, the "Who's Who in Tucson" coalition retooled the committees'
designs and marketing slogans to persuade the local electorate to climb
onto the urban renewal bandwagon.[2]

As early as 1939, the Chamber of Commerce had proposed that the
mayor and city council form a committee to investigate a "federally-
assisted slum clearance program" in response to the passage of the Federal
Housing Act of 1937. These efforts culminated in 1939 with the passage
of an Arizona law, entitled Powers and Duties of Cities and Towns to

Undertake Slum Clearance Projects.[3] Although no plans were drawn up at that time, and no structures razed, sections of la calle became targets of new city designs to infuse "order" and "American" culture into the area. Although the state's eighth urban renewal initiative, the Pueblo Center Redevelopment Project was the first to move beyond the planning stage and the first to be implemented.[4]

That city officials and policies accelerated la calle's decline for more than two decades has gone all but unrecognized. The destructive consequences of this intentional neglect made it easier for the city to sell its urban renewal plan both to federal housing authorities and to the local electorate. By the 1960s, the neighborhoods in and near la calle met all the institutional guidelines that qualified them to be designated "slums."

An East Side Community Center?

After World War II, boosters launched a series of efforts to convince Tucsonans that they needed a new community center to host a variety of entertainment events, particularly conventions, to attract new visitors and investors.[5] In 1953, the Tucson Chamber of Commerce formed the Community Center Committee, headed by the owner of the Ghost Ranch Lodge, Arthur N. Pack. Its members included hotel owners, bankers, lawyers, investment brokers, architects, retailers, service club members, and people with interests in the arts.[6] "The tourist," Pack's committee made clear, "is the major factor in delineating the need [for such a center]. His expenditures in Tucson are the city's greatest single source of income and he must be furnished with adequate opportunities for recreation and entertainment."[7]

After consulting with planners and architects, the committee asked the city to reserve forty acres of vacant land near Randolph Park (now Reid Park) for a "multi-purpose auditorium." The site they proposed would locate the Community Center some three miles east of downtown on the eastern edge of the city in 1953 but in what would be considered midtown today. To gauge support for such an endeavor, Pack conducted what he called a "referendum," mailing questionnaires to Chamber of Commerce members. Although 480 (80 percent) of the 600 respondents approved of the Randolph Park location, influential voices continued to push for a "central downtown location."[8] Coincidentally, another Chamber of Commerce committee, calling itself a "tax study group," explored the possibility of Pima County seeking federal aid for a community center downtown. That Arizona legislators had not yet passed enabling legislation to permit such collaboration did not faze the committee, which confidently declared this "not an impossible hurdle."[9]

In the meantime, key Chamber of Commerce members leading the drive to build a convention center downtown expressed their dissatisfaction with the results of Pack's referendum. "Businessmen appeared quite naturally anxious," recalled Pack, "that any future project be located within walking distance to the downtown area." Reacting to the objections of these influential Tucsonans, Pack's committee decided to take "a second look at the slum area close to downtown, which is no credit to Tucson at the present."[10]

Soon after the federal housing authorities established a national Urban Renewal Office in 1954, the Arizona state legislature passed laws enabling municipalities to partner with the federal government in slum clearance programs, to conduct studies to determine their housing and redevelopment needs, and to float loans or municipal bonds to finance their renewal projects.[11] This windfall opportunity for redeveloping Tucson's core changed everything. The Chamber of Commerce turned its full attention downtown. As Pack later explained, "Inasmuch as a large number of Chamber members favored a downtown location, it was deemed advisable to investigate the possibility of a site [for the community-convention center] in an Urban Renewal area."[12] Thus 1954 marked the end of discussions on locations other than downtown for such a center.

In 1960, another offshoot of the Chamber of Commerce, the Tucson Civic Center Planning Group, financed *A Community-Convention Center for Tucson*, a report for the mayor, city council, and the "people of the city of Tucson."[13] In language strikingly reminiscent of tourist promotional literature, the 79-page document stressed the need to locate the new center downtown but failed to mention, even in passing, that a large community existed in the area under consideration.

Intentional Neglect

Most houses in the near-downtown neighborhoods of la calle had been built between 1860 and 1890, when, as in the 1960s, Mexican Americans made up the majority of their population.[14] Owners made few improvements to their homes until the first half of the new century, when they converted former stables and carriage houses into carports or additional housing. Wood-burning stoves provided homes with heat, and thick adobe walls and high ceilings kept them cool. City developmental services began to install water mains around 1912, when most private wells were abandoned. Electricity and telephone services also became available to residents around 1912, but most continued to depend on kerosene lanterns for lighting, and few could afford to have telephones. With rising demand for affordable housing, property owners turned larger homes into boardinghouses and small apartments, providing themselves with additional income and further increasing the area's population density and number of renters.[15]

In the late 1930s and early 1940s, the city put in sidewalks and curbs, which required, however, that trees and shrubs be removed from in front of the houses, giving the neighborhoods a starker, less lived-in feeling. By this time, most houses had electricity, and some residents had installed indoor plumbing. Evaporative coolers began to make an appearance, although water heaters remained a rarity. By the 1950s, the vast majority of adobe houses, now many decades old, had suffered severe weathering and by the 1960s, for reasons discussed below, few property owners were investing in home improvements.[16] From as early as May 1941, when the Ladislas Segoe survey team had begun knocking on their doors,[17] each urban redevelopment plan had sent a message to home and business owners in la calle that the city fully intended to level their neighborhoods. And each round of deliberations only drove that message home.

A 1961 city document plainly warned property owners that investing in improvements "would be a step against the tide in the area."[18] Carlos Robles, an attorney who represented some residents in urban renewal condemnation proceedings, highlighted the intentional neglect of city officials and their role in hastening the area's descent into disrepair. La calle residents, he recalled, "were told not to improve their property because it had no future. . . . These people had been under the threat of condemnation for a decade."[19] Anna Montaño claims that her grandmother, who owned a cluster of apartments, applied for building permits to upgrade her plumbing, but city officials repeatedly rejected her requests.[20] Don Laidlaw, chief urban renewal officer for the Pueblo Center Redevelopment Project, recalled that "during the 1950s, [and] before the new project got started [in 1966], there was some zeal on the part of building inspectors to rein in improvements, because the conclusion had been reached that everything was gonna get torn down—why spend public money on buying back improvements?"[21]

Public statements by city officials denigrating the appearance of buildings and physical conditions in the neighborhoods in and around la calle conveyed the clear impression that their eventual destruction was an inevitable part of the natural order of things. In 1964, two years before voters approved urban renewal, media reports indicated that city officials had curtailed collection of trash and refuse, reinforcing and reinscribing perceptions of la calle as a "filthy" place. A woman with a large trash pile behind her house apologetically told reporters, "I've called and asked [the city's sanitation department] to take it away, but they never seem to get here."[22]

"Slumming"

After World War II, events moved quickly in favor of urban renewal, particularly after the passage of the Federal Housing Act of 1949. This legislation established a national urban renewal policy that "promised to clear out slums and revive the downtown economy [of cities across the nation] by attracting new businesses and middle-class residents back to the urban core."[23] By this time, the ethnic separation apparent at the turn of the century had become more pronounced as tucsonenses from the lower classes gravitated to the neighborhoods downtown. In 1949, the Citizens' Housing Committee alerted the mayor and city council to the prospect of a drastic increase in the population density of the urban core, where the influx of "low-income" people would cause living conditions to worsen.[24] Planners had designed the Tucson Freeway, now known as Interstate 10, to pass through Mexican American neighborhoods in the southern and western sections of the city. This freeway project destroyed close to 500 dwellings. Not surprisingly, faced with restrictive covenants in other parts of the city, most of the displaced tucsonenses moved back to familiar territory in or near la calle.

The barrios that boosters characterized as impeding economic growth and tainting the city's image also embodied a past and a people with their own distinctive culture and traditions. That this mattered little, if at all, to the urban development coalition is evident in a 1961 *Tucson Daily Citizen* editorial, which articulated a vision of the modern urban core as nonresidential: "City records and the street signs say it is Meyer Avenue, but nobody ever calls it that. It is Meyer STREET. Was, is and probably always will be. It's yesterday's Tucson, in the shadows, now, far removed in the minds of our citizens from the proud and respectable canyon of concrete and glass that is our downtown today."[25]

The editorial made no direct reference to Mexican people or spaces but clearly implied that they belonged to yesterday, just as the future belonged to the modern and respectable citizenry. Historian William Deverell's view of Anglo attitudes toward Mexican people in Los Angeles applies here: "Such [exclusionary] visions are but the expected product in a city constructed *precisely* around racial categories and racial exclusion. Los Angeles is not so much a city that got what it wished for. It is a city that wished for what it worked diligently to invent."[26]

Although institutional neglect actively contributed to turning large parts of la calle into a slum, city officials seemed oblivious to the role they had played in actually worsening the poverty there. This became abundantly clear in 1964, when Don Laidlaw invited city officials and reporters to join him on a tour of the barrios just south of the central business district so they could experience and see for themselves the "deteriorated" conditions there. The photograph that appeared in the *Tucson Daily Citizen* shows the officials, most in suits and ties, walking through some of the worst parts of the city. Its caption, "City Officials Go Slumming," reflects the paper's foregone conclusions about the neighborhoods.[27]

The largely uninhabited area Laidlaw had chosen to tour and the *Citizen* to photograph seemed calculated to expose the neighborhoods' most unattractive features, to emphasize the contrasts between modern, "respectable" Anglo American men in impeccable business attire and outdated, crumbling "Mexican" structures on the verge of collapse. The newspaper portrayed city officials as outsiders in a remote landscape, completely unfamiliar with their surroundings. In reality, however, they were just a few blocks away from their city hall offices and would only have had to look out their windows to see the area where they now stood.

Although the officials never bothered to get the area residents' opinions of the pending renewal project, they were quick to offer their own. "Peering through the broken window of a condemned adobe apartment building," the *Citizen* reported, "Mayor Lew Davis saw broken wine bottles, feces, ripped bedding and old clothing littering the floor. 'Whew,' he said with a frown. 'It may be condemned but it's still used from time to time.'"

In the course of the tour, Luis Martínez approached the officials and told them of an apartment complex sorely in need of repairs. Martínez also told them the owner ignored tenants' requests and inflated their rents. When a member of the city council asked him to name the owner, "Martínez mentioned a prominent Tucsonan. There was an embarrassed silence." Rather than expose the offending landlord, however, the newspaper chose to protect his identity. At the end of the tour, the evaluators came to a predictable conclusion for a city where the poor were held responsible for their deteriorated living conditions and where landlords and officials, no matter how derelict in their duties, were held blameless. In the words of one tour member: "We've got to get going on this urban renewal project." "No one disagreed," the paper reported.[28] Instead of asking the constituents they met—and had been elected or appointed to serve—who had allowed things to deteriorate to such a state or demanding that trash be collected and building codes be enforced, city officials continued to overlook the area's major problems.

The 392-Acre Project

The Federal Urban Renewal Act of 1954 mandated that cities develop a "workable program" for development. Three years later, the City of Tucson under Mayor Don Hummel, the local Real Estate Board and the Home Builders Association candidate, prepared a report for what they called the Old Pueblo District, 392 acres of the most densely populated, predominantly ethnic neighborhoods in the city.[29] They submitted their project application to federal housing authorities, who approved it and awarded the city $151,000 for surveys and planning.[30] In May 1958, the city hired William J. Bray as assistant city manager in charge of urban renewal and two months later opened its first urban renewal office downtown. Federal authorities placed a five-year time limit on this project, making May 8, 1963 the critical completion date.[31]

In 1958, the Old Pueblo District stood as "one of the largest and most ambitious renewal projects in the U.S." Although federal officials suggested that the project be broken up into two or three separate ones, city officials insisted on a "single long-range project." Initial, "highly tentative" plans indicated that city officials hoped to relocate families near their former homes by constructing low-cost housing on the extreme southern side of the targeted urban renewal area.[32] According to 1958 estimates, 1,310 families lived in the designated area. More than 600 had lived there for five years and nearly 400 had lived in the same houses for more than ten years. A newspaper report on the area observed that these families "like[d] the convenience of the section, located near downtown. They also like[d] to live in and around their families and friends."[33]

In 1961, Mayor Hummel appointed the Citizens' Advisory Public Information Committee (CAPIC), which in turn asked Urban Renewal Officer and Assistant City Manager S. Lenwood Schorr to prepare a report explaining the "mechanics" of urban renewal to the people. Banking executive Mundey Johnson and Dean Sidney W. Little of the College of Fine Arts at the University of Arizona, both members of the Tucson Regional Plan Board, chaired this committee. An architect, Little actively supported urban renewal as a "vehicle whereby Tucson could recover her position as a city of charm and beauty."[34] According to the CAPIC report, *Urban Renewal: A Teamwork of Private Enterprise and Government for Slum Clearance and Redevelopment of the Old Pueblo*, far fewer families faced relocation—850—than had been estimated in 1958, these being "predominantly of Mexican-American ancestry," even though 1,500 structures were targeted for destruction.[35]

The committee's report highlighted conditions in "the heart of our city," which it described as ridden with crime, fire hazards, and high rates of juvenile delinquency. It argued that all Tucsonans were affected by these conditions and that the entire city unfairly subsidized this area through property taxes.[36] As urban renewal proponents would claim in subsequent redevelopment campaigns, the report maintained that the neighborhoods near downtown used more than their fair share of services, that law enforcement and fire departments spent more of their energies there than elsewhere in the city, and that the cost of these services exceeded the property tax revenue received from the neighborhoods. "It's your pocket book!" the 1961 report reminded Tucsonans. "You now subsidize this blight." As for the cost of the proposed renewal, the "city's investment will be returned many times and in many ways."[37]

To qualify for federal assistance in 1962, the city council declared the project area a slum and redevelopment "necessary in the interest of public health, safety, morals or welfare of the residents of the City of Tucson."[38] Using Scottsdale, an affluent, suburban community near Phoenix, as a model, the project introduced plans to build Old Pueblo Village, a shopping complex designed to appeal to tourists, and offered a "limited" amount of housing for former residents of the area. It also called for construction of an industrial park, a nine-acre shopping area, and a civic and cultural center. Once completed, the planners proclaimed, the 392-acre project would make Tucson "the Southwest's outstanding cultural magnet and tourist attraction."[39] The city would acquire properties in the targeted area through the power of eminent domain. It would then condemn and raze the structures on them and resell the land to private developers "who [would] renew it according to the Urban Renewal plan" (see fig. 5.1).[40]

The federal requirement to build public housing for those displaced caused many influential real estate agents and the Home Builders Association to balk. They believed that this amounted to "nothing more than socialism," and they insisted that "private enterprise," not the government, should provide whatever housing the city needed.[41] Indeed, the public housing requirement proved to be a major obstacle to approval of the project. The biggest obstacle, however, would be William Mathews, editor and publisher of the *Arizona Daily Star* and one of the city's leading power brokers.

Although generally pro-growth and anti-industry, Mathews cautiously monitored city spending on new development projects. He objected to the Old Pueblo District Project because he believed it would destroy

> a part of the city inhabited by those of Mexican heritage means [where] Mexican customs have prevailed in most of this district for scores of years . . . when the advocates of urban renewal plead that structures are too near property lines and that family dwellings are intermingled with business and industrial areas, they forget old Mexican customs. . . . The pamphlet the city administration has published pleads that the area has a wasteful street design. That was the way the Mexicans built their villages. Must the people of Tucson destroy this remaining area of former Mexican life just because the streets are too narrow and buildings old? . . . Maybe someday Tucsonans would look back at urban renewal and wonder why they authorized such a project which wiped out at one stroke what remained of Mexico in Tucson.[42]

The 1962 Plan

In response to the objections of William Mathews and others, in February 1962 city officials quietly whittled the ambitious project down

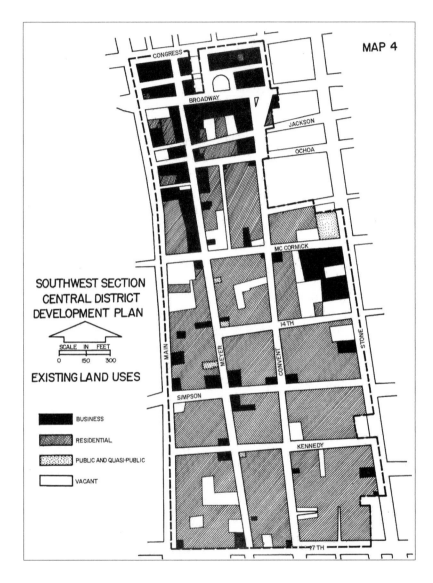

Figure 5.1. A map of the 392-acre urban renewal plan that confirms the high retail activity in la calle. In 1966 the Pueblo Center Redevelopment Project leveled the area north of 14th Street. (City of Tucson, *Redevelopment Plan*, pt. 2, map 4)

to seventy-six acres—less than one-fifth its original size. A new group emerged to "urge the enactment" of the modified plan—the Citizens Urban Renewal Enterprise (CURE)—whose members included the same major players who had been involved in previous citizens' committees.[43]

Three months later, the city held a public hearing, as required by the federal government, in anticipation of submitting the project to the voters for their approval. A divided group of 800 Tucsonans attended. CURE chairman Arthur Pack emphasized that the new committee "was completely independent of [other] citizens' urban renewal committees" and that they supported the renewal plan "on the basis of our own study and analysis." Mayor Lew Davis, Urban Renewal Director S. Lenwood Schorr, and architect Edward H. Nelson also voiced their support for the plan. Those speaking against the plan included citizens who feared it would increase their property taxes, but others voiced different objections. Dan McKinney, for one, argued: "It is an abuse to condemn one man's land and sell it to another at a planned loss and then only a richer man can afford to occupy it after the area had been rebuilt." Luis Martínez, a business owner on Meyer Avenue, who had earlier asked touring city officials to address a slumlord's unjust treatment of tenants, dismissed the city's claim that minimum housing codes could not be enforced as "so much hooey." To "cure" and improve the area, he declared, the city had only to order its fire and building inspectors to do their jobs. Tucson rancher Phil Clarke questioned both the city officials' intentions and the so-called standards they had relied on to declare certain areas in need of razing. He demanded to know what had happened to the extensive "slums" identified in the original 392-acre project now that the city had reduced it to less than eighty acres: "Did they evaporate into thin air?"[44]

In a surprise move, on May 8, 1962, the mayor and city council decided to kill the project, suspend the urban renewal process, and instead concentrate on "clean[ing] up the slums through enforcement of housing codes."[45] The people living in the urban renewal area, one council member explained, were "entitled to the enforcement of all laws, rules, and regulations that will afford them a decent way of life."[46] Nevertheless, neither the mayor nor the council ruled out any future urban revitalization projects. Urban renewal advocates had learned important lessons in 1962. The next project would steer away from any public housing provisions.

The city had passed a housing code in 1957 that had set minimum standards for all dwellings. Tucson had also hired its first housing inspector that same year. Admittedly, the inspector did not target any particular section of town before 1962. Instead, he followed up on complaints throughout the city. On the day the city announced its intention to "clean up the slums," the *Tucson Daily Citizen* asserted that the area south of downtown all the way to 22nd Street "had been a slum for thirty years and little had been done to correct conditions there" and that it "had been left in limbo awaiting the urban renewal project which was supposed to sweep it clean for new development."[47]

To "banish the blight," the city hired another inspector in 1962 but adopted no development plan. Nor did it propose ways to improve the living standards of neighborhood residents in and near la calle by providing much-needed municipal services, such as regular trash pickups, or by helping owners repair and upgrade their properties. Instead, the city's inspection and demolition efforts worked to make poverty in the area more visible and to confirm what urban renewal proponents had claimed about the downtown neighborhoods for the last five years.

In September 1963, the city demolished most of the housing units in Gay Alley and ordered the few that remained to be "fixed up."[48] This left a large tract of vacant land in the midst of la calle. That year, building inspectors targeted 118 of the most dilapidated units near downtown and managed to demolish 21 of them. Although city officials claimed to have brought 38 units into "compliance," some, perhaps many, of them were simply boarded up as unfit for human habitation, in compliance with standard procedure in such cases.[49] The brief "banish the blight" campaign left entire sections in and near la calle as vacant lots—which grew weeds and, in the absence of city services, accumulated trash—or as uninhabited buildings, which building inspectors then condemned and had boarded up. The entire process served to reinforce perceptions of decay and dilapidation, sending strong visual signals to both area residents and Tucsonans in general that la calle and the neighborhoods near downtown had indeed become slums.

Build America Better Committee

Despite the official decision to table urban renewal in May 1962, the city's main development advocates in the private sector continued to demand action that would address the "dire needs of the Tucson area."[50] Eight months later, in January 1963, the Tucson Board of Realtors invited an outside "advisory team," the Build America Better Committee of the

National Association of Real Estate Boards, to devise a redevelopment plan "as a Community Service to the city of Tucson."[51]

The advisory team called itself "a group of disinterested observers from across the nation invited to help the city chart a course for the improvement of neglected areas." Its chairman, R. Gordon Tarr, who, like Segoe and Faure, hailed from Cincinnati, declared as his main goal to "present an action program capable of winning the essential support to progress." Despite being hired by a group of private individuals, Tarr and his team had unlimited access to city government documents, services, and staff.[52]

The team's final report, *An Action Plan for Tucson*, issued late in 1963, is a study in contrasts. In visual and textual representations, it sets new against old, progress against adobe. One photograph sets "The Good Life" opposite a picture of an outhouse (see figs. 5.2 and 5.3). The report builds to its central contrast—those who lived in adobe houses with those who lived in the suburbs: "A thousand people a month settle in Tucson seeking happiness in a modern land of health and opportunity while others born in the city go home each night to mud huts a stone's throw from the central business district."[53] Surprisingly, the report did not shrink from holding city agents responsible for having neglected certain neighborhoods: "Tireless housing and building code enforcement," it asserted, "would have made large-scale demolition unnecessary in many old city areas." It also recommended rehabilitation of some of the poorer areas in the city through "house by house inspections."[54]

On one point in particular, the Build America Better advisory team minced no words. It determined that South Meyer Avenue, la calle's main commercial thoroughfare, had "no future," so it "should be cleared of present structures and completely redeveloped." If done with "careful planning," the team assured Tucsonans, this could "open the heart of the city to view by creating a magnificent new entrance from the freeway to downtown."[55]

One team member, Guy Hollyday, recommended revitalization because the failure of previous redevelopment programs had "cast a cloud over the whole area. The owners sit back and do nothing because they think the city is going to do it for them."[56] Another, Allan Moore, highlighted the committee's advisory role and urged that resolving the city's problems not be left up to outsiders and that realtors "of your community should work as a liaison group between the city committees and the citizens of the city."[57]

Tucson—Study in Contrasts

Figure 5.2. Comparing suburban prosperity with the poverty near downtown. (Build a Better America Committee, *An Action Plan for Tucson*, 5)

Build America Better's indictment of South Meyer Avenue had severe consequences. When the citizens' Committee on Municipal Blight (COMB) introduced a new urban renewal plan to the mayor and city council in November 1964, they used the advisory team's 1963 report to support the

Figure 5.3. Comparing the isolated "problem" areas with the busiest downtown intersection. (Build a Better America Committee, *An Action Plan for Tucson*, 53)

need for destroying not only South Meyer Avenue but also much of the surrounding area.[58]

The Pueblo Center Redevelopment Project

By 1964, urban renewal had again moved to the top of the city's agenda. Behind the scenes, advocates invited the regional director of federal urban renewal in San Francisco to Tucson. Getting right down to business, the director declared the neighborhoods in and near la calle "the most fantastically bad slum area in the country," "a threat to [property owners], to increasing land values, and tax revenues," and "destructive of your property, your community and the downtown climate." He recommended "getting rid of" them.[59]

In November 1964, the mayor and city council decided to "unanimously reexamine the possibility of an Urban Renewal project in the Meyer [Avenue] area." That same month, COMB unveiled its *Pueblo Center Redevelopment Project.* "The downtown area needs a shot in the arm," the new project's report would argue, and the proposed "Community Center [and] cultural facilities will do that."[60] The city again ignored the many people who lived in the urban renewal area, promising instead to make downtown more attractive by replacing them and their businesses with "a good cultural base." The project proposed by COMB would "reenergize" downtown by razing an established, densely populated area to the south. As the report made clear, planners hoped to populate the downtown area with a new breed of people: "Change the environment and people will want to live in high density apartments in the downtown."[61]

Former Mayor Don Hummel, who had first supported then abandoned the 1962 project, reemerged to promote the new, COMB-promoted project because "such a program would . . . return land to its highest and best use and provide [the] downtown area with room for growth." "With an urban renewal plan would come jobs," he added.[62] It is important to note that this push for urban renewal occurred as the city faced an economic downturn, which provided promoters with rhetorical ammunition to garner support. In 1963, Hughes Aircraft, the city's major private employer, had laid off more than 50 percent of its employees, and construction in the city had come to a standstill.[63] After a "leveling-off period," wages, agriculture, business income, and the rate of population growth all experienced a decline.[64] As evidence of the increase in unemployment, the local newspaper reported that when the City of Tucson announced five job openings for laborers, 1,100 applied.[65] For its part, COMB promised that urban renewal would bring "instant industry" to cure the city's economic woes.[66]

The year 1965 proved a landmark for national housing policy. The passage of the Housing and Urban Development Act of 1965 strengthened the link between the federal government and municipalities. In addition to offering more fiscal aid, this new legislation strengthened a federal-local alliance that had been evolving since the New Deal. As part of his Great Society, President Lyndon B. Johnson also created a new cabinet position, the Department of Housing and Urban Development (HUD), to ensure that housing and urban issues would have a stronger voice in his administration and the federal government.[67] In a bureaucratic system known for taking its time, Tucson's urban renewal process in the mid-1960s stands out. The federal government approved the city's application in a record one month and five days on March 6, 1965.[68]

In Special Provisions for Disadvantaged Persons of the 1965 housing act, HUD articulated its goal of aiding the poor and disenfranchised by making housing more accessible. The department promised lower rents and more public housing. It also touted a new Federal Housing Administration, which would place greater emphasis on lower-income families.[69] On paper, HUD's goals appeared to be an earnest effort to bring equity to housing and, in so doing, to help remedy pressing social problems. Although formulated in and administered from Washington, D.C., Great Society programs also sought to empower local communities.[70] By empowering Tucson's city officials, however, the Federal Housing Administration (FHA) in effect empowered the local elite to implement its own objectives rather than those of the entire community.

On November 8, 1965, at a public hearing convened by the city council, Roy Drachman and City Manager Mark Keane outlined the new urban renewal project. Some 400 people, most of them "coat and tie" businessmen, attended the two-and-a-half-hour gathering in the main ballroom of the Pioneer Hotel. Thomas Via, chairman of COMB's planning subcommittee, an active member in the Tucson Regional Plan, and president of the Tucson Electric Power Company, stressed "tight control" in order to avoid mistakes in implementing the new project. Keane also promised that the project would preserve six homes as historic sites in the renewal area.

Previous press reports noted that nearly 400 families had applied for the 160 units at La Reforma, Tucson's main public housing complex, and been placed on a waiting list. Indeed, according to Housing Director C. W. Chambers, the list would have been much longer, but "many families don't apply because they feel it is hopeless."[71] To garner support from realtors and builders for the pending project, Phil Richardson, chairman of COMB's subcommittee on housing, announced at the November 8 hearing that the Pueblo Center Redevelopment Project provided no public housing and asserted that there was "adequate low-cost housing in the community for the relocation of families in the project area."[72]

Most of the audience spoke out in favor of the new project. One high school student asked, "As tourists come through and see the slums, do you think they'll come back? As they see the litter, the garbage all over the street do you think they'll come back?"[73] Representatives from the Chamber of Commerce, Tucson Trade Bureau, Central Trades Council, Tucson Broadcasters Association, Tucson Festival Society, and symphony organizations all endorsed the project. At the end of the meeting, Mayor Lew Davis asked for a straw vote. When only a handful in the audience refused to stand and endorse the project, the mayor exclaimed, "I am most encouraged—in fact, elated!" Thus COMB's urban renewal project became the City of Tucson's official plan.[74]

On January 18, 1966, urban renewal proponents experienced another triumph when Pima County voters approved $8.1 million in bonds for a new integrated court and office complex on Pennington Street between Church and Warner avenues.[75] To make way for the new county complex—integrated into the city's larger designs to transform downtown but not officially a part of urban renewal—the city demolished the Alianza Building and a large number of structures on West Congress. The money from this bond election also subsidized a joint city-county underground parking garage north of Congress in the Presidio area.

One month later, on February 26, 1966, HUD announced it would award the city $4,865,000 to begin implementing its Pueblo Center Redevelopment Project.[76] The announcement could not have come at a more opportune time, only days before the scheduled March 1 special election. Close to 5 million federal dollars proved a large incentive for local voters to approve municipal bonds for the new urban renewal project.

The federal government promised to pay two-thirds of the city's costs.[77] City officials planned to borrow $15 million: $8 million dollars to acquire the various properties in the designated area and another $7 million to raze the structures and install new streets and sewers. They expected that the sale of cleared land to private developers would yield about $4.5 million. After deducting this amount and federal grants totaling $7 million, the net debt owed by the city would be $3.5 million. Local urban renewal officials promised voters that, thanks to fees generated by the proposed underground garage and other anticipated revenues, the actual cost to city taxpayers would be minimal.[78]

The Bond Election: March 1, 1966

Although the promotional campaign focused mostly on rallying support for the new community center, which loomed large and consumed most of the debate, it was not in fact on the ballot. Voters were asked to mark yes or no on permitting the city to borrow up to $14 million in short-term, low-interest loans from the federal government. Their approval would allow the city to acquire properties in the designated eighty-acre renewal area through negotiated purchase or condemnation under the power of eminent domain.[79]

Although voter approval of the initiative gave city officials the green light to pursue their plans to transform the area by acquiring properties, destroying structures, and laying the groundwork for future construction, it did not authorize the city to build anything. Since the proposed community-convention center had received much media coverage, days before the election the city council made it clear that it "remained unanimous in its commitment to proceed with the center as soon a financing method can be selected," but because voter sampling had indicated that urban renewal supporters might have second thoughts about the community center's $9 million price tag, and because city officials had not yet found a way to pay for it, the council decided not to put the center on the ballot. Roy Drachman urged voters not to be deterred by urban renewal's fiscal problems: "Approval of the urban renewal project is the next logical step. When we have this under way the mayor and council can make a carefully reasoned decision as to how to proceed with the final step—construction of the community center."[80]

As he had in 1962, a week before the election, the editor of the *Arizona Daily Star*, William R. Mathews, urged the electorate to vote no on the new initiative. Although he used his editorial mostly to complain about the city council, he recognized the gravity of leveling an area that housed a large number of residents: "People will be removed from their homes to other quarters that the city must provide. Then their homes will be demolished. . . . Many people with little means will suffer grievously in thus being uprooted from their homes." Mathews warned that "all of the land will lie idle until the city finds a way to finance a convention center."

He also expressed distress at "the complete destruction of what is called the Mexican district of Tucson." True to his fiscally conservative nature, Mathews advised taxpayers to think about the urban renewal costs and to be leery of attempts to portray the entire area as a slum. Many who lived within the delineated area but outside the worst sections of South Meyer Avenue, Mathews insisted, "cannot be called slum dwellers. Every building is very old, but it is being used for either a home or an office."[81] Nevertheless, by 1966 Mathews's power had begun to wane. The large number of new arrivals who had moved to the city and the increasing numbers of Tucsonans who turned to television for information and news had diminished his power to sway an election.

In response to Mathews's criticism, architect Edward H. Nelson, a member of the Citizens' Committee on Urban Renewal and an urban development promoter since the late 1950s, highlighted the "unsanitary and dangerous" conditions in the targeted area. Nelson's visions of the future stood in stark contrast to the Mexican culture that prevailed in the area. As he saw it, the community-convention center would appeal to new people and a new culture: "It is a place where singers, athletes, Boy Scouts, square dance people and others can come. True, it will be used for conventions. But it is essentially for community things."[82] Urban renewal thus promised Tucson's suburbanites and visitors a new space where they could feel safe to indulge in and celebrate their "American" culture.

In direct opposition to the *Star*, the *Tucson Daily Citizen* gave the Pueblo Center Redevelopment Project its blanket approval. The editor addressed critics who claimed that urban renewal had failed in other cities by arguing, "Most of the ill-starred projects started with wholesale razing of densely populated slums." He declared Tucson's urban renewal project exceptional because it intentionally excluded provisions for low-income housing. Other cities had failed, according to the editor, because they had "relocate[ed] thousands of persons in new residential units, which quickly became high-rise slums." In comparison to these public housing projects, the eighty-acre urban renewal area in Tucson "is sparsely populated. It has many vacant lots. It includes already condemned and abandoned structures." He also reminded the electorate that a "number" of historic buildings would be "saved and restored." He concluded his editorial by urging Tucsonans to approve the project, to "think of it as a positive program to provide public facilities the city needs. Local government needs more office space, more space for police and courts and other essential services. Think of the project as an economic stimulus."[83]

Although the bonanza of close to 5 million federal dollars and the dip in the economy may have swayed voters to approve the proposed urban renewal plan, other factors may have distracted Tucsonans from examining the finer details. The debate took place in the midst of the city's most famous murder trial. Charles H. Schmid, known as the "Pied Piper of Tucson," stood accused of murdering two young women. Nationally known attorney F. Lee Bailey came to Tucson to defend Schmid, and the case received extensive national attention.[84] The day after the election, instead of announcing the vote, the headlines read, "Jury Finds Schmid Guilty."

Most city officials were ecstatic with the returns, especially longtime urban renewal advocate Mayor Lew Davis, who declared them "a good omen for Tucson. We will now proceed with programs introduced in the last few years that mean that people of Tucson are in favor of progress." He also thanked members of the citizens' committees "for getting the facts before the people."[85]

At the time of this special election, 55,000 real property owners were eligible to vote, yet only 17,427 chose to. As triumphantly as the mayor portrayed the results, they did not represent an electoral mandate. Although 10,193 voters voted for, and only 7,129 against, the urban renewal plan, less than 20 percent of eligible voters—and less than 4 percent of the city's total population—gave urban renewal their approval.[86]

Relocation

After the election on March 1, 1966, city officials quickly began to acquire properties. Out of the eighty-acre project, only 50 acres of land needed to be purchased; the rest was made up of streets. Once acquired, the vacated structures remained empty until their scheduled demolition. The city appraised properties, and the owners could either accept the "fair market price" or attempt to negotiate for more money. If the issue could not be resolved amicably, the city would use its power of eminent domain to acquire the property through condemnation at the price it last offered. The former owner was then free to file a lawsuit in superior court. It could take up to three years before the court decided whether the city owed the former owner—now the plaintiff—more money. If the plaintiff lost and the court set a price lower than what the city had paid, then he or she needed to return the overpayment.[87]

The actual demolition of structures began in May 1967. Over the next two years, 269 structures, some of them multiple-occupancy dwellings or businesses, were destroyed.[88] The city managed to relocate "118 individual householders, 142 families, and 105 businesses."[89] In the end, official estimates reported that 735 residents had to leave their homes. Mexican Americans accounted for 63 percent of those displaced, African Americans for 27 percent, Anglo Americans for 9 percent, and Chinese Americans for the remaining 1 percent.[90]

Recognizing the plight of tenants, HUD and the Tucson Urban Renewal Office offered them both monetary and physical assistance in relocating. The number of people who did not seek any sort of relocation assistance is not included in the public records and is hard to estimate. Statistics vary, but one report from the U.S. urban renewal commissioner suggests that 13 percent of those who lived in the area targeted by renewal had "either moved out of the city or disappeared."[91] Some, like Pedro Gonzales's family, refused relocation assistance outright.[92] One elderly former resident recalls that when city officials offered her family assistance, she asked them, "What help can you give someone when you're throwing them out of their house?" The woman's husband could not bear being relocated and died two months later. "If the city wants to kill old people," the woman declared, "they should shoot them and not take their houses, families, and friends away from them."[93]

Many downtown residents resisted relocation, but few pursued legal remedies. Among the few, Elmer Cobb and his wife, owners of the Old State Bar, filed an unlawful-eviction suit against the city for $200,000 in 1968. The Old State Bar stood in the way of the realignment of Main Street and the city's new sewer project. Municipal agents took possession of the property and moved the contents of the business to storage.[94] According to published reports, city officials boasted that "in the hundreds of relocations we made . . . Cobb was the only tenant we had to evict forcibly."[95] Although city agents may well have used, or threatened to use, physical force in only that one instance, force is inherent in the power of eminent domain, and there can be little doubt that residents who had not freely decided to move were indeed forced to do so.

At eighty-seven, Mexican American Leonides P. Wall refused to leave the home she had lived in for forty-three years. As Keith Carew reported, "Her husband had died there, all their children were born there, and she didn't want to leave her lifetime friends." She also refused to leave because a large palm tree planted by her deceased husband would be destroyed along with her home. Although she did indeed lose her house and the income she received from the few attached apartments, in order to expedite her leaving, the city moved the tree and replanted it in an area where she could visit it.[96]

Between 50 and 60 percent of the property owners accepted the initial offer made by city appraisers. A few filed for reappraisals in the hopes of receiving more money for their properties. Monica Flin, the owner of El Charro Restaurant, which had been in business for some thirty years in the area of La Placita, sought damages in superior court for the "grossly inadequate" sum that city officials had paid her for her property (see fig. 5.4). Flin had been given $58,500, but had paid $60,000 for the property twenty-five years earlier. Her property had been appraised without considering the new downtown structures that would have enhanced its value. Flin admitted she had accepted the money city officials offered her, but she later came to believe that "the settlement was made through fraud [and] mistake [based] on her own [limited] mental capacity and total lack of real estate experience to fully understand the transaction." In 1968, when the city appraised her property and negotiated with Flin, she was eighty-two years old.[97]

Virginia Gamez, an eighty-four-year-old widow, sued the city to obtain more money for her home and three rental units. When city officials offered her $5,000, she asked for $48,000—and another $25,000 in punitive damages when she filed her lawsuit. A superior court jury awarded her $7,100, less than one-sixth the value she placed on her properties. Decisions such as these convinced many property owners that taking legal action against the city was futile. However, in a surprising turn of events, a month after the Gamez case a Pima County superior court judge ordered the city to amend its property appraisals. Previously, they had based their valuations on the amounts the properties were worth *before* urban renewal. The judge ruled that the construction of the newly built city hall and county government complex north of Congress had to be taken into account in the appraisals. His ruling enhanced property values for the city as current owner, but came too late to ensure that former owners received fair value for their properties.[98]

"The area has just plain declined economically and physically over the last ten years," Don Laidlaw explained in October 1967. "A piece of property that may have been worth $10,000 about twenty years ago is

Figure 5.4. El Charro Restaurant, located in La Placita at 140 W. Broadway. (Courtesy Special Collections, University of Arizona Library; Tucson Urban Renewal, roll 9 C, no. 3)

now worth maybe $5,000. . . . This is a concept which is awfully hard to explain . . . to a different culture."[99] Most residents had to purchase homes in more affordable areas, often far from downtown. According to Laidlaws's administrative assistant, Phillip B. Whitmore, some area residents did not fully comprehend the inevitability and imminence of forced relocation once voters had approved the new project in March 1966. They "really didn't believe urban renewal was a finality. They thought it was something which would happen in the remote future."[100]

Despite outreach efforts by Laidlaw to inform residents of the city's plans to relocate them (one attempt even featured mariachis on a corner, who performed while Laidlaw dealt with what he called the "evident failure of communication"), many residents remained unapprised or misinformed about the relocation.[101] Renters made up the vast majority of residents in the target area. Because, however, the justice system served only property owners in condemnation proceedings, renters had no legal recourse.[102] Thus no court records document their dissatisfaction.

Moreover, there were no newspapers in the 1960s that focused on the tucsonense community. When and what residents of the targeted area came to learn about urban renewal, other than through Laidlaw's outreach efforts, seems unclear. Most came to understand the force of eminent domain the hard way. Exclusionary politics as well as cultural and language barriers discouraged area residents from fighting back. Many lacked previous experience fighting city hall. Unfamiliarity with and fear of law enforcement due to past experiences were other deterrents. Attorney Carlos Robles observed that "most [residents] wanted nothing to do with the law. They feared it. . . . When the city threatened [legal action] if they didn't move, they left without going to court. They thought there was something criminal about courts. They did not understand that these were civil cases."[103]

Historically, Mexican people in Tucson looked to the Catholic Church for guidance and leadership. Their lives revolved around the security offered by their predominantly Spanish-speaking barrios and the nearby church, Saint Augustine's. Alva Torres and a few others recall that some of those relocated told her that the priests from the cathedral encouraged them to "accept their fate and not to fight the inevitable."[104] City officials distinctly understood this relationship and capitalized on the Church's moral authority in the tucsonense community. In cases where people refused to move, relocation authorities brought a police officer and a local priest as a "disinterested . . . interpreter and mediator" to persuade people to leave their homes.[105] One such priest, José Hurtado, later came to regret his complicity in this removal process: "I think the city could have handled it much better. The people got lost in legalities and technicalities. . . . I don't know, maybe the Church should have gotten more involved."[106]

The Catholic Church, however, had a vested interest in ensuring urban renewal's success. Two weeks before the scheduled 1966 election, Bishop Francis J. Green announced plans to link Saint Augustine's renovation with urban renewal. "Because of the urban renewal program and the possible transformation of the area," he explained, "renovation of the cathedral will complement and blend in with the development of the area." The Diocese of Tucson worked with the city to acquire 77,000 square feet of vacant land, made available when adjacent dwellings were demolished, to expand its cathedral and parochial school.[107]

The Tucson Community Center

Even as they removed residents and cleared the land to accommodate what would finally be called the Tucson Community Center (TCC), city officials had not found a way to fund its construction. At the beginning of 1969, construction proceeded on the proposed local city and county offices, but a large tract of land, site of the future TCC, sat vacant in the middle of the project area. Newspaper reporter Don Robinson put a positive spin on this landscape oddity: "A 40-acre plot of barren ground in downtown Tucson stands out as 'a symbol of progress' for the city as it ploughs its way into 1969." And even though it would likely remain undeveloped for some time, to Robinson the tract represented a distinct improvement over the "streets, alleys, and vacant lots that were decorated with trash and [the many] buildings infested with vermin."[108]

In the meantime, the Chamber of Commerce had succeeded in persuading state legislators to allow cities in Arizona to enter into long-term lease-purchase agreements so that they could construct auditorium-convention centers (see fig. 5.5). A private, five-member nonprofit corporation, the Community Center Authority, was formed in 1965 to finance construction of the TCC. This group would issue $15.5 million in revenue bonds ($12.3 million in 1969 and another $5.2 million in 1970), enough to pay for construction of both the new center and a new police and fire headquarters located nearby. The City of Tucson had contracted to pay back the principal and interest on the bonds and any other expenses incurred; but it would not claim ownership for another thirty years. Instead, under a lease-purchase agreement with the Community Center Authority (owner until then of the multibuilding complex), the city would use revenue generated from the center to make rental payments and defray any other expenses.[109] Groundbreaking festivities for the TCC were held on May 12, 1969, when the mayor proudly announced, "This is the day all of us have waited for."[110] City officials insisted on calling the TCC a community center because "civic center" "convey[ed] an image of governmental bureaucracy 'including the jail house,' as opposed to a fine place for conventions and cultural and sports activities."[111] *Arizona Progress*, a monthly report issued by one of the state's largest banks, praised city officials' decision to use "community" because it provided "some insight to the philosophy governing its creation." Although hosting conventions would of course be a primary purpose of the new center, *Progress* found its "overriding purpose" to be "serv[ing] the cultural,

Within the image:
PARKING GARAGE "Nearing Completion"
COURTS BLDG. "Under Const."
GSA BLDG. "Under Contract"
POLICE & FIRE BLDG. "Under Contract"
HOTEL "Under Contract"
COMMUNITY CENTER "Under Const."

Figure 5.5. Structures under construction, circa 1970. (Courtesy Special Collections, University of Arizona Library; Views, Tucson, 1970, Downtown Development)

and the sporting, and the entertainment needs of the entire Tucson Metropolitan community."[112] This comment, and others like it throughout the push for urban renewal, suggests that many in the dominant culture held the ethnic populations in the renewal area responsible for depriving the "entire" community of such a resource. Thus a 1961 city report claims, "We do not live in a neighborhood only but in a *total* city, it is the interest of every Tucsonan to have a sound downtown area. . . . It is our cultural, commercial and political nerve center. It has been said that 'A City whose central core is not the favored shopping place of the entire region around it . . . is destroying itself . . . and in the process of destroying the suburbs too.'"[113] This sentiment, also evidenced in the composition of the city's citizens' committees, indicates that when many referred to "community," they actually meant those from the suburbs and the dominant culture.

The $17.6 million Tucson Community Center, which included a music hall and performance arena, opened on November 6, 1971 (see fig. 5.6).

Figure 5.6. A view of the Tucson Community Center and surrounding parking lots, circa 1971. (Courtesy Arizona Historical Society, Tucson, MS 1255 f. 135 [B])

A small theater opened later. Back patting, handshaking, and public speaking abounded at the ribbon-cutting event, which drew five hundred city leaders and reporters. Mayor James N. Corbett declared, "This is a great living testimony made possible by this community." Howard A. Shift, chairman of the city's planning and zoning commission called it "absolutely magnificent." "It's been a long time coming." Construction workers were still putting the finishing touches on the Music Hall, where Arthur Fiedler, who arrived to cheers aboard a fire truck for the ribbon cutting, would perform a few days later.[114]

On the evening of Monday, November 8, Fiedler started off the TCC's first official performance in the Music Hall with "The Star-Spangled Banner," a moment *Tucson Daily Citizen* reviewer Sue Giles described as "goose-pimply."[115] More than 2,000 people attended the concert, with the women arriving in formal gowns and fur coats and the men in tuxedos and dinner jackets.[116] Dan Pavillard, also a *Citizen* reviewer, described

Figure 5.7. The Ice Capades at the TCC in November 1971. (Courtesy Special Collections, University of Arizona Library; Tucson, Community Center, Ice Capades, Nov. 1971)

Fiedler and his Pops performance as "something out of Disney, swooping, splashing and exploding in a shower of sparkles." Fiedler concluded his program with "76 Trombones." Cries of "More!" from the audience led to three curtain calls and two encores of "Hey Jude" and a rousing rendition of "Stars and Stripes Forever."[117]

The following day, the first event in the new performance arena, the Ice Capades, would hold many spellbound (see fig. 5.7). The newspapers described the $7.7 million, 65,000-square-foot arena as big enough to accommodate a three-ring circus.[118] Its floor could be readily converted from a skating rink to a hardwood court or "rodeo sawdust" to accommodate a wide variety of events. For the arena's inaugural extravaganza on November 9, decorators had decked it out with lavish quantities of red, white, and blue. The mayor introduced Governor Jack Williams, who told the 7,000-strong crowd that the community center belonged to "the people" and that it represented "tomorrow."[119] The *Citizen*'s entertainment critic, Micheline Keating, reported that the "ice has a nice informality that makes everyone feel at home. It is cheerful and gay," like a "family room." "The costumes, glistening with newness, provide the frosting on the show."[120]

In 1971, the City of Tucson paid about $1.2 million a year to the Community Center Authority. Optimistic officials looked to the TCC to "be of substantial economic benefit to Tucson." Conventions promised to bring in more than 25 percent of the city's lease-purchase payments, with "shows, meetings, entertainment, extravaganzas, pageants, concerts" expected to bring in the rest.[121]

City officials were not moving into uncharted territory as they implemented their urban renewal visions. Other cities had destroyed low-income neighborhoods close to their downtown areas in an attempt to revitalize them—and failed. Jane Jacobs's *The Death and Life of American Cities*, published in 1961, gave local urban renewal advocates ample time to grasp potential problems. Jacobs urged cities to explore other place-based alternatives to improve "slum" areas without destroying them. "Marked with the planners' hex signs," Jacobs wrote, the poor "are pushed about, expropriated, and uprooted much as if they were the subjects of a conquering power."[122] Under the headline "From Right and Left: What Urban Renewal Critics Have to Say" a month before the urban renewal bond election, the *Citizen* cited the comments of sociologist Herbert J. Gans, who called for the end to the "practice of punishing the poor."[123] Local boosters and city officials paid no heed. Instead, throughout their promotional campaign, they portrayed their urban vision as exemplary and their renewal plan as designed only to improve conditions and meet "the needs of residents of the area."[124]

But from the rubble of urban renewal emerged a new way of thinking about history, older structures, and preservation. Deeply affected by the destruction of la calle and its nearby barrios, Alva Torres and the La Placita Committee fought to preserve a Mexican American place in Tucson and to defend a more inclusionary version of its history.[125]

6

The La Placita Committee
Claiming Place and History

> They cheated everybody and built something [La Placita Village]
> that for years did not make them money because they did not do
> it right. When you do something wrong, it comes back to you,
> and that's what the city did. La Placita would have been a natu-
> ral asset to the city. People could have come out and seen how the
> city once was. Our grandchildren and tourists would have loved
> it. It's like we had a little diamond and we gave it away for a zircon.
> I love Tucson, and the buildings are not the people, but they are
> part of a story that you try to save.
>
> —Alva Torres, December 2002[1]

Alva Torres's conversation with Rodolfo Soto in the midst of urban renewal raised her consciousness regarding space and history. Torres remembers it as a "baptism with fire," which came to affect every facet of her life. She began to make the connection between "the city's attempt to show that an area was devastated" and the efforts of city officials to "get their hands on money and build a community center."[2] But even though sections of la calle and its surrounding barrios had already been demolished when she moved to save history in April 1967, the bulldozers had not yet reached La Placita.

Recognizing that urban renewal threatened not only buildings but also memory, Torres initiated a public battle to preserve both a place—a Tucson landmark—and an essential part of Southern Arizona history. At the core of the debate over urban renewal lay conflicting visions of the past Tucsonans wished to celebrate and the future they hoped to construct. The La Placita Committee, consisting mostly of women, emerged to challenge what it saw as the cultural elitism inherent in urban renewal policies. Led and organized by Torres, this grassroots organization, armed with a heightened historical consciousness, became urban renewal's earliest and most formidable foe.

The effects of urbanization in Tucson have been uneven, and the motivations for designating some areas as undesirable and justifying unequal public services for Mexican Americans have often been relegated to the background when discussing plans for the city's development. Previous chapters have underscored how dominance became inscribed in the making of place.[3] Understanding these dynamics sheds light on the challenges the La Placita Committee faced in its public struggle to defend places and representations of the past that portrayed Mexican people as active contributors to history.

In their speeches and reports supporting urban renewal, promoters affirmed the city's commitment to preserving significant historic sites. Once the electorate had approved the Pueblo Redevelopment Center Project, however, planners began to modify and expand their construction plans. Far from being arbitrary, the city's early preservation efforts were laden with cultural and racial meanings evident in the battles over space and memory. For some U.S. cities that witnessed intense civil rights activism, the late 1960s ushered in an appreciation of diversity and pride in cultural differences. In contrast, Tucson's urban redevelopment put ethnic homogeneity and modernity first in order to attract tourists.

Tucson's Public Square

La Placita, originally called La Plaza de la Mesilla, dates back to the first years of Anglo settlement. Like most of Tucson's early celebrations, the annual festival of Tucson's patron saint, San Agustín, took place in La Placita. Spanning two weeks, it began on August 28, San Agustín's feast day, and culminated with the Mexican Independence celebration on September 16. Oxcarts of pomegranates, sugarcane, and quinces from Sonora, fireworks, music, Yaqui dancers, and riders on horseback all converged on the center of town for the festivities. Young women in traditional Mexican attire would parade their animals around the plaza as a "circus gaiety" took over the city. Couples would make their private intentions public by promenading around La Plaza, followed by watchful chaperones.[4] Nevertheless, in the early 1900s, with increasing social and legal restrictions, primarily on gambling and alcohol consumption, the festival waned in popularity.[5]

The San Agustín Church, which also served as a convent and school, had been built in the plaza area in 1868. After annexation by the United

States, Southern Arizona became part of the Diocese of Santa Fe. Officials of the Catholic Church, who presided over the finishing touches to the church, increasingly asserted their institutional control. They soon decided that "the old church [had] ceased to serve its community."[6] In 1898, on completion of the new Saint Augustine's Cathedral, currently located on Stone Avenue, Father Peter Bourgade sold the old church. The church building became first a hotel, then a brothel, then a garage, and finally a taxi stand.[7]

In 1929, speaking for the Business and Professional Women's Club of Tucson, Gertrude E. Mason declared that the former San Agustín Church represented "practically our last chance to save for our generation and those to come, some of the charm of old Tucson." She envisioned restoring the building and turning it into a community center, which "would add to our city, make a hometown of it," and attract tourists. Her appeals were rebuffed by an unnamed but powerful businessman, who, the *Tucson Daily Citizen* reported, "had decided that the historic value of the building was 'not worth 5 cents.'"[8] When workers began to dismantle it in 1936, the last owner of the church building, automobile dealer Frank C. O'Rielly, suggested that its stone remnants be "dump[ed] into the nearest bank of the Santa Cruz River."[9]

Despite the destruction of the old church, however, Mexican Americans and at least some Anglos continued to gravitate to La Placita for socializing and celebrations. "It was kind of the central area of town," Roy Drachman recalled at age eighty-three. "There were several businesses in La Placita. I remember the rounded park with the kiosk [gazebo] in the center, and the several benches around the park. . . . Many fiestas were celebrated there like the 4th of July, 16th of September, [and] 5 de Mayo." Adela Brady remembered that "we used to have music there every Saturday, every Sunday. . . . Había sitio donde tocaban, cantaban y se paseaban [There was a place for playing music and singing and strolling around]."[10] Pedro Gonzales recalled that, even as late as 1967, there "was always something happening at La Placita. Yes, there were special fiestas but it was [also] an everyday thing. We used to just hang out" (see fig. 6.1).[11]

In 1942, the Alianza Hispano-Americana organized a patriotic parade through the streets of la calle, which culminated in a fiesta, complete with speakers, most in Spanish, talent contests, mariachis, and dances at La Placita. Here, to demonstrate tucsonenses' loyalty and support for the war effort, the Alianza sold war bonds and defense stamps, promising to

Figure 6.1. A celebration at La Placita. (Courtesy Arizona Historical Society, Tucson, PC 214 f. 65 [D])

match every dollar spent, up to $40,000.[12] Indeed, because only Congress Street separated La Placita from their hall, the organization held most of its outdoor celebrations there.

In an uncharacteristic and unprecedented move, the Tucson Rodeo Committee proposed to stage its 1944 fiesta at La Placita—to bring it "back to life." "War or no war, the modern Pueblo is going to recapture the 'jaripeo,' or rodeo, spirit in February 1944, cementing Latin American friendship and goodwill," the committee announced, borrowing language directly from Franklin D. Roosevelt's Good Neighbor Policy.[13] With the 25,000 "Spanish-speaking people of the community" parading through the plaza and with "dancing in the streets, [the] gaily garbed citizens in the true Charro and China Poblano costumes of that day will add the authentic touch of a town that has not forgotten entirely its rich past."[14]

The Rodeo Committee assigned the task of ensuring that tucsonenses participated in the fiesta to the Alianza. In striking contrast to previous civic celebrations, the committee arranged to encourage tucsonense visibility, and most of the city's leading tourism boosters participated in this effort. In a new approach to marketing the city's image, the Rodeo Committee promised to sustain cultural aspects that distinguished La Placita: "What is most important, La Plazita [sic] will not sink into oblivion at the close of the festivities; it will take an important place in Tucson's postwar plans, creating a Mecca for tourists yet to come, one that will surpass the famed Olivera Street in Los Angeles, providing a future industry of handicraft and tourist entertainment that has helped make this city famous throughout the nation."[15]

Needless to say, tourism lay at the core of the 1944 Rodeo Committee's goal of incorporating events at La Placita into their Fiesta de los Vaqueros. Indeed, the tourist industry had taken on a new hemispheric emphasis, which reflected global events. According to historian Alex Saragoza, Mexico had started marketing key Mexican destinations to tourists in the 1930s. When war broke out in Europe, tourists throughout the United States wanting to visit a foreign country but also to escape the "turmoil across the Atlantic" increasingly traveled to Mexico, and the Mexican tourist industry reaped the benefits. The trend continued with the postwar economic boom, when people from the United States, equipped with widely distributed guidebooks, traveled to Mexico in their automobiles.[16]

Thus, in 1944 the Tucson Rodeo Committee hoped to capitalize on the increased flow of Mexico-bound travelers by staging a fiesta in Tucson that "involv[ed] the entire population, emphasizing the romance of the early Mexican atmosphere."[17] Using their new, albeit onetime, marketing strategy, they hoped to sell a "Mexican" Tucson, which required that they briefly welcome tucsonenses into the civic fold to add authenticity to their fiesta. Indeed, the Rodeo Committee seemed even to apologize for the consequences of their adherence to the Anglo fantasy heritage: "As the years rolled by the rodeo took on a Western cowboy aura, dropping the characteristic charm of fiesta time, as La Plaza was almost forgotten and the dancing and visiting between neighboring families and friends became a thing of the past." For the 1944 fiesta, every item sold bore a tag with a picture of the former San Agustín Church, and the Spanish language dominated in the performances, films, and music. Not only did the Rodeo Committee invite visitors to visit la calle so they could experience Mexican culture in Tucson, they also provided free taxi rides to "view the historical portions of the Old Pueblo."[18]

Figure 6.2. A parade of children at a La Placita festival, circa 1962. (Courtesy Arizona Historical Society, Tucson, PC 214 f. 65 [C])

Formed in 1950, the Tucson Festival Society also recognized that La Placita's cultural qualities could lure certain segments of the tourist market. Although its stated primary goal was to promote the region's cultural assets, the society also sought to promote "economic progress" in the city. To this end, it wanted to "extend the Tucson winter season beyond its traditional limits: The festival planners, who envisage a late-March preliminary program and the actual festival Apr. 6, 7 and 8, have come up with a most workable blueprint for an extended and enlarged tourist season. . . . The cultural heritage of our region deserves such a memorial. The economic future of our community demands it."[19]

Through a series of local events, the Festival Society revived older traditions and cultural forms. Out of these came the Fiesta de La Placita, which featured Mexican entertainment, dancing, and music. A parade of children dressed up in Mexican and Spanish costumes ended at La Placita and kicked off a weekend of activities (see fig. 6.2). Although this two-day celebration was an official Festival Society activity, tucsonenses took responsibility for staging it, thus assuring high attendance. Various

Figure 6.3. Ronquillo's Bakery, located behind the Plaza Theatre in La Placita, circa 1966. (Courtesy Special Collections, University of Arizona Library; Tucson Urban Renewal, roll 9 E, no. 3).

Mexican American organizations sponsored game and food booths as a means of raising funds for their clubs and organizations. The Fiesta de La Placita continued until 1969.[20]

As the commercial and ceremonial center of la calle for more than a hundred years, the area around La Placita defied and inverted the local economic and social hierarchy. La Placita and its surrounding businesses provided tangible evidence of a place that survived and thrived due to the Mexican people's patronage, solidarity, and loyalty. On its perimeter stood the Belmont Hotel, El Charro Restaurant, Ronquillo's Bakery, some small specialty shops, the Rosequist Gallery, the Zepeda Shoe Shop, La Plaza Theatre, and Half-Moon Chinese Food—all operating in 1967 (see fig. 6.3).[21] The commercial and entertainment vibrancy of this space reflected Mexican American success and entrepreneurship, past and present. The gazebo, semicircular plaza, and surrounding businesses that together formed what most tucsonenses considered La Placita represented the intersection of place, community, and identity to much of the tucsonense community. As la calle's public square, it marked Mexican Americans' quest for autonomy, fostering deep feelings of belonging in tucsonenses. Josephina Lizárraga recalls that, when she moved to Tucson from Mexico in the late 1950s, she would go to La Placita, eat at El Charro Restaurant, take a stroll—perhaps shop and then go to the movies at La

Plaza. She looked forward to these nights out with her husband because it "reminded her of being back in Mexico."[22] No other area in Tucson served as a focal point for Mexican and Mexican American culture, history, and economic advancement.

Replacing Historical with Commercial Space

In April 1965, the Historical Sites Committee, appointed by the mayor and city council a few years earlier and chaired by Isabel Fathauer, a strong crusader for historic preservation, announced the sites it believed merited preservation and restoration.[23] The committee included on its list a number of structures north of downtown and a few noteworthy sites in la calle. It recommended preserving the John C. Frémont House, at 145–153 South Main Avenue, because the explorer, presidential candidate, and fifth territorial governor was said to have lived there in 1881. In the same block, at 195 South Main Avenue, the house of Captain Jack Burgess (a prominent soldier, Indian scout, mining engineer, and civic promoter) also made the committee's list, as did the Sabino Otero House, at 219 South Main Avenue, constructed in the early 1860s and "considered the best remaining example of Mexican style architecture." In listing the "La Placita area," the committee noted that the area "served as a favorite spot for celebrations for many years," but pointedly refrained from citing any specific structures, businesses, or streets.[24]

The city's commitment to a "definite blueprint" for preserving key sites is reflected in a February 1966 article by *Tucson Daily Citizen* reporter Dan Pavillard, who began his story by stating, "If anyone thinks no one cares about Tucson's heritage, specifically its old, historic buildings, let him dare crank up a bulldozer within earshot of one of the monuments." That said, Pavillard went on to report that city officials had reduced the number of historic structures they hoped to preserve and restore to five: four north of Congress and only one—the Frémont House—in la calle. And of these five, only the Frémont House remained a priority. Six others, determined to be "historically valuable" but "architecturally unsound" and including the Otero House, had been removed from the list. From Pavillard's passing mention that "also to be preserved is the gazebo (bandstand) in La Placita Park on West Broadway," one can safely conclude that city officials did not see the larger La Placita area as a cohesive unit worthy of preservation.[25]

Indeed, in La Placita's case, the city's commitment to "efficient" street patterns clearly trumped its commitment to historic preservation. Because planners expected large numbers of people to be drawn to the new global community center, they viewed unimpeded access to the area as critical. Accordingly, they designed major traffic corridors to move traffic east-west and north-south, and they recommended removing the smaller streets. The planners also expected an influx of pedestrians and incorporated a number of foot bridges "to encourage visitors to circulate freely" between the central business district and the Community Center. Clearly visible from the freeway, the new concrete buildings were "to provide major landmarks and a striking entrance to the Downtown area."[26]

The 1965 plan called for development of a "Special Commercial area," between Congress Street and Broadway, and between Main and Church, to "be of special character not provided in the Business District, and oriented toward both the community at large and the visitors to the Community Center specifically."[27] This left planners and designers tremendous leeway to create a place that would appeal to suburbanites and tourists.

A 1966 *American City* article described what COMB envisioned for the La Placita area: "La Plazita, where early Tucsonans held festivals, will be retained and enlarged and the gazebo will be restored. Pedestrian overpasses will connect the shops to the government plaza and community center." As part of the area's "enlargement," COMB called for the creation of new arts and crafts specialty shops, restaurants, and offices.[28] Evolving urban renewal plans increasingly began to stress "quality development," a focus that would have severe consequences for the old La Placita.

The City of Tucson owned the semicircular park in the center of La Placita. In 1966, urban renewal planners recommended replacing the original La Placita site with 13,000 square feet of "exclusive and privately owned sidewalks and landscaping."[29] They proposed that Broadway be shifted south and widened to serve as a major east-west thoroughfare cutting directly across the plaza itself. In its place, the Pueblo Center Redevelopment Project proposed a multimillion-dollar modern concrete shopping, office, and restaurant complex—La Placita Village—to complement the city's new Community Center and larger urban renewal plans (see fig. 6.4).

Figure 6.4. An example of the type of shoppers that planners envisioned would gravitate to the La Placita Village. They promised "jewelry, optical, and sewing shops, men's wear, ladies' boutiques and food specialty shops." For architectural features, they envisioned "Numerous iron balconies, courtyards with large potted plants, interesting light fixtures and gaily colored umbrellas for outdoor dining will add a touch of old Mexico." (*La Placita Village*, 10)

"Baptism with Fire"

At first Alva Torres believed city officials when they expressed a commitment to preserve historically significant sites as an integral part of their
urban renewal agenda. Distracted by family responsibilities, she did not
really *see* the destruction that had already begun in the city's oldest sections. Torres had always had strong ties to la calle. Like most tucsonenses, she often socialized, attended celebrations, and shopped there.
She had worked in a la calle clothing store, Lyric Outfitting, before her
marriage to Arthur Torres, an electrician, in 1953, three years after grad-
uating from high school. Unlike most tucsonenses of her generation,
however, Torres attended the University of Arizona, where she received
a two-year liberal arts degree. Living in the Armory Park area a few
blocks from La Placita in 1967, at this writing, Torres remains an active
member of Club Mavis, a Mexican American women's social club she
joined at the age of fifteen. When interviewed, she recalled the numerous fiestas at La Placita, where she often managed her club's booths. For
her and many other tucsonenses, these fiestas strengthened personal
and community bonds. In celebrating the saints' feast days, Mexican
Independence, and the 4th of July, they mostly celebrated themselves.
Torres had always considered la calle a vital part of Tucson, and La
Placita an indispensable part of la calle (see fig. 6.5).[30]

   With no prior experience in local politics or in dealing with city hall,
Alva Torres's approach to saving La Placita demonstrates a surprisingly
refined political sense.[31] She began by contacting the editor of the *Arizona
Daily Star*, William Mathews, because she believed he wielded substantial influence. Although not particularly friendly, Mathews listened
while she outlined her new mission. When she asked him, "Instead of
destroying everything, why not at least save La Placita?" he told her that
a group called the "San Agustín's Placita Committee" or the "San Agustín
Committee" had been assigned the task of dealing with citizen concerns
about La Placita. Mathews suggested that Torres talk to Don Laidlaw,
the chief urban renewal officer at city hall, and that she "tell him Bill
Mathews sent you." Without Mathews's referral, Torres felt that Laidlaw
might have ignored her.[32]

   Instead, in early October 1967, Laidlaw met with Alva Torres. He
described the meeting in a memo to inform COMB and others at city
hall of a potential obstacle: Torres, he said, "stated her understanding
that the hour was late, but she added that she was determined to make

Figure 6.5. Alva Torres took this photograph of her three children and a family friend at a La Placita festival in 1963, four years before she became a historic preservationist. (Courtesy Alva B. Torres)

every effort to see that certain other objectives were achieved . . . to retain substantially the same street pattern and almost all the buildings. . . . She stated that this was the Tucson Mexicans knew and stated further her belief that the area should be preserved more or less as it is."[33] Like Mathews, Laidlaw suggested that Torres meet with the San Agustín Committee. She suspected she was "getting the runaround," but, fearing that La Placita's days were numbered, she decided to meet with the committee anyway. The first member she contacted, Thayer Painter, seemed interested and supportive: "I would like you to come [to a meeting that night], Painter told her, "but I have to check with some of the other members. It is a closed committee, but I really like your plan; I like it better than what we have." At this point, however, Torres did not have a definite plan.[34]

Torres expected to encounter bureaucratic obstacles in her efforts to save La Placita but not such blatant exclusion, and on such a personal level, as she did from the San Agustín Committee. "Who are you to get involved?" the group's leader asked her in a telephone call. "Where do you get the authority?" Caught off guard, Torres replied, "I was born here, this is my town, I have as much right as anybody else, and I think I have a good idea." As it turned out, the San Agustín Committee never invited her to their meetings.[35]

The committee's strong affiliation with Saint Augustine Cathedral, which stood to benefit from the proposed demolition of adjacent structures, prevented it from challenging urban renewal.[36] Moreover, it made no attempt to garner community support for the preservation of La Placita. Indeed, there is no record that the City of Tucson ever formally appointed the members of this so-called citizens' committee.[37] Belonging also to both the Tucson Festival Society and its subcommittee in charge of the La Placita Fiestas, they stepped in to ensure that they would have a plaza, in whatever form the city decided, for their annual downtown event. The fact that Mathews and city officials considered San Agustín Committee members to be "official" representatives of the larger public needs speaks to their influence and their ability to legitimize themselves.

Although a few of Tucson's Mexican American elite sat on the San Agustín Committee, most members were well-connected Anglo Americans who also belonged to the Tucson Festival Society, with a commercial interest in showcasing local arts and culture. The committee expressed its "willingness for planners to make necessary changes in the area," provided the Tucson Festival Society could still hold its annual La Fiesta de La Placita in "a plaza-like commercial area."[38] Committee members insisted on retaining the name "La Placita" for the area, but, far from fighting to save the original La Placita, they supported replacing it with a new plaza, one that would highlight a contrived "Southwest" heritage, reminding visitors of "another world."[39]

The La Placita Committee

Alva Bustamante Torres came from an established tucsonense family. In this time of crisis, she turned to her staunchest allies, her large network of family and friends.[40] As her first act in trying to save La Placita, Torres formed a prayer group. Here she shared Rodolfo Soto's and her concerns with her family and friends and persuaded them to get involved by praying. Armed with their shared Christian beliefs and commitment to saving history, these Mexican American women (most were Catholic, but

several Methodists took part as well) would become the core of the La
Placita Committee. They prayed for God to intervene and to grant Torres
strength and direction.[41]

In the spring of 1967, Torres set out to talk to business owners around
La Placita. She struck up a conversation with Jane Rosequist, the owner
of an art gallery at 18 South Convent Avenue. In 1945, Rosequist and
her husband had converted eight adobe row houses into a framing
shop and later began to sell paintings and sculptures, whereupon urban
renewal officials informed her that she had to move.[42] Although Torres
had not envisioned forming a political group before this encounter, she
impulsively told Rosequist, "I'm going to have a meeting and I'm going
to invite some people to come. I want to form a committee to save La
Placita." "Well, *you're* interested," said Rosequist, "but probably nobody
else is. Who are these people? What makes you think you can do anything? Other people have tried." Six months before, Rosequist herself
had tried but failed to move her gallery to the Otero House to ensure
the house's preservation.[43] Torres told her she could do it "because I have
already set up a prayer group to pray for me and La Placita." This sparked
Rosequist's interest, and she became much more supportive.[44]

Understanding the limits of individual effort and living in a political era that promised change, Torres also understood the advantages
of a collaborative and collective effort. More important, she knew she
needed more than a prayer group to stop the bulldozers. She held the
first informal meeting of the Society for the Preservation of Tucson's
Plaza de la Mesilla, soon to be called the La Placita Committee, in her
home. According to Torres, the group welcomed all who were interested
in saving La Placita and the surrounding area no matter what their background or ethnicity. Because Torres invited people she knew and these
were mostly tucsonenses, they made up the bulk of her group. Although
its membership hovered at about twenty, the committee became the city's
most vocal public critic of urban renewal.[45]

Rosequist had suggested that Torres get in touch with Alene Dunlap
Smith, who also had an interest in historic preservation. Smith brought
a different political perspective to the La Placita Committee. She had
moved to Tucson from Waterloo, Iowa, in 1946 and had gained political experience as a member of the League of Women Voters. Smith, who
lived in the former Samuel Hughes House and had a strong appreciation of history, complemented Torres's political drive. The two women
formed a lasting friendship.[46]

Spearheaded by Smith and Torres, the committee launched a letter-writing campaign to influential people to gain support. The letters provide insight into the group's goals and ideology, particularly regarding tucsonenses' role in their city's history and what they perceived as urban renewal's "hidden" agenda, as well as the importance of historical memory. Thus, in December 1968 Torres wrote to Mayor Jim Corbett:

> As Mexican-Americans we see the project of our preservation of La Placita as one of great importance to our ethnic group. We would like to see the Plaza de la Mesilla and the surrounding area developed as a representation of our heritage and culture and as a contribution of this ethnic group to the City of Tucson. We do not wish to impose our ways on Tucson, but neither can we stand by and see the last authentic remnant of our identity with the Old Pueblo be utterly destroyed.[47]

Torres's linking of place and collective ethnic identity corresponds to that described by historian Dolores Hayden: "Identity is intimately tied to memory: both our personal memories (where we come from and where we have dwelt) and the collective or social memories interconnected with the histories of our families, neighbors, fellow workers, and ethnic communities."[48] Decades before, the cherished San Agustín Church had been demolished to make way for a bus terminal. Urban renewal now threatened to obliterate the greatest repositories of Mexican American memories remaining in la calle and its surrounding barrios—not just La Placita but also grocery stores, clothing stores, and entire streets in the area.

In the civil rights spirit of the late 1960s, the La Placita Committee insisted that local and federal government agents heed their demands because its members represented a minority group that had suffered discrimination.[49] Committee members publicly proclaimed themselves citizens in a system and society they perceived as undemocratic. They did not, however, represent the fundamental interests of la calle's residents, nor did they try to alleviate the economic burdens of those forced to relocate. Indeed, for the most part, the committee's rhetoric and goals did not express a commitment to economic justice. Although its letters to elected and appointed federal officials often highlighted the social costs of urban renewal, the committee focused primarily on historic preservation, casting it as compensation, at least in part, for the unfair burden borne by those displaced. Thus, in an October 1967 letter to a regional urban renewal officer, the committee wrote: "The people who are affected by Urban Renewal in being relocated in residences as well as many small businesses are also Mexican-American. It is therefore logical and just that our wishes be given fair consideration. The part of Tucson which is in reality the OLD PUEBLO is being completely destroyed. Of the 80.2 acres involved, the Plaza represents less than three acres."[50]

When she wrote Lady Bird Johnson, Torres appealed for help as a mother and made historic preservation a gendered issue: "We are pressed for time. . . . As a native of Tucson I feel [saving La Placita] would be a reflection of our heritage and cultural background and we, as parents, should retain this area for our children. . . . In Arizona we do not have a single authentic Mexican plaza to reflect this heritage which helped build the Southwest. Please, Mrs. Johnson, help us."[51] For Torres, much of what it entailed to pass on "heritage and culture" to future generations took place in the domestic sphere.

Torres perceived attacks on La Placita as attacks on the history of the Mexican people who had built and lived in Tucson. In a letter to Congressman Morris Udall, she cited the indifference of local officials and identified the city's hidden agenda: "It is not enough that many citizens of Mexican descent who have lived in the area for many years are being relocated and being caused some financial hardships since most are pensioners, but it appears to us that the main effort is to destroy once and for all any identification with the Mexican-American community."[52]

As one of the many tucsonenses sending letters of support to the committee, Irma Villa wrote: "For years it has been proven that people were supposed to be proud of their cultural background, but if symbols of this cultural background are destroyed in the name of progress there is very little that the people of today and our future generations have to be proud of."[53] Such sentiments confirm the power of place, which historian Dolores Hayden defines as "shared time in the form of shared territory," and which bonded the La Placita Committee members as they rallied to gain supporters.[54] In letters outlining the committee's goals and announcing the dates of forthcoming meetings, each personally signed by its secretary, Ann Montaño, the committee invited influential individuals to attend: "We hope to make a coordinated community effort to preserve this historic area in Tucson and would appreciate an opportunity to discuss it with you at this meeting."[55]

At the first official meeting of the La Placita Committee, held at the Pioneer Hotel in Tucson on June 15, 1967, Rodolfo Soto, an amateur historian, made a presentation, "The Preservation of a Memory in the Midst of Progress," which was intended to remind his audience of fourteen of Tucson's origins. Most of the men took it upon themselves to gather information that would date the buildings in La Placita. Alva Torres committed herself to preparing a list of the advantages of preserving the old structures. The committee also drew up a list of people who might be interested in its efforts and who were to be personally invited to future meetings.[56] This approach proved effective: nearly a hundred people attended the committee's next official meeting at El Charro Restaurant on Friday, August 11, 1967.[57]

Many la calle residents forced by urban renewal to relocate and leave their friends and neighbors were angry and resentful. "We saw it all go down," Leticia Jacobs Fuentes remembered in 1997. "It was bad. . . . People weren't very happy. They'd been there all their lives. It was quite a trauma for us, for everybody. . . . We were a happy family there. We lost that neighborhood."[58] Many others felt betrayed by a city that had masterminded the destruction of their community and historic spaces. Some, like Rodolfo Soto, harbored private feelings of fear, loss, disappointment, and resentment. These types of nonconfrontational sentiments characterize what James C. Scott calls "hidden transcripts," which he describes as a "critique of power . . . [a] discourse that takes place 'offstage,' beyond direct observation by powerholders."[59] In this distressed and dislocated community, Alva Torres broke the silence and voiced its previously muted but widely shared discourse.

Grounded in resentment and disillusionment with the status quo, Torres turned these "hidden transcripts" into a public issue—so much so that city officials called a special meeting to address the "good deal of controversy . . . being generated over the questions of preserving La Placita."[60] Through Torres's leadership and actions, the preservationist concerns of many tucsonenses finally found public expression.

Not surprisingly, the local papers did not give much coverage to La Placita Committee activities. Indeed, they ignored these persistent and visible preservationists even when they stood on various downtown street corners, gathering signatures for a petition in 100-plus temperatures. Their petition demanded that the city implement their plan to save the La Placita area. Working street corners, grocery stores, and numerous gatherings during the hot summer months, they gathered support and signatures, collecting over 8,000, mostly from Mexican Americans, evidence that the committee had significant tucsonense support.[61]

The committee's demands are best outlined in its four-page "Plan for the Preservation, Restoration and Uses of the Plaza de la Mesilla Area, within the Pueblo Center Redevelopment Area," presented to the mayor and city council along with their petitions in September 1967. In it, the committee demanded that the city declare the Plaza de la Mesilla area and its surrounding structures a "Historic Area for the City of Tucson, Arizona" and "provide for authentic restoration" of structures that dated back to the nineteenth century. The committee feared that the old structures would be destroyed and replaced by new ones designed to mimic them. Recognizing the importance of religion to the area, the plan called for construction of an Inter-faith Chapel, as well as a museum and historical library. Committee members hoped that the chapel would be built on the site where the old San Agustín Church once stood. They insisted in their plan that the plaza remain an open area so that the festivals, celebrations, and public meetings of the past would continue, that only the gazebo, the new chapel, and the museum be allowed in this open area, and that a "perpetual restriction against [constructing] any other buildings" be enforced. The plan also provided alternate street designs that would keep La Placita area "entirely" intact. Finally, it presented a request by the committee that the city include a "750 seat theatre suitable for both movie and legitimate theatre productions in Spanish" as part of the new construction near La Placita.[62]

The committee insisted that its plan be "considered as a whole, a unified plan [and] that it [was] critically important to save everything authentic in such a uniquely historic area, continuously successful for over 100 years."[63] Clearly, committee members had a different vision of the downtown area than urban renewal planners. At the core of their demands and proposals lay the hope that Mexican Americans would continue to gravitate to the downtown area despite the demolition of large sections of la calle. To compensate for the loss, they proposed new structures and cultural sites.

As bold as the committee's demands were, it did not have the funds to take on the rehabilitation of the old structures or even to assist in it. It aimed to make its proposals for La Placita public, get as many people as possible to support them, and force the city to adopt them. Its plan had asked city officials "to explore fully all possibilities for the use of Federal, State and Foundational Funds available for historic restoration and development."[64] The committee did not consider this an unreasonable request because city officials had enthusiastically provided substantial support and funding avenues for the restoration of the Frémont House, named after territorial governor John C. Frémont, an icon of the U.S. conquest of the West.[65]

The committee recognized the obstacles it faced in persuading city officials to deviate from their renewal plans. "The problem at heart," Alva Torres pointed out, "centers around the alignment of a street."[66] She insisted that if the project's Broadway route were shifted only "ten feet to the north," most of the plaza would be saved and a new chapel could be built on the site where the old San Agustín Church once stood.[67] The committee went so far as to commission a civil engineer and University of Arizona professor, Donald L. Woods, to redesign the area "with the goal of integrating [its plan] into the urban renewal project." In Woods's blueprint, Broadway would be shifted slightly to the north of the city's proposed realignment. Although his alternative plan integrated the key aspects of the committee's social and political agenda, Woods admitted that "if the movement of traffic was the ultimate priority, then the city's designs were the best."[68]

Torres and the La Placita Committee also tried to go around city officials, appealing directly to President Lyndon B. Johnson. In his reply on the president's behalf, however, Deputy Assistant Secretary for Renewal Assistance Robert E. McCabe made his department's deference to local authorities abundantly clear:

> It is my understanding that the Urban Renewal Plan does provide for the preservation of the Plazita itself and, where economically feasible, for the preservation of certain structures which are determined to be of historic significance. . . . I have also been informed that the Community Redevelopment Office of the City of Tucson has been working closely with the Tucson Heritage Foundation, the Tucson Historical Sites Committee, and the Arizona Pioneers Historical Society in determining which structures may be preserved. Thus far it has been determined that four buildings of historical architectural significance will be preserved and will become part of an art center. In addition, the Frémont House and the Otero home, which are of historical significance to the City of Tucson, probably will be preserved.[69]

Although national guidelines required federal oversight of local urban renewal projects, McCabe insisted that "the determination as to which buildings in a project are to be retained is a local decision. As you are

Figure 6.6. The proposed rerouting of Broadway across La Placita: (1) the kiosko, or gazebo (2) La Plaza Theatre (4) El Charro Restaurant (5) Rosequist Galleries (6) the Greyhound Bus Depot. (Drawing by Paul Mirocha)

probably aware, urban renewal is a local program. Projects are conceived, project objectives are established, and plans are prepared, approved and implemented by the locality."[70]

Later in September 1967 the committee's actions caused Don Laidlaw to bring the two organizations involved in La Placita's future to the table to address their "differences of opinion" and "approaches" and to chart some semblance of "peace." At this meeting, Laidlaw sided with the San Agustín Committee, which supported La Placita Village and "want[ed] to preserve the location as a historic site to create around la Placita a distinctive and charming commercial area. . . . The city staff has agreed on all points with these objectives. We feel they are feasible" (see fig. 6.6).[71]

Although Laidlaw voiced a readiness "to consider the alternative," he and his staff's commitment to what they considered "feasible" prevented them from considering any alteration of their realignment of Broadway ("this part of the proposed plan for the area cannot be changed").[72] Laidlaw released a letter he had sent to Torres to the *Tucson Daily Citizen*, presumably to demonstrate his public commitment to negotiating. The newspaper published a portion of his concerns and priorities: "Because of changes in elevation (topography) between Church and Main and requirements for pedestrian circulation throughout the redevelopment project, and because of requirements for utility installations, the street pattern as presently designed could not be altered without substantially disrupting service, public safety, efficiency and economy of the redevelopment as a whole." In this letter, Laidlaw asked Torres seven questions: Which property owners wished to remain and "use their buildings in accordance with the redevelopment plan"? If buildings could be rehabilitated and brought up to building standards, how much would it cost? Were the property owners "ready" to take responsibility for these costs? Did the owners have the "necessary funds" to undertake such a project? What would the buildings be used for? What rents would be charged? What would the exterior of the buildings look like?[73] Laidlaw requested that the La Placita Committee secure "letters of intent" from the area's building owners that addressed these questions before he and his staff would consider the committee's proposed plan. The cooperation of building owners proved critical because, typical of the rest of la calle, most businesses rented their properties, including Ronqillo's Bakery and La Plaza Theatre. El Charro Restaurant and the Rosequist Gallery, which actually owned their properties, stood as exceptions. In framing these questions, Laidlaw clearly placed the burden of structural rehabilitation on private property owners to meet the stipulations of the city's federally sponsored urban redevelopment project.[74] The city offered neither funding nor tax incentives to help with the rehabilitation of structures.

Laidlaw insisted that "the street pattern as presently designed is necessary to meet requirements for vehicular and pedestrian safety. . . . I must conclude that in spite of specific benefits to the commercial area that might result from the modification of the street pattern, the overall requirements of the redevelopment project would prevent our considering at this time the revision of the street system in the vicinity of Broadway and Church." The City of Tucson had paid planners and consultants large sums of money to design the new La Placita Village complex, it had already secured federal funding to subsidize the demolition of all structures in the designated urban renewal area, and now it put enormous pressure on the members of the La Placita Committee to accept the city's plan.[75]

The inflexibility of urban renewal planners on the location of Broadway, the City of Tucson's stated refusal to take fiscal responsibility for the proposed restoration, and deadlocked negotiations with property owners and renters caused the committee to modify its plan and make a major concession: "If Broadway MUST transverse the original Plaza site, then the street should be moved further North, if at all possible and certainly no further South."[76] Overwhelmed and recognizing that Broadway would be rerouted to cross the La Placita area to accommodate the proposed new La Placita Village, committee members decided to pursue an alternative strategy—to preserve as much of the plaza area as possible.[77] As committee president, Torres acknowledged in an open letter published in the local papers in 1968 that her group's battle to save all of La Placita had come to an end. She thanked Laidlaw, the mayor, and the city council for accepting a few minor amendments to the Pueblo Center Redevelopment Project, and she also thanked the 8,062 people who had signed the committee's petitions for their support. She highlighted what her committee did manage to save, noting that "a small part of the Plaza de la Mesilla in the final plans where none was previously planned" will be incorporated into the new La Placita Village.[78]

The intense energy Alva Torres put into the petition drive and into saving at least some of La Placita made her physically ill, so ill she had to be hospitalized. When it came time, in September 1967, to submit the petitions to the mayor and city council, she could not attend.[79] Torres never recovered from the battle to save La Placita. The demolition of each additional structure caused her great pain: "It was as if they were killing one of my kids."[80]

"I think we failed," Torres lamented in 2002. "We were successful in making urban renewal a public issue. . . . But we were not able to preserve [the] environment that made La Placita special, and we should have been able to save it."[81] Nevertheless, thanks to the La Placita Committee's intervention, in the place where Congress and Broadway intersect—an area surrounded by concrete buildings, some many stories high—a small, triangular patch of green grass still exists. For Torres, it is the "most attractive area downtown." Although earlier designs would have moved the gazebo to the center of the new La Placita Village, the committee's efforts forced the city to leave it in its original spot (see fig. 6.7). There its age and authenticity stand out against the modern "Southwest" structures of the new complex.

Even after the La Placita Committee abandoned its plan, Alva Torres continued to walk the area and monitor construction of the village. She watched as Monica Flin relocated; she kept vigil on the construction around the Samaniego House, one of the two houses south of Congress that city officials chose to preserve.[82] In 1970, when a section of the

Figure 6.7. The cars parked to the left of the kiosk indicate that this photo was taken before the construction of La Placita Village, circa 1971. Congress and Broadway separate the kiosko (one of the few vestiges left of La Placita), from the County Buildings in the background. (Courtesy Special Collections, University of Arizona Library; Tucson, Views, 1970, Pima County Administration Building)

building that had once been home to El Charro faced demolition, she wrote city officials another letter. Her words echo her extraordinary historical vision:

> It is the last remaining edifice in Tucson where many of us often went to enjoy ourselves with our loved ones. Not one other building standing in Tucson is of as much value in a non-monetary way as this one. . . . Personally I place a great value on intangibles. Intangibles are after all the only indestructible forces or energies left to us. . . . Please do not begin to measure in money what it would cost to restore the "El Charro" building, otherwise you will probably give up. . . . In order to save an important spirit in the "Old Pueblo," first you must love it—if you do not, I doubt that anything I can say will make you want to save it.[83]

La Placita Village

By 1971, city officials had destroyed nearly all the structures that surrounded La Placita. The gazebo and the semicircular park were now surrounded by barren land. While builders put the finishing touches on
the Community Center, Phillip B. Whitmore, the newest urban renewal
director, began to "feel" the market for commercial developers to build
La Placita Village. By this time, city officials had removed most of the
people from la calle and its surrounding barrios, and the downtown area
seemed eerily vacant. "Until now," Whitmore said, "the value of the site
to a developer has been marginal. But, things are beginning to fall our
way." He predicted that commercial interest would "increase as the hotel
and center near completion."[84]

La Placita Village, a $10.2 million, three-acre complex that included
200,000 square feet of new office, shop, cinema, and restaurant space in
five different levels "decorated in an authentic Southwest style" opened
on May 3, 1974.[85] Mariachis wandered through the new complex, as did
jazz musicians, barbershop quartets, and clowns. If the defeat of the La
Placita Committee and the destruction of most of La Placita failed to
remind tucsonenses who attended the opening of their "historical erasure," then the staged reenactment of the capture of Tucson by U.S. cav-
alry should have. According to press reports, the "highlight of the day
was the re-enactment of the arrival in old Tucson of the Mormon bat-
talion on December 16, 1846." To this were added "authentically garbed
Tucson Mountain Men showing interested groups what was worn by the
stalwart explorers who first brought the sound of the English language to
what is now Pima County."[86]

The Tucson Historic Committee

If there is a positive side to the La Placita tragedy, it is that significant
steps were taken to protect other historic sites from the ravages of urban
renewal and development in Tucson. To this end, the La Placita Committee
eventually forced the mayor to create a new preservationist organization,
the Tucson Historic Committee. With it, the former outsiders became
insiders, who directly affected local policy. Alva Torres served on this committee for six years.[87] The Tucson–Pima County Historical Commission,
which was established in July 1974 and remains an active and powerful

voice in historic preservation, can be traced back to the efforts of Torres and the La Placita Committee.

In 1972, committee members successfully lobbied for passage of the Historic Zone Ordinance, which still protects older structures from destruction or dramatic alteration.[88] Today, the gazebo of La Placita, the wishing shrine El Tiradito, and the Sosa-Carrillo-Frémont and Samaniego houses, among other structures, have Arizona Historical markers that specifically mention Mexican American contributions to local history, in both English and Spanish, something that Alva Torres insisted upon.[89] In defending their Mexican American heritage, the members of the La Placita Committee fostered a more enlightened and inclusive historic preservation agenda and consciousness, embodied in the City of Tucson's historic preservation ordinance.

Torres understood that representations of the past play a vital role in how individuals and communities perceive their present and envision their future. She and her fellow La Placita Committee members shared a common identity, a common investment in the past, and a common hope for a more inclusive future.[90]

Clearly, "pride of identity and self-determination" characterized the committee's organizational ideology.[91] Like many tucsonenses, Torres and her committee members never forgot the historical relationship between La Placita and the nearby, now-demolished San Agustín Church. This memory would eventually prompt them to push to have a chapel built there. Serving a collective memory grounded in a sense of place and belonging, the committee had sought to save a site recognized by tucsonenses as an important shared cultural, historical, and public space.[92]

Historians of the United States generally recognize organizations such as the Daughters of the American Revolution (DAR) and the Mount Vernon Ladies' Association, which have furthered a master narrative based on American exceptionalism as traditional women's historic preservationist groups.[93] The emergence and impact of the Society for the Preservation of Tucson's Plaza de la Mesilla, better known as the "La Placita Committee" (1967–74), complicates their understanding of layered claims to space. The members of the committee, predominantly women of Mexican descent, recognized the need to preserve public sites that testified to the personal and collective significance of Mexican Americans in the history and development of Tucson and the surrounding area. They recognized the importance of representations of the historical role of tucsonenses both to identity formation and as a counter to pervasive misperceptions about Mexican people. And they demanded that the history and at least some physical evidence of their ancestors' extensive tenure in Southern Arizona be preserved even though this challenged the manufactured local narrative and conflicted with the images and notions of the Anglo fantasy heritage. Despite bureaucratic obstacles and a lack of institutional support, the La Placita Committee resisted historical dispossession to claim a dignified place for Mexican Americans in the local and national imaginary. Its political activism raised crucial issues regarding the role of Mexican people in Southern Arizona's past, present, and future.

The Politics of Memory

> I didn't want to move . . . and finally my husband said, "Well, we're
> gonna move the phone, maybe that'll move you." So he did. He
> moved the phone . . . he took out the bed. . . . But I didn't want to
> move. They had a hard time getting me out.
>
> —Leticia Jacobs Fuentes, last resident of
> Sosa-Carrillo-Frémont House,
> May 1987[1]

In the historic preservation debates of the 1960s that arose in Tucson,
commemorating one site most often meant consigning another to obscu-
rity. Unlike members of the La Placita Committee, individuals closely
associated with the power structure actively participated in invent-
ing and defending a narrative that commemorated an Anglo American
hero in Tucson. Although many older and historically significant sites
associated with Mexican Americans in the building of Tucson called
for preservation, the cultural meanings that defined a pioneer identity
in this narrative erased Mexicans and Mexican Americans as historical actors and contributors. In the campaign for urban renewal, especially as historic sites in the targeted area were actually demolished, one
structure, the Frémont House, named after Territorial Governor John C.
Frémont, received powerful institutional support for its restoration and
preservation.[2]

In 1964, influential Anglo American citizens organized what amounted
to an advocacy group, the Tucson Heritage Foundation. The group conspicuously constructed a vision of the past in which they felt invested,
one that celebrated their heritage in the form of an American hero. They
sought to educate the public about a history not through writing but
through manipulating the landscape. Although their personal motivations were in some respects similar to those of the La Placita Committee,
members of the Heritage Foundation, in close cooperation with the

Arizona Historical Society, were able to dictate public policy and manipulate like-minded local, state, and national agencies to preserve a site that glorified their Anglo American heritage.

As the first major successful historic preservation project in the city, the Frémont House relied on the dominant culture's established understandings as to who warranted "pioneer" status and who merited commemoration for their contributions in the past. Heritage Foundation preservationists highlighted their public role as savers, indicating that they, too, saw themselves as pioneers, blazing paths that connected local history to the larger narratives that emphasized American exceptionalism. And as savers and pioneers, they staunchly rebuffed criticisms that they were misrepresenting the city's history and marginalizing the role of Mexican Americans in that history.

Constructing a Pioneer Identity

In 1884, influential locals in Tucson formed the Society of Arizona Pioneers, the predecessor of the Arizona Historical Society. During the early years, this organization did not engage in historical site preservation. Its members concentrated instead on promoting narratives that publicly confirmed their identity as pioneers and on constructing their version of Arizona's history.

The arrival of the Southern Pacific Railroad on May 20, 1880, greatly affected the town, which had previously felt isolated and on the outer margins of the nation. To many, the railroad served as a vital link to the rest of the country.[3] Indeed, its arrival signaled that Tucson had reached a level of "civilization" that early settlers had struggled so hard to achieve. As founder of the Arizona Historical Society, Charles D. Poston pronounced that settlers who arrived after the railroad could "scarcely claim to be pioneers."[4] Historian Alexandra Harmon puts such pronouncements in perspective: "Reminiscing pioneers were usually grinding axes besides the ones they had used to clear the wilderness. . . . They sought to impress newcomers with the sacrifices that had made it possible for everyone . . . to enjoy the amenities of civilized life."[5] Throughout the West, the construction of a pioneer identity became closely linked to ideas of citizenship, independence, and whiteness. In the popular and historical literature, Native Americans were never recognized as pioneers, in large part because they and the Western environment were perceived as untamed obstacles to the progress associated with Anglo American pioneers.

In the Southwest, the presence of Mexican people added another layer to the pioneer saga. Places like Tucson had long histories of Indian, Spanish, and Mexican settlement. Who, or what groups, would history credit with planting the seeds of future civilization? An examination of the official seal of the Society of Arizona Pioneers (selected in 1887 and on display in the society's administrative offices in midtown Tucson) makes it fairly clear who the society thought that should be (see fig. 7.1). Featured prominently in the center of the seal are what appear to be Anglo Americans arriving as a family in a covered wagon from a land unseen but crowned with light beyond the mountains. Ahead and to one side of the wagon strides the husband-father-patriarch, carrying a rifle and leading his oxen, wagon, wife, and children. Behind him walks a miner, carrying a pick, with a packhorse and (presumably) the miner's mule tethered to the rear of the wagon. Crouching in the cactus-studded foreground are what appear to be hostile Indians in feather headdresses. The image implies that pioneers ushered in new technology and civilization to the desert wilderness. In contrast, the Indians, living as they are shown in a natural, unaltered desert environment, had not developed or used the land. Their bows and arrows emphasize the dangers pioneers faced and therefore the courage and bravery of Anglo American settlers. That the Indians are hiding at the very edge of the seal speaks to their "backwardness" and "treachery" but also confirms their marginal role in the pioneer experience.

Mexican people and Mexican artifacts are conspicuously absent from this seal, whereas in point of fact even the earliest Anglo American settlers found an established and self-reliant Mexican community in Tucson. The historical presence of Mexicans goes unrecognized in this seal and in western iconography generally because it "complicates" the pioneer legend described by historian Linda Gordon: "The challenges [pioneers] met and conquered (or endured) came from two sources: The roughness of the natural environment and the coarseness of its 'natives.'"[6]

That Spaniards and later Mexicans had settled much of the Southwest debunked the pioneer narrative that Anglo Americans came to a barren land inhabited only by Indians. Indeed, that Mexicans joined forces not only with various Indian bands but also with Anglo American settlers to battle the Apaches and paved the way for future settlement are well-documented facts.[7] Such collaborations challenged the often repeated

Figure 7.1. The seal of the Society of Arizona Pioneers. (Photograph by the author)

and glorified narrative that Anglo Americans single-handedly "tamed" Arizona. "The Arizona pioneers owed much to the Apache," writes historian Sonnichsen in recounting this narrative. "Without him, there would have been none of those dangers and vicissitudes they loved to talk about, none of the bloody revenges they defended. . . . [T]here probably would have been no pioneer society to claim credit for bringing civilization to the savages."[8]

Historical claims to a pioneer identity or ancestry gave Anglo Tucsonans the right—and the authority—to govern, to write history, and to publicly bestow upon themselves recognition for "civilizing" the area. "Indeed," argues Gordon, "a substantial part of what pioneering *meant* was racial: that which had to be braved, endured, and transformed was the low civilization of the earlier inhabitants."[9] Mexican American men from Tucson's elite who had achieved entrepreneurial success comparable to that of most Anglo Americans were invited to be three of the society's fifty-nine founding members. These men had made their fortunes, had lived in Tucson, and had contributed to the history of the city and region for decades before most of their Anglo counterparts. Yet such facts were seldom acknowledged. In keeping with ethnocentric and exclusionary notions of the time, Anglo historical accounts recognize the Welsh immigrant Sam Hughes as the Father of Tucson.[10] The use of "father" is not accidental here: it signifies a patriarchal claim to property and power sanctioned by history. Native Americans and Mexican Americans, grouped together as members of the "lower civilizations" regardless of culture or class, have been institutionally excluded from recognition as pioneers. After celebrating its seventy-sixth anniversary and undergoing the first of two name changes, the Arizona Historical Society journal, *Arizoniana*, asked, "What is a historical society supposed to do for its state?" At the society's first historical convention, held in 1959, the guest speaker informed members that "every city and state in America has in some degree been guilty of sacrificing its historical places and things on the altar of progress. . . . A community which has bulldozed its historic sites into oblivion must create images of the past in the shape of monuments and replicas if it is to 'regain its soul.'"[11]

Inspired to look for their "soul," as well as their own personal connection to the past, some present at the convention formed the Friends of Fort Lowell in April 1960 to preserve the deteriorating army post, abandoned in 1891.[12] In a similar vein, in August 1962 the Arizona Historical Society dedicated the state's first commemorative historical bronze marker near Florence to honor Charles D. Poston, who arrived in Tubac around 1854, as the Father of Arizona.[13] The cultural forces that motivated the Friends of Fort Lowell and that made Poston's historical marker a reality foreshadowed the Frémont House preservation effort.

In pursuing its historic preservation goals, the Heritage Foundation hoped to showcase the role of John C. Frémont in making the West a part of the United States, a major qualification in civilizing a region according to the pioneer legend. Many books had chronicled Frémont's adventures and accomplishments, thus conferring historical legitimacy on him as a "true" American pioneer.

John C. Frémont

Starting his career as a second lieutenant in the U.S. Army Corps of Topographical Engineers, Frémont gained national recognition as an explorer. "The Pathfinder" sketched out and publicized the westward routes that countless others, including Brigham Young and later the Gold Rushers, would follow. His knowledge of Western topography made him a valuable asset to an expansionist nation and president in the first half of the nineteenth century. His father-in-law, Senator Thomas Hart Benton, introduced him to President James K. Polk. In meetings with Polk, Frémont shared his maps, experiences, and knowledge about Mexican territory.[14] Daniel Webster also invited the Pathfinder to dinner to talk about California. It thrilled Frémont to know that the two of them shared similar desires. "You know my opinion to have been, and now is," Webster told him, "that the port of San Francisco would be twenty times as valuable to us as all Texas."[15]

Like Polk and Benton, Frémont firmly believed in Anglo superiority and felt that California remained "unused" by Mexico. "Americans, it was argued," writes historian Reginald Horsman, "were not to be blamed for forcibly taking the northern provinces of Mexico, for Mexicans, like Indians, were unable to make proper use of the land. The Mexicans had failed because they were a mixed, inferior race with considerable Indian and some black blood. The world would benefit if a superior race shaped the future of the Southwest."[16] The man whose life would be the focal point of Tucson's preservation efforts 100 years later desired Mexico's northern territory because "its great forests and fertile lands, the fish that crowded its waters, the noble harbor and great commerce that waited for it, were all unused; lying in waste like an Indian country, as in great part it was."

Frémont's connections with those in power would prove beneficial when the Pathfinder later made some gigantic political blunders.[17] Lieutenant Colonel Frémont arrived in California just in time to encourage and participate in the Bear Flag Revolt in 1846 and to be appointed military commander of the Territory of California. But when Frémont disobeyed orders and exceeded his authority, General Stephen W. Kearny had him arrested for mutiny. A court-martial found Frémont guilty, and the army discharged him. President Polk pardoned and reinstated him, however. In 1850, realizing that his future lay beyond military service, Frémont resigned from the Army and entered politics (although he would later serve in the Civil War as a major general, resigning once more in 1862).[18]

President Rutherford B. Hayes appointed Frémont governor of the Territory of Arizona on October 8, 1878. In just over three years, widespread anger over his extended absences from Arizona forced him to step down.[19] His corrupt financial dealings in speculative land, railroad, and mining schemes would bring him to ruin, and Frémont died disgraced, penniless, and devoid of political clout in 1890. Nevertheless, when, some eighty years later in Tucson, critics brought up Frémont's unsavory side, Executive Director of the Arizona Historical Society Sidney Brinckerhoff dismissed them by saying, "As we all know, there were a number of U.S. presidents whose records may leave something to be desired, but who are nonetheless honored because they were our presidents."[20] Brinckerhoff's remark expresses an important tenet of institutionalized political power: former officeholders are worthy of commemoration irrespective of the quality of their service.

Sabino Otero

In contrast, the Oteros could not match the national prominence of John C. Frémont. Their claim to regional fame derived from their early settlement and economic success in Southern Arizona. The Spanish government awarded the first land grant in present-day Arizona to Toribido Otero in 1769. Located in Tubac, Arizona, some forty-five miles south of Tucson, the land grant remained in the Otero family well into the twentieth century. The Oteros had the added distinction of being in the cattle business in Arizona longer than any other family. Despite continual attacks by Apaches, Toribido herded cattle from Sonora into Southern Arizona, and his descendants, the most famous being Sabino Otero, continued this tradition.[21]

After the Gadsden Purchase, Apache raids increased in number and severity, resulting in financial setbacks for the family's freighting and cattle businesses. This prompted Sabino to move from Tubac to Tucson, where he built a house on 219 South Main Avenue in 1861 to provide his family a safe haven. Sabino ended up conducting most of the family's business in Tucson, and a member of the Otero family continuously occupied the home into the late 1960s.

As a cattle magnate, Sabino Otero represents one of the few members of the Mexican American elite who managed to hold on to, and even increase, his financial fortune when Southern Arizona became part of the United States. Like Leopoldo Carrillo, Otero spoke English, understood written contracts, and successfully integrated himself into the new economy and society. Strong evidence points to Sabino's philanthropy in developing the Tucson area. He also assisted a major local hospital in times of economic need, donating $6,000 in 1900 and another $24,000 in 1914.[22] The Oteros would later give the city the land occupied by the wishing shrine and current historical landmark El Tiradito.[23] Although there are no books written about Sabino Otero, and he left no memoirs, it is clear that he played a valuable role in the growth and development of Tucson and Southern Arizona. Many Tucsonans attribute the name of Sabino Canyon, on the eastern edge of the city, to Otero, who is listed as one of the early Mexican American members of the Arizona Historical Society.[24]

The Otero House

In one of several seeming exceptions to the historical claims of the Anglo American narrative, preserving the house built by Sabino Otero had been an official city priority from the very beginning of urban renewal. Indeed, city documents acknowledged its importance by declaring: "The Otero house, built with strong hand-cut beams from the nearby Santa Rita Mountains in 1861, characterizes the sturdiness of Arizona's pioneers."[25] Olga Otero Litel, Sabino's great-granddaughter, felt a deep attachment to the house and had attended urban renewal and city council meetings to keep abreast of developments affecting its fate. Litel had also met with the mayor and Don Laidlaw, whom she had come to trust. In a private, closed-door meeting, they had assured her they would preserve the house and leave it in the same location.[26] Unfortunately, the hundred-year-old home stood in the way of new plans to increase the size of the auditorium in the proposed new community center. Despite private and public promises—at a citizens' committee meeting that barred both the press and the public six months after the urban renewal bond election—city officials decided to take down and relocate the Otero House. They claimed that keeping the house in its original location "could disrupt the balance of the project" and announced that it would be easier to relocate the Otero House than to come up with alternative plans.[27]

Intent on forcing the city to keep its promises, a few historically-minded Tucsonans converged on a city council committee meeting. Sidney Brinckerhoff of the Arizona Historical Society put the matter bluntly: "Location is considered as important as the building itself in preserving a historical site."[28] Jane Rosequist, who owned and operated an art gallery near La Placita, offered to purchase the Otero House, pay the restoration costs, and make the house into a new art gallery. She responded to fiscal concerns by saying, "This would not cost the city a cent. If you tear it down and rebuild, it will be very costly."[29] In declining Rosequist's offer, however, city officials assured the public that "project funds" would pay for relocating the building.[30]

Olga Otero Litel felt betrayed. Driven by her desire to save her great-grandfather's home, Litel decided to fight city hall on her own terms and formulated a plan she felt would force city officials to reconsider their decision. She kept a vigil near the house, waiting for any sign that signaled its impending destruction (see fig. 7.2). On May 8, 1969, the day the city planned to take down the house, Litel, pregnant and leading her three small children, climbed onto the bulldozer scoop and refused to move. She devised this plan because she felt sure that her actions would attract the news media and win support from her friends in city government. Litel vividly remembers that some people ridiculed her throughout her more than five hours of protest. Finally, exhausted and in tears, she gathered her children and went home. The next week, she had a miscarriage, which she later attributed to her disillusionment with the city, the humiliation she had suffered that day, and her bereavement at the loss of her great-grandfather's house.[31]

The day after workers dismantled the Otero House, the *Tucson Daily Citizen* printed two photographs, one titled "Sabino Otero Home Goes under Shovel" and the other, "Mariano Samaniego Home—Is It Next?"[32] Luckily, the original house, built in 1878 by the successful nineteenth-century politician Mariano Samaniego, did not stand in the way of urban renewal or any expanded changes, as the Otero House and La Placita had. Although it did not figure in early urban renewal plans, with the removal of the Otero House, the city made preservation of the Samaniego House a priority. Even in supporting its preservation, however, Don Laidlaw discounted the house's Mexican past.

Figure 7.2. Olga Otero Litel took this photograph on the day before the demolition crews arrived in May 1969. (Courtesy James Litel)

Preserving this "very definite contribution to Tucson's cultural heritage," he declared, would "strengthen greatly the city's ties with its *Spanish American history*."[33]

The Tucson-Frémont Connection

Meanwhile, the city's commitment to the preservation of the Frémont House raised troubling questions. How much time did John C. Frémont actually spend in Tucson? Did Frémont ever live there? Some reports indicated that Frémont never spent a single night in what some now called the "Frémont House"; others speculated that he did spend a night but in another house. Since Prescott had its own Frémont House, it strongly opposed establishing another one: "You people down in Tucson have been getting all the publicity and funds for YOUR Frémont House, and there are some historians who say the governor never even spent a single night in the place."[34]

The Frémont-Tucson connection did not surface until 1958, when Tucson opened its first urban renewal office and the *Arizona Daily Star* began highlighting the old homes near downtown that might face destruction. As part of that effort, local reporter Alex Parker found an 1881 directory that listed Frémont as living in Tucson at 245 South Main and that noted, "Governor Fremont resides one-half of the year in Tucson, the other half in Prescott."[35]

When, however, Parker tried to find the house on 245 South Main, he learned that no such address existed. Reasoning that the address numbers had been changed, Parker and his assistants overlaid an 1883 map on more recent maps, scaled off the estimated location of "245 South Main," and confidently declared they had "rediscovered the Fremont House" at 149 South Main. "The approach worked perfectly," the reporters elatedly proclaimed, "and we quickly rediscovered the Fremont House. This was 4:30 p.m. Tuesday, August 19, 1958, and Christopher Columbus was no prouder than we were at this moment."[36]

The house they had "rediscovered," however, had always been known to tucsonenses as the Carrillo House. Leopoldo Carrillo's family had continuously occupied it since 1878. As a boy, Carrillo had moved to Tucson from his native Sonora around 1840. He became an entrepreneur and would own own more than a hundred properties and build the city's first two-story office building. The natural springs of his Carrillo Gardens provided enough water to allow desert dwellers to luxuriate in greenery and even to sail small boats.[37] Carrillo bought the property at 149 South Main from a member of the Sosa family and built the house there between 1879 and 1880.[38]

The last Carrillo descendant to live in the house, Leopoldo's granddaughter Leticia Jacobs Fuentes, greeted the reporters who knocked on her door in 1958. She would live there until forced to move in 1968, when the city acquired the property through the power of eminent domain.[39] Although Fuentes resisted the move, others had set their sights on her home even before the electorate had approved urban renewal (see fig. 7.3).

Tucson Heritage Foundation

In 1960, Arizona Historical Society President Harold Steinfeld appointed members to the society's new Committee on the Preservation of Historic Sites, predecessor to the Tucson Heritage Foundation. Chaired by Ann-Eve Johnson, the committee immediately set about saving the recently "rediscovered" home of Arizona's fifth territorial governor.[40]

Shortly after the incorporation of the new foundation as a nonprofit in 1965, Harold Steinfeld pointed out that, whereas the Arizona Historical Society served the entire state, the Heritage Foundation would concentrate only on Tucson landmarks. "Cries are raised on every side

145 S. Main - Moving Day - 12/15/68
Left to Right: Henry Fuentes, Leticia Fuentes, Herman Camacho and
Alfonso Jacobs, Jr.

Figure 7.3. Leticia Jacobs Fuentes finally leaves her home. (Courtesy Henry Fuentes Jr.)

to save this and save that," Steinfeld said, "but no group so far has had authority to do anything but talk. The Tucson Heritage Foundation has authority to act, and we will act just as rapidly as we are able to obtain funds for our purposes."[41]

As political insiders from Tucson's elite, founding members of the Heritage Foundation served on the city's various citizens' committees, and most also served on the Arizona Historical Society Board. In addition to Steinfeld, they included Clare R. Ellinwood, Ann-Eve Johnson, Carlos Ronstadt, and William A. Small Jr. A prominent local rancher and businessman, Ronstadt also headed the Chamber of Commerce's Water Resources Committee and served as a member of the reactivated Tucson Regional Plan.[42] Copublisher and half-owner of the *Arizona Daily Star,* Ellinwood shared many social commonalities with William Small Jr., who would take over his father's newspaper, the *Tucson Daily Citizen,* in 1966.[43]

In October 1965, the Heritage Foundation met at Johnson's home and elected Carlos Ronstadt president. Ronstadt declared the group a "permanent organization, whether or not the urban renewal plan is adopted." The official representative of the city's Historical Sites Committee "welcomed the role of the Heritage Foundation as a parallel organization. . . . The city committee can gather evidence of historical importance but has no funds, and the foundation would fill a definite need by fund-raising." Ronstadt made it clear that his foundation aimed to preserve the "one-time home of General John C. Fremont." He expressed his hope that "another organization would undertake to acquire the Sabino Otero home" because "at present the Heritage Foundation has no funds for a second project."[44]

Holding an assortment of offices in the Heritage Foundation, Ann-Eve Johnson represented the strongest voice for saving the Frémont House. A member of the Arizona Historical Society Board for a number of years, she also served as board president in 1968.[45] Johnson claimed that her ancestors were pioneers, and that her family had lived in Tucson for many generations. Her grandfather Jacob Samuel Mansfield helped write the city's first charter and played an active role establishing the University of Arizona. Johnson grew up hearing pioneer stories and remembered being "told about . . . the early hardships and the good times. . . . We were always taught to be proud of our Jewish, Danish, and English heritage."[46]

By the time she became the chief Frémont crusader, Johnson had chaired various charity and community boards, as well as the state's Republican Party from 1956 through 1962. She also cochaired Barry Goldwater's 1964 presidential campaign in Arizona.[47] Since John C. Frémont had been the first Republican Party candidate to run for the presidency, saving the Frémont House became a partisan and personal crusade for Johnson and her fellow Heritage Foundation members. It gave them the opportunity to highlight both their political beliefs and their pioneer ancestry.[48] In 1966, the Heritage Foundation selected Professor Emil W. Haury as its new president. A noted archaeologist and expert on Southwestern and Mexican Indians, the professor had chaired the Department of Anthropology at the University of Arizona from 1937 to 1964.[49] As a recognized expert, Haury lent legitimacy to the Heritage Foundation's Frémont House crusade.

Before the Frémont House–naming controversy, several Heritage Foundation and Arizona Historical Society members voiced their support for the La Placita Committee. "I cannot imagine that a national shrine, such as Independence Hall, would be moved to some new location, or wholly reconstructed because it was in the way of modern developments. Although Tucson's landmarks have only *local* significance, they should be similarly safeguarded," Emil Haury wrote to the committee's president, Alva Torres, after attending a committee meeting at El Charro Restaurant.[50] Sidney Brinckerhoff also formally endorsed the La Placita Committee's goals, meeting often with Alva Torres.[51]

As chair of the City of Tucson's Historical Sites Committee in 1966 and someone who in its first years worked closely with the Heritage Foundation, Isabel Fathauer wrote a letter to the editor insisting that the city "retain" La Placita and "restore" both the Otero and the Frémont House. She pointed out that "many citizens voted for the Urban Renewal Project because they had some assurance" those structures would be preserved. "We owe it to our Spanish American citizens," Fathauer added, "to save the Otero House, a landmark to their culture and ours. The present is built on the past and the future on both, and we need historic continuity in the growth and progress of our city."[52]

By the early 1970s, as they became invested and passionate in their efforts to save the Frémont House, these historic preservationists changed their positions on which ethnic group merited recognition. By May 1970, the Heritage Foundation had already informed city officials that it hoped to buy the house. At a meeting presided over by city council member Robert Royal, Haury requested that "the adjoining land on which the Otero House stood," some fifty feet south of the Frémont House and vacant since the Otero House had been removed, also be put up for sale. City officials had dismantled the house, promising to reconstruct it later. Both Haury and Fathauer cited the "cost and the need for a garden to enhance the Fremont House" as reasons for not rebuilding the Otero House on the adjoining land.[53] In an ironic reprise of a charge leveled against the Frémont House, they also argued that the Otero House lacked "authenticity."

The Heritage Foundation's influence over both city government and the Arizona Historical Society became evident in the next stage of events. In October 1970, Director of Community Development Thomas Via wrote the Arizona Historical Society that he had been "authorized by the Mayor and Council to negotiate a contract with the Heritage Foundation for the restoration and maintenance in perpetuity of the [Frémont House]."[54] The city moved quickly to grant the Heritage Foundation's request.

During the last months of 1970, the Heritage Foundation, the mayor, and the city council had received letters from the Tucson Corral of the Westerners, a local group of historically minded individuals, the La Placita Committee, and Mary Acosta, president of a charitable organization known as La Noche Plateada, supporting efforts to restore the "Carrillo-Frémont House."[55] Nevertheless, in February 1971, as one of the "two top priority items" that he expected his Tucson lobbyist to push for in Washington, D.C., Mayor James N. Corbett pointedly spoke of securing federal funds to preserve the "Frémont House."[56] The next month, Corbett's lobbyist reported that it would be easier to obtain public restoration funds if an official government body held title to the house.[57] Shortly thereafter, Director of Community Development L. E. Woodhall informed the city manager that the Heritage Foundation and the Arizona Historical Society "have agreed it would be better for the Society to take title to the Frémont House than for the Foundation to do so. This is because the Society, as a public body, may seek federal funding for restoration."[58] Representing both the society and the foundation at a meeting of the mayor and city council later in March, Ann-Eve Johnson made it clear that the foundation would "'put in writing' its willingness to finance restoration" and that it would "assume responsibility for the restoration, even if the other group were to receive possessory right."[59]

That is precisely what happened. The mayor and city council voted to transfer the Frémont House deed to the Arizona Historical Society, a public and state agency.[60] And the Arizona Historical Society, in turn, transferred responsibility for restoration and preservation to the Heritage Foundation.[61] The division of ownership and restoration responsibilities may seem complicated, but it was in effect no more than a formality: the same people controlled the boards of both the Heritage Foundation and the Arizona Historical Society; they merely changed hats to meet different funding requirements.

Weeks before, in early March, reports of a controversy over the house's name had started to appear in the local newspapers. Should the house be named after Leopoldo Carrillo, who had been "one of the oldest and most prominent citizens and property owners of Tucson," or after General Frémont, who "lived in the house for only a short time"?[62] As the new owner of the house, the Arizona Historical Society immediately moved to have it listed in the National Register of Historic Places. The City of Tucson had applied for this listing in July 1970, referring to the site as the "Carrillo-Frémont House."[63] After numerous closed-door, off-the-record conversations, however, Arizona Historical Society Director Sidney Brinckerhoff managed to get the Carrillo name deleted.[64] The National Park Service formally accepted the revised application and listed the Frémont House in the register on June 3, 1971.[65]

Despite city cooperation and support for the Frémont House project overall, the Heritage Foundation encountered some discontent over its efforts. A few city officials, dissatisfied with the pace of the restoration, pressed the foundation to have all work completed by the time the community center opened. One city council person even suggested that the Frémont House be relocated. Anti–Frémont preservationist sentiments remained muted, however, for fear of political repercussions: "There might be a lot of pressure from 'history buffs.'"[66] Indeed, some of those "history buffs" angrily complained when flooding caused damage to the floors and walls of the house in December 1970.[67] City construction workers immediately changed the drainage patterns and encased the house in plastic to protect it.[68]

That city officials submitted to Heritage Foundation demands to save a dubious piece of Tucson's pioneer legacy confirms the power of coalition politics and substantiates historian Michel-Rolph Trouillot's observation that "the production of historical narratives involves the uneven contribution of competing groups and individuals who have unequal access to the means of such production."[69] Unlike the La Placita Committee, the Heritage Foundation was granted bank loans to start and pursue its project even before the arrival of federal funds. Some supporters felt so strongly that they donated large sums to save the Frémont House.[70] Passing up an opportunity to highlight the many layers of Tucson's history, the Heritage Foundation steadfastly refused to include "Carrillo" in the name of the house despite strong historical reasons for doing so. An archivist hired by the foundation found that Carrillo, though "on the list of founding members" of the Society of Arizona Pioneers, was "not an officer."[71] Even if he had been, it is highly doubtful the Heritage Foundation would have agreed to include his name.

The Historic Tucson Committee

Most Tucson residents learned on June 22, 1971, that the Frémont House had been listed in the National Register of Historic Places from the local papers, which also reported that the Carrillo name had been removed from the application.[72] The Historic Tucson Committee organized in response. At its first meeting on August 2, the new committee, many of whose members served on the La Placita Committee, elected Mary Acosta as chairperson and drafted an open letter to the Arizona Historical Society. Acosta warned reporters not to portray her committee as "anti-Fremont" and as "attacking the work of the Society." Instead, it simply wanted the society to "set the record straight" on the Frémont House name.[73] In its letter to the society, the committee declared that dropping the Carrillo name "not only distorts history, but can be interpreted as a direct affront to the Mexican-American community." It went on to point out that the city had applied for federal funds to restore the house "under the name Carrillo-Fremont" and that "the name 'Fremont' was added recently and is incidental to the house's long history."[74]

An Anglo American woman, Mary Acosta had often felt like an outsider in her small and cliquish Ohio hometown. Once in Tucson, she married Dr. Ruben Acosta, a Mexican American. Despite being a physician's wife, she immediately became the target of disparaging remarks and discrimination simply because of her last name. Concerned that her children would encounter hostility in Tucson and motivated by her antipathy to any type of discrimination, she began to speak out and act to preserve Mexican American history.[75]

Arizona Historical Society Director Sidney B. Brinckerhoff responded to the committee's letter by insisting, "The real significance of the house historically is that it was the Frémont residence. That's why we saved it. There have been four governor's homes in Tucson and only the Frémont house is left." In an effort to draw attention away from the name change, he declared that "our real problem now is to save and restore the house, and if this furor keeps up we may not be able to save it."[76]

On August 4, in a show of solidarity, the Arizona Historical Society's directors voted unanimously to approve the "John C. Fremont home as it appears in the National Register of Historic Places." A society press release announced the next day that the directors had decided to "continue the name of the house without Carrillo," and noted that "it has always been the Fremont House. We will merely continue the name." Although President Harry Montgomery claimed that the society's board had held various discussions on the matter before determining that "nothing could justify adding Carrillo to the name of the house as a historic site," James Officer later determined that the board minutes did not contain "any mention or discussion of a controversy in Tucson over the name." As a compromise, however, the directors decided to attach a Spanish phrase—"Casa del Gobernador"—to the site's official name.[77]

When Acosta and the other Historic Tucson Committee members learned of this through the local media, they were stunned. Brinckerhoff had promised them that the board would make no decision about the house's name at its meeting. Acosta declared that the issue was "not closed" and that her group resented being manipulated.[78]

Reminding committee members of the society's "current efforts for restoration of Tucson's historical street names, most of which reflect Spanish or Mexican influence," Montgomery expressed his dismay at their objections: "It distresses me that the efforts of our society to preserve a small fragment of Tucson's colorful and romantic history have been interpreted as 'a direct affront to the Mexican-American community.'"[79] Both Brinckerhoff and Montgomery cast the Historic Committee in the role of troublemaker and potential impediment to the historic preservation process.

President Montgomery suggested that the Historic Committee give up its Frémont House fight and turn its attention elsewhere. "We hope that [the committee's] deep interest in historic site preservation will continue," he went on to say, "and lead to the preservation of other fine historic homes in Tucson, including two Cordova houses, the Bonillas house and the Samaniego home." The society was prepared to help in these efforts, but would not spearhead them.[80]

"As for the naming of the house," Brinckerhoff argued in a similar vein, "it is already done. I would suggest a major expenditure of energy and talent in the direction of saving some other great old homes in Tucson, a number of which belong to prominent Mexican-Americans and which bear their name. We would be happy to join that preservation effort."[81] That same day, he sent a memo to society staff ordering them to "refrain from discussing or expressing opinions, publicly or in the Arizona Historical Society building, regarding the Fremont name."[82]

With Montgomery, owner of the Phoenix-based *Arizona Republic*, at the helm of this preservation effort, it is not surprising that both of Tucson's major newspapers supported the society's decision. The *Citizen* called the drive to restore the Carrillo name a "waste of time and civic enterprise. It is a kind of last-minute nit-picking that frustrates the serious and well qualified efforts of the Arizona Historical Society to do its proper job."[83] The *Star* declared that the naming of the house was simply "not an instance of ignoring Tucson's splendid Mexican-American heritage." To deflect any charges that members of either the society or the foundation had racist motivations, the paper assured its readers that "they are the same people who are proud to live on streets called 'calles' and avenues called 'avenidas.' . . . It is time a foolish quarrel is ended."[84]

Having been involved with the La Placita Committee, most Historic Committee members felt angry that, after all their efforts to preserve a small part of Mexican American history in Tucson, an elite group of insiders had received institutional, local, and statewide support to advance an exclusionary version of Tucson's history. Edward Carrillo Jacobs, who was the grandson of Leopoldo Carrillo and who had been born in the house on South Main, became the strongest voice for the restoration of the Carrillo name. Although active in Democratic Party politics for thirty years and once the party treasurer for Pima County, in relation to Heritage Foundation members Jacobs remained an outsider.[85]

Refusing to abandon its battle, the Historic Committee paid to run a quarter-page advertisement in the local papers outlining its cause.[86] Its members also sought to take advantage of their personal relationship with the Democratic mayor, James Corbett. On September 7, 1971, the Historic Committee, headed by historian and Franciscan priest Father Kieran McCarty, a personal friend of Corbett's, delivered its lengthy plea to the mayor and city council. After asking that his committee be made a permanent committee of the City of Tucson, McCarty called it "a step in the one and only right direction." "We should be overjoyed," he said, "that the impetus for its formation has come in great part from our Mexican-American community, which represents in time nearly two-thirds of the history of the Old Pueblo."[87]

Speaking to me in February 1999, McCarty stated his conviction that both the society and the foundation had disrespected the Mexican

American community and its history. He also felt that his position at the Franciscan Mission and his relationship with the Mexican American community required that he get involved. He admitted that his close relationship with fellow Catholic Jim Corbett played an important role in getting the city to cooperate and make this predominantly Mexican American organization responsible for the city's future historic preservation agenda.[88] It is also likely that Mayor Corbett used this decision to placate and silence the more vocal dissenters who continually and openly challenged the Arizona Historical Society's naming of the Frémont House and its historical authenticity.

On September 7, 1971, the city council moved unanimously to adopt Ordinance 3712, which established "a Historical Committee for the city of Tucson" (the Tucson Historic Committee).[89] Its formation proved a triumph for former members of the La Placita Committee, who were now empowered insiders. Two-thirds of the members of the new citizens' committee identified themselves as Mexican American, unprecedented for a city committee in Tucson. Alva Torres, always at the forefront of historic preservation, served as a founding member (see fig. 7.4).[90] Torres summed up the Frémont House controversy:

> The Arizona Historical Society must be commended for the very difficult fight it put over the years to save the house in the first place. But equally important to the people of Tucson and to all Americans who come to our city is the proper recognition and example of the role Mexican Americans played in laying the foundation for what Tucson is today.[91]

The inclusionary and more locally driven historic preservation agenda of the new committee contrasted sharply with that of the city's former historical committee, disbanded two months before, which devoted its energies to preserving "structures or sites associated with important events which are symbolic of some great idea or ideal of frontier people."[92]

The new committee immediately ordered the city clerk to investigate the appropriateness of the Frémont name. He informed them that, as legal owner of the house, the Arizona Historical Society could name it whatever it chose.[93] In a compromise and in recognition of the new committee's political influence, however, the Heritage Foundation allowed the Historic Committee to contribute to the official plaque's wording.[94]

Figure 7.4. La Placita and Tucson Historic Sites Committee members and supporters at Alva and Arturo Alberto Torres's Wedding Anniversary in 1970. (Courtesy Alva B. Torres)

The official dedication of the John C. Frémont House, Casa de Gobernador, took place on April 7, 1972 (see fig. 7.5). The governor, mayor, and city notables attended. Brinckerhoff, Johnson, Haury, and Montgomery, who had led the drive to preserve the house, were invited to say a few words. First Lady Pat Nixon cut the ribbon in a ceremony jointly hosted by the Arizona Historical Society and the Tucson Heritage Foundation.[95] The plaque detailed the house's multilayered and inclusive history:

> This home, the only remaining residence of a Territorial governor, was occupied in 1880–81 by Major General John C. Frémont, famed explorer and 5th Territorial governor of Arizona. Built in the 1850's by José María Sosa, it was acquired by his son-in-law Michael McKenna in 1875 and by Sra. Jesús Suárez de Carrillo in 1878. The Tucson Heritage Foundation restored the house as an example of Mexican-American architecture, 1850–1880. Listed in the National Register of Historic Places.

Figure 7.5. Top: the Leticia Jacobs Fuentes home, circa 1966 (courtesy Special Collections, University of Arizona Library; Tucson Urban Renewal, roll 7 D, no. 4). Above: the Sosa-Carrillo-Frémont House Museum (photograph by the author).

A few days later, the *News-Gazette*, a short-lived independent local weekly, asked, "Why were all the Spanish surnames eliminated [from the house's name] and only the Anglo 'Fremont' remains?" Objecting to the lack of Mexican Americans in the official dedication ceremony, the paper declared: "Frankly, we're not satisfied. First, we don't accept 100 percent of the so-called history. Second, the Mexican-Americans, Arizona's true pioneers, have been slighted." An informal survey conducted by the *News-Gazette* during the height of the controversy found that 75 percent of respondents opposed the officially designated name of the house.[96]

City officials never rebuilt the Otero House, as they had promised. The wooden structural members were hauled away to a city storage yard. In need of nineteenth-century building materials to accentuate the Frémont House's "authenticity," workers turned to the "strong hand-cut beams" and other materials from the now-dismantled Otero House.[97] Years later, when the Arizona Historical Society was expanding and renovating its museum on Second Street, John Koch, a former urban renewal real estate specialist, reminded the society that wooden remnants of the Otero House still sat in a city storage yard. From these, the society built a porch onto the museum patio.[98]

The Tucson Historic Committee acted to ensure that the damage caused to historic sites and structures by urban renewal could never happen again. In 1972, it drafted and successfully lobbied for adoption of Historic Zone Ordinance 3815, which made it possible to save, among a number of other structures, the Samaniego, Cordova, and Bonillas Houses.[99]

The Heritage Foundation had predicted in 1969 that the Frémont House would draw many tourists: "Because Fremont is such a well-known national as well as Arizona figure, local and tourist interest in the house-museum will be extremely high. The economic value to Tucson of the preservation and development of this home will be extensive, and the national publicity will certainly be of value."[100] Alene Smith of the La Placita Committee emphatically disagreed. "If in Tucson as a tourist," she said, "I would not be intrigued in the least to include [the Frémont House] on my itinerary."[101] Typical of most of the city's efforts to bring visitors and shoppers back to the downtown area as it went forward with urban renewal, the Frémont House attracted neither visitors nor locals and remains empty most of the year.

The Frémont House episode was by no means unique. "Considering the enormous impact that Hispanic culture has had upon the United States, especially in the Southwest, West, and lower Southeast, it is surprising to learn that Hispanic cultural heritage is under-represented in the National Register," lamented the National Park Service in 2002. Of the 67,000 properties listed in the register for that year, only 73 (just over 0.1 percent) were nominated for "Hispanic ethnic heritage."[102]

8

Conclusion

The Heritage Foundation's success in preserving the Frémont House in the early 1970s confirms that Tucson's economic elite had the power to define institutionalized meanings to spaces. In its various manifestations over many decades of the city's history, the Anglo fantasy heritage played a key role in the spatial and social marginalization of Mexican Americans. The discrimination that persists to this day denied the Carrillo, Otero, Torres, and many other longtime tucsonense families access to the power needed to save their community and their place in history.

The Continuing Quest to Shape History

When asked in 1997 how he felt about urban renewal, former Mayor James N. Corbett said he harbored no regrets about destroying the downtown neighborhoods in and around la calle: "I never quite figured it out [what critics of urban renewal wanted to save], if they were talking about the bars on West Congress . . . the derelicts and drug users on Meyer Street . . . the Gay Alleys . . . the slumlords owning properties down there. I'm sure some areas could have had a second look—there could have been some. But it was not in the [city's] best interest."[1] Underlying Corbett's assessment is his internalized understanding of history, and his own family's history in particular. Coming as he did from a family who had arrived in Tucson in the nineteenth century, and whose members, as "pioneers," were credited with helping to build Tucson, Corbett asserted that he, "of all people, had the right to decide on a bold stroke of change for the future."[2]

The long and involved urban renewal process, which Pedro Gonzales has called "brown removal,"[3] underscores the persistence of local image makers in seeking to create an "imagined community" of upscale shoppers downtown. By leveling la calle, Tucson lost a large body of consumers who had contributed to the central business district's economic vitality and who had constituted a large source of the city's tax revenues. In 1994, anthropologist James E. Ayres wondered "what Tucson would be like if the city had the vision to take the $7.1 million plus from the [federal government] and had really done a 'renewal' by rehabilitating all of the 250 historic buildings that were viable." Ayres calculated that "enough money would have been available to provide $30,000–$60,000 for each building—more than enough for the time. Think of the property tax base that would still exist today. Except for the Samaniego House, the 80-acre urban renewal area produces no taxes."[4]

Just south of the Tucson Community Center, a small neighborhood stands as testament to what might have been had civic leaders decided to upgrade and renovate the buildings of la calle and its surrounding barrios. During the urban renewal process, anticipating a likely increase in property values, speculators moved in to acquire properties south of 14th Street in the path of the proposed Butterfield Freeway.[5] By the time city officials shelved construction of the freeway, however, a growing number of mostly well-to-do Anglo Tucsonans interested in restoring and preserving older adobe structures had already taken up residence in a barrio they found "eclectically, unpredictably, joyously" distinctive.[6]

Through gentrification, Anglo Americans became the inheritors of the oldest barrio in Tucson, called Barrio Viejo or Barrio Histórico. In 1988, hoping to win recognition and praise for their restoration efforts, new residents organized a house tour, but they encountered criticism and outright hostility. Indeed, the tour "provoked emotions that had been dormant for many years," wrote Carmen Duarte in the *Arizona Daily Star* on October 11. "It pitted those developing the area [against] those who say developing eventually will displace people."[7] "Vandals" spray-painted "racial slogans" on some of the structures, Lourdes Medrano Leslie had reported in her *Star* article of the day before, which featured a few photographs of the slogans, such as "Gringos out of the barrio" and "This barrio belongs to La Raza." One of the main organizers of the house tour attributed the graffiti to people who were "misinformed about what the barrio is about."[8] But, in fact, most tucsonenses living in or near the area had personally seen how the interplay of politics and economics transformed the old barrio into an expensive, "desirable" housing development for Anglo outsiders. To many, the gentrification of this old tucsonense neighborhood represented another episode in the city's history of exiling Mexican Americans from their own communities. The "vandals" who wrote, "Barrio Viejo is now Barrio Gringo," were acutely aware of this shift in power.[9]

In a manner reminiscent of historic preservation efforts elsewhere in the city, some of the more prominent Barrio Histórico preservationists began to offer a version of history that disparaged the old barrio in order to highlight their intervention and role as "savers." This version allowed them to construct a role for themselves as modern-day "pioneers" in the master narrative.

An earlier *Star* article on the house tour began by noting: "Twenty years ago, there were whorehouses down here. This was the red-light district."[10] Evangelina Cota, who lived on South Meyer Avenue in a home built by her grandfather more than one hundred years ago, responded angrily: "Twenty years ago, old ladies sat outside their homes and talked to each other. There were no hookers here."[11] Another longtime resident, Judy Bernal, added that "Chicano youth have enough problems overcoming day-to-day [challenges] without reinforcing negative connotations about their culture or their backgrounds."[12] These tucsonenses and many others understood that their history and the history of the barrio were inseparably linked and that portrayals that demeaned their places also demeaned Mexican Americans.

Barrio Histórico preservationists, like the members of the Heritage Foundation before them, defended the historical authenticity of older documents that were often based on much-exaggerated Anglo American claims of bringing progress and civilization to Tucson. Because quotations painting the old barrio as disreputable came from the Tucson directory, the new preservationists considered them undisputed facts. This imagined version of history validated their role in civilizing a formerly "Otherized" place.

In a related episode of historical manipulation, *Tucson Daily Citizen* columnist John Bret Harte rose in 1978 to defend the Heritage Foundation's preservation efforts, asserting that the former home of Leticia Jacobs Fuentes and her family, "once elegant but by then badly run down, had been serving as a brothel before the city acquired it for demolition as part of the Community Center complex. But it was a fine example of territorial architecture, and its association with John C. Fremont . . . gave it historical significance."[13] Belen Camacho, Fuentes's daughter, countered by offering her family's history and association with the house. She listed the name of each member and the dates each had lived in the house. Her mother, Leticia Fuentes, had inherited the house from her father in 1940 and had lived there until forced to move in 1968. "I don't know where [Harte] gets his information from," Camacho wrote, "but in no way was this great house ever used as a brothel."[14] Instead of offering a retraction or an apology, however, the *Citizen* printed an editorial response directly below Camacho's letter. There must be some truth to the story, the paper's editor insisted, because of the indisputable integrity of an anonymous source. "There is a strong oral tradition locally that the John C. Fremont House . . . was used as a brothel prior to its acquisition by the city during the urban renewal program. Unfortunately, the person often remembered to have substantiated this information is deceased. When the house was so used is not pinned down specifically in popular recollections."[15]

Decades later, in a bitter irony not lost on tucsonenses, narratives that had been used to justify destroying many of their places in and around la calle were used to justify "saving" still others and, in effect, to continue the urban renewal process by dislocating people of color in the name of progress.

The Sosa-Carrillo-Frémont House

In 1991, the Tucson–Pima County Historical Commission prepared to celebrate its twentieth anniversary. After revisiting the contentious Frémont House–naming debate, the commission wrote the Arizona Historical Society to "request, in the interest of historical accuracy, a correction in the naming of the house in question from the John C. Fremont House to the Sosa-Carrillo House." Approved unanimously by the commission's members, this recommendation would have been considered treasonous by the society's directors twenty years before. In the same letter, the chair of the commission, Joana D. Diamos—pointing out that "it was never established that John C. Fremont spent one night in the house"—declared, "The time has come to restore the historical name to the house."[16] At an Arizona Historical Society Board meeting with commission members as well as Carrillo and Sosa descendants, Leticia Fuentes, the last resident to live in the house, pleaded with the board to include "Carrillo" in the house's name.

Arguing against any proposed name change in September 1992 on behalf of the Heritage Foundation, attorney Peter Johnson (son of the by then deceased Ann-Eve Johnson) told the society's directors that the naming debate had come to emphasize "history of ownership" at the expense of the "original commemorative purpose" of the foundation's restoration project. The Heritage Foundation no longer claimed that Frémont ever lived in the house. Rather, Johnson maintained, "it was crystal clear that John C. Fremont leased the structure, that he was Governor of the Territory of Arizona at the time it was leased, it was used as a residence for his daughter." They also questioned the validity of the "other history," meaning the house's affiliation with Mexican Americans, and charged that Leopoldo Carrillo never owned the property. In the foundation's opinion, Johnson told them, the fact that the Frémont House "was the only remaining structure in Tucson . . . related to the seat of government of Arizona as a Territory" constituted "the single and compelling reason for saving [it]." Indeed, they insisted, "The house was not saved for any other reason." He warned the society's directors that if the house were not recognized, or even "celebrated," as such, "an important lesson to the children of this community [would] not [be] taught." They also warned them of the dangers of historical revisionism, "when the mere passage of time obscures the original purpose and allows a different focus and interpretation to be given by those who are then in a position to do so."[17]

Former Heritage Foundation President Emil W. Haury also spoke out against the name change, arguing that the Frémont name symbolized an "illustrious and historic" past. "In my view," he argued further, "to change the name in this late hour would not reflect positively on Heritage Foundation's prime reason to save and commemorate the house." As a compromise, Haury suggested that the house retain the Frémont name but that the plaque be updated to read "was rented in 1880–1881 for his family."[18]

As a sign of a new day and greater cultural sensitivity, however, the society's directors decided to do what Mary Acosta and the La Placita Committee had asked for in 1971: to "set the record straight." In September 1992, the "Frémont House" officially became the "Sosa-Carrillo-Frémont House." Having determined that the Frémont name had less importance, the directors voted to place it after the other two names.[19]

Miscalculations and Transformations

Among the last of la calle's prominent historic structures was the La Plaza Theatre, which the city demolished in 1969. With the destruction of nearby neighborhoods, as well as supporting retail and food establishments, business had dramatically declined. Manager Abe Campillo remembers that when he asked city officials to assist him in relocating the theater, "They said it did not fall in with their plans."[20] In 1969, La Plaza was the only indoor Spanish-language movie house in the entire state. To his credit, Urban Renewal Director Donald Laidlaw did try to find another site for the theater but with no success.[21] Nor did city officials consider dedicating, in whole or in part, any of the new smaller theaters near the center's performance arena or in La Placita Village to Spanish-speaking films. On its last night, La Plaza held a *despedida* (farewell) and invited mariachi groups and other artists from throughout Southern Arizona. "They said they wouldn't miss it for the world," Campillo recalled. "You see, most of them grew up around or had performed at the Plaza."[22]

A 1971 *Citizen* editorial warned that, unless its facilities were used, "the 17-year-old dream of a Community Center could turn into a financial nightmare." The editor called for a "return" on the city's investment, arguing that city taxpayers had "every right to expect the center to show an operating budget [in the black] in the not-too-distant future."[23] Even though it was built next to the center, the $11 million hotel that opened in 1973 failed to draw tourists, this despite repeated renovations under different owners and names (Braniff International, Holiday Inn Broadway, Radisson Hotel City Center, Hotel Arizona). Faced with clear evidence that the downtown was dying, the city council took a tremendous financial leap in 2007, approving construction of an entirely new downtown hotel for $300 million, once again to "revitalize" the area.[24]

City officials created the La Placita Village complex in 1974 in the belief that it would attract tourists. Their projections for its contrived historic and retail sites proved wrong. They declined to meet the La Placita Committee's demands; they ignored warnings that a Mexican marketplace devoid of Mexican people could never succeed. Civic boosters' determination to transform the city's image had convinced them that the only route to achieving the racial homogeneity they desired was to infuse the area with "American" culture.

Despite the promotional campaigns, which included giving out "La Placita Lives!" T-shirts and bumper stickers in 1977, La Placita Village turned out to be a commercial disaster: the shops and movie theater multiplex "bombed." "After 25 years of a bad case of the blahs," the *Star*'s Rhonda Bodfield reported in 1999, the newest complex owners painted the concrete buildings bright colors in an effort to "draw on Hispanic influences to make the project more welcoming. Some of the wounds

Figure 8.1. La Placita Village on a Saturday afternoon. (Photographs by the author)

from urban renewal will never heal, but we can try to recapture some of the flavor that was here" (see fig. 6.4).[25]

When, however, yet another set of owners suggested moving the historic La Placita gazebo in 2006, the Star voiced its clear opposition. "La Placita was named for a place that no longer exists except in the memory of some elderly residents," it reminded Tucsonans. "At a time when the city's population was small and predominantly Hispanic, it was a commercial center and the plaza where people met. . . . The gazebo . . . is a reminder, a touchstone that is mainly part of a memory culture. It's a connection to a story that most Tucsonans have never experienced but that they may have heard from their grandparents."[26] That the gazebo remains, and in its original location, is a testament to the steadfast resistance of the La Placita Committee and its quest to preserve tucsonenses' space and history.

From the very beginning, the transformed downtown could not compete with commercial development on the expanding edges of the city when it came to attracting suburban consumers, nor could it bring back those consumers driven from the area by urban renewal. Civic boosters, city leaders, and planners, despite the millions spent on construction and promotion, failed to make good on their promises. When their commitment to downtown revitalization failed to bear fruit and their profits began to suffer, two of the three biggest local department stores—Steinfeld's and Levy's—relocated to suburban malls; Jácome's lingered on at its Stone and Pennington location until 1980 before closing its doors. But even the stores that moved could not compete in the new economic environment they had helped to spawn They were swallowed up by national chains.

As historian Lizbeth Cohen sees them, urban renewal failures across the nation "testify to the importance of preserving a mix of commerce and diversity of consumers to protect cities from [the] internal restructuring of any commercial sector or the shifting loyalties of any particular group of customers." "We might rightfully ask," Cohen goes on to say, "what obligations [urban renewal boosters] had—and still have—to the urban citizens whose tax dollars have underwritten their postwar development."[27]

Four years after the Tucson Community Center's grand opening in 1971, Roy P. Drachman stepped in, not to apologize and offer explanations for where policies and designs had gone wrong but to suggest a new project. "There has been much written and spoken," he said, "regarding our downtown area and the need for its revitalization. There is no question that our central city area is not enjoying good financial health and, in fact, it is sick." Addressing the vacancies and lack of commercial activity in the new La Placita Village, he admitted that the complex was "not much short of being a disaster, and there is little to be hopeful about." Drachman's solution for revitalizing Tucson's downtown involved privately funded housing: "If a way could be found to cause several thousand families, mostly non-minorities, to move into the areas surrounding downtown, there would again be enough shoppers to support many retail stores, restaurants and other commercial enterprises."[28]

About the same time, those directly involved in implementing plans for the Tucson Community Center revealed just how little "return" city planners had expected. Thus, in 1976 the city's chief urban renewal architect, Bernard J. Friedman, recalled: "The idea was to develop a center on 'a human scale'—constantly buzzing with a variety of activities and linked to La Placita Village and the government offices downtown. Designers hoped to attract noon-time lunchers to the carefully landscaped grounds, complete with a 'desert creek' with boulders providing the constant background sound and sights of rushing water. . . . Nobody expected it would ever make a profit."[29] And, in 1977, former urban renwal director Philip Whitmore told the *Citizen*, "Now, when we say [the community center] worked, we mean it was produced. We don't necessarily mean it worked in terms of economics."[30]

In 1988, because national conventions had "virtually ignored" Tucson, city officials decided to expand the Tucson Community Center facilities. At a cost of $24.2 million, they added more exhibition space, increased the size of the ballroom, and provided additional parking. In keeping with the "new look," they decided to change the center's name to the "Tucson Convention Center."[31]

To some Tucsonans, the Tucson Convention Center and its associated cluster of buildings are emblematic of the city's skewed political and economic policies. That the decision to build them also encouraged the development of a gentrified barrio immediately to the south of the performance arena adds to deeply felt impressions of policies mired in injustice and loss, deliberately calculated to marginalize Mexican Americans and other ethnic minorities as disposable and unwanted threads in the civic fabric. To many, the center's concrete structures and the land they occupy represent an active place of memory and arouse feelings that go far beyond nostalgia.[32] As we have seen, those memory-driven feelings have also influenced local politics and the fate of other urban development projects, as they do to this day.

Many things have changed in Tucson since urban renewal's implementation. Most important, the city's Mexican Americans have themselves changed. Panchita Leon outlines how things used to be: "The people were still timid. . . . At that time there was no one to speak up. They [city officials] made the plans—and nobody from the barrio knew it."[33] Pedro Gonzales, a child of ten when city officials forced his family to relocate, speaks to the different times and generations: "Back then people used to fight for their rights, but they got intimidated by the system. But I'm not. I'm not afraid of the system or the government. . . . We know now that they can't do that to us anymore. . . . I am not saying I am educated, because I didn't go to the University. But we know how the system works."[34]

Back in 1970, when planners and urban developers were pushing the Butterfield Freeway, which would have cut through what remained of her barrio, El Hoyo, Leon reacted because "we've got our roots here." She and other barrio residents succeeded in stopping the proposed freeway dead in its tracks. Fellow protester Rosendo Pérez recognized that "any threat to the barrio is a threat to the Mexican-American culture. . . . There were a lot of us people that they used to call dumb Mexicans—they tried to push it over on us. But the tide has turned."[35]

Also around this time, the more radical Chicano movement surfaced in Tucson in the form of the People's Coalition, which demanded that the City of Tucson serve the needs of tucsonenses and the poor. When coalition activists realized that their picketing, staging rallies, and blocking traffic were not drawing media attention, they moved their protest to the city's main tourist attractions. Visitors could not escape seeing their signs and hearing their chants of "Tourists, go home!" and "People sí, tourists no!" Coalition leaflets informed visitors that "the only concern of Tucson city government was for tourists rather than the local residents." One of its leaders, Salomón Baldenegro, outlined the coalition's strategy: "Tourists are the backbone of Tucson's economy. If we talk to them, then they can exert pressure on the Chamber of Commerce, and then on the businessmen of Tucson."[36] Not surprisingly, the protesters made the front page of the *Citizen*, and city officials immediately moved to negotiate with them.[37]

Continued newspaper retrospectives, repeated downtown revitalization projects, and Tucsonans who remember the past keep urban renewal alive in the collective consciousness of tucsonenses. According to one local historian, memories of the areas destroyed have reached "mythic proportions."[38] As Tucsonans discussed Rio Nuevo, the newest downtown revitalization plan, approved by voters in 1999, comparisons to the Pueblo Center Redevelopment Project inevitably arose. Tucsonenses have kept a critical eye on any developments proposed for the downtown area. At the first meeting to discuss the Rio Nuevo Project, four hundred people showed up, causing Project Director John Jones to marvel, "The amount of participation is unprecedented in my 20 years as an urban planner in Tucson." Although city officials and developers have attempted to "get the word out" in a variety of ways, some citizens insist they have not tried hard enough. At a Rio Nuevo public hearing, Angie Quiroz protested that "more meetings could have been held in the barrios. Planners should come to the people, not the other way around."[39]

In 2002, when asked about the newest revitalization plan, Raúl Rodríguez, who had shined shoes at La Placita Village for seventeen years, expressed his support for new housing that would bring people back to the downtown area because "the barrio was a good place to live, and it remains so." He recalled that his mother made tortillas for some Mexican restaurants forced to move by urban renewal. "The city made a big mistake," Rodríguez concluded. "Now it needs to make it up."[40]

Similar sentiments were express at a meeting of the Rio Nuevo Project Subcommittee in 2008, where Daniel Gamez García demanded a more just way to conduct comprehensive development projects in Tucson. His mother's family had lived in the urban renewal area. "The problem was with the injustice that took place," García recounted. "What I mean by that is, those families, and not just my family, were . . . forced out. Their houses, their homes, their land was deemed unlivable, meaning that the city . . . chose not to give them the opportunities to develop their homes. . . . So it is not an issue of our people being displaced and being unhappy and disgruntled. It is a matter of doing what we have to do. . . . We saw what history did to us. We are asking for history *not* to repeat itself again at this present time and [under] this present Council."[41]

Replying to García at that same meeting, the two city council members present agreed that collective memories of urban renewal did indeed still play an important role in local politics and that they could not "undo what happened" and would approach new projects.[42] City councilwoman Regina Romero, a child of Mexican immigrants, promised in both Spanish and English to remember history in future revitalization projects: "La ciudad de Tucson tiene mucha historia y necesitamos recordar la historia y no repetir los errores que lo hemos hecho antes. Y no lo vamos a hacer. The City of Tucson has a long history, and we need to remember history and not repeat the mistakes we have made in the past. We do care, and we will do everything possible in a very creative way to make sure that we have the diversity in our downtown that we deserve to have as a city."[43]

The promise to remember history is hard to keep in a city where plans to revitalize downtown make headlines almost daily. One can only hope that Tucsonans consider the past as they formulate new ideas for the future and examine thoroughly any plans that promise to "reju-vante" older neighborhoods. Where do we direct new generations of Tucsonans who hunger for a sense of their ancestors' contributions to the history of their city? Historian David Glassberg makes clear, "A sense of history locates us in society, with the knowledge that helps us gain a sense of *with whom we belong*, connecting our personal experiences and memories with those of a larger community, region, and nation" (emphasis in original).[44]

This discussion underscores that more than forty years later the subject of urban renewal retains its political currency. In a city where downtown redevelopment projects make the news almost daily, new urban ideals are often debated and hotly contested. Proposals that promise to embody an inclusive history, however, are hard to keep in a city whose economy is so strongly dependent on reinvention and myth. Seemingly, the vast majority of Tucsonans do envision a more vibrant downtown but the formula for securing one remains a mystery. One can only hope that Tucsonans remember la calle as they devise new plans for the future.

Notes

Introduction

1. Mexican Americans, some of whose families had lived in Southern Arizona before it became a part of the United States, and who claim this area as their home, then and now, identify themselves as "tucsonenses." A multilayered interrelationship between region and ethnicity and a strong historical and cultural connection with Sonora, Mexico, form the core of this distinctive and unifying identity. See Cynthia Radding, *Wandering Peoples: Colonialism, Ethnic Spaces, and Ecological Frontiers in Northwestern Mexico, 1700–1850* (Durham, N.C.: Duke University Press, 1997); and Thomas E. Sheridan, *Los Tucsonenses: The Mexican Community in Tucson, 1854–1941* (Tucson: University of Arizona Press, 1986), for more on this regional identity. I use "Tucsonans" to refer to people of all ethnicities who claim Tucson as their home (and who sometimes call themselves Tucsonians), and "Mexican people" to refer to Chicanas/os, Mexican nationals, and those from earlier generations who may have identified themselves as "Spanish."

2. Alva Torres, audiotaped interview, December 6, 2002, Tucson.

3. Susan A. Crane defines "collective memory" as that which a people remember, or their personal "lived experience" and historical memory as the "preservation of lived experiences" that are institutionally and professionally commemorated or remembered through museums, exhibits, texts, historical markers, and so on. "Writing the Individual Back into Collective Memory," *American Historical Review* 102, no. 5 (December 1997), 1372–1385.

4. Many other inner cities across the United States, and ethnic communities in particular, became targets for "rehabilitation" as the federal government partnered with municipalities to implement urban renewal. See James Robert Saunders and Renae Nadine Shackelford, *Urban Renewal and the End of Black Culture in Charlottesville, Virginia: An Oral History of Vinegar Hill* (Jefferson, N.C.: McFarland, 1998); June Manning Thomas and Marsha Ritzdorf, eds., *Urban Planning and the African American Community: In the Shadows* (Thousand Oaks, Calif.: Sage, 1997); John M. Goering, Maynard Robison, and Knight Hoover, *The Best Eight Blocks in Harlem: The Last Decade of Urban Reform* (Washington, D.C.: University Press of America, 1977); John F. Bauman, *Public Housing, Race, and Renewal: Urban Planning in Philadelphia, 1920–1974* (Philadelphia: Temple

University Press, 1986); Herbert J. Gans, *The Urban Villagers: Group and Class in the Life of Italian-Americans* (New York: Free Press of Glencoe, 1962); and Thomas J. Sugrue, *The Origins of the Urban Crisis: Race and Inequality in Postwar Detroit* (Princeton, N.J.: Princeton University Press, 1996).

5. There are few historical works on urban renewal in Tucson. Michael Logan, *Fighting Sprawl and City Hall: Resistance to Urban Growth in the Southwest* (Tucson: University of Arizona Press, 1995), focuses on Tucson and Albuquerque with only passing mention of the TCC and sheds welcome light on the institution of urban renewal and especially on the conservative politics associated with it and with growth issues. Margaret Regan, "There Goes the Neighborhood: The Downfall of Downtown," *Tucson Weekly*, March 6–12, 1997, in addressing what urban renewal meant to Tucson's Mexican American community, critically examines the process. Regan makes use of a variety of interviews to highlight residents' attachment to their neighborhoods and to argue that city planners failed to achieve their goal of revitalizing the downtown area. Keith Carew, Adolfo Quezada, and Priscilla Altuna, "Urban Renewal's Dispossessed," *Tucson Daily Citizen* (hereafter *Citizen*), December 12, 1970, A-1, and "¡Ole!" section, pp. 1–12, stands out as a valuable, timely investigation of urban renewal in Tucson, including interviews with those relocated and some city officials that were conducted shortly after relocation and demolition had taken place. See also "Tucson's Barrios: A View from the Inside," special report, *Arizona Daily Star* (hereafter *Star*), July 16, 1978, 1–27, which includes tucsonenses' reflections about urban renewal and the area destroyed; Janet Mitchell, "Vanished Tucson," *City Magazine*, May 1989, 44–48; Donald H. Bufkin, "From Mud Village to Modern Metropolis: The Urbanization of Tucson," *Journal of Arizona History* 22 (Spring 1981): 63–81; and Patricia J. Clark and Martha M. Fimbres, "A Study to Identify and Access the Psychological Ramifications Inherent in the Process of Relocation Regarding Census Tract I in Downtown Tucson, Arizona" (master's thesis, Arizona State University, 1978), which illuminates the human tragedy brought about by urban renewal.

6. For more on Sonoran-style row houses, their history, and their unique design, see Anne M. Nequette and R. Brooks Jeffery, *A Guide to Tucson Architecture* (Tucson: University of Arizona Press, 2002).

7. Archaeological evidence also indicates that the Tohono O'odham and Pima Indians, who had long inhabited the Tucson area, were rather recent arrivals. Margaret Regan, "What's to Become of Tucson's Birthplace" in *Tucson Weekly*, June 27–July 3, 2002. Declarations about the "oldest continuously inhabited city" are always controversial. This distinction has also been bestowed on other areas, such as Ácoma in New Mexico, founded 1100–1250. See the *Columbia Encyclopedia*, 6th ed. (New York: Columbia University Press, 2001). See also http://www.bartleby.com/65/ac/Acoma.html. For more on Indians of the region, see William Kelly, *Indians of the Southwest: A Survey of Indian Tribes and*

Indian Administration in Arizona (Tucson: University of Arizona, 1953); Eric V. Meeks, *Border Citizens: The Making of Indians, Mexicans, and Anglos in Arizona* (Austin : University of Texas Press, 2007); Ned Blackhawk, *Violence over the Land: Indians and Empires in the Early American West* (Cambridge: Harvard University Press, 2006); Edward Holland Spicer, *Cycles of Conquest: The Impact of Spain, Mexico, and the United States on the Indians of the Southwest, 1533–1960* (Tucson: University of Arizona Press, 1962); and Clare V. McKanna Jr., *White Justice in Arizona: Apache Murder Trials in the Nineteenth Century* (Lubbock: Texas Tech University Press, 2005).

8. Fay Jackson Smith, John L. Kessell, and Francis F. Fox, *Father Kino in Arizona* (Phoenix, Arizona Historical Foundation, 1966), 14, 44.

9. Thomas Edwin Farish, *History of Arizona*, 8 vols. (San Francisco: Filmer Brothers Electrotype, 1915–18), 1:321, and Sheridan, *Tucsonenses*, 30, 275n24. Mesilla, New Mexico, the second major settlement in the Gadsden Purchase area, was swiftly occupied by U.S. forces in 1851.

10. I use "Anglo American" or "Anglo" to refer to someone of Euro-American descent—even though many of the people I am grouping together under this designation did not trace their roots to England—to reflect a usage widely accepted by Tucsonans in the past. Indeed, most civic boosters, whatever their ethnic background (so long as they were of European but not Spanish descent), freely associated themselves with the idyllic and heroic Anglo American model. As C. L. Sonnichsen notes in *Pioneer Heritage: The First Century of the Arizona Historical Society* (Tucson: Arizona Historical Society, 1984), 11, "The 'Anglos' themselves included immigrants from England, Wales, Germany, France and Switzerland. Anyone was eligible who had helped tame the territory."

11. James E. Officer, "Sodalities and Systemic Linkage: The Joining Habits of Urban Mexican Americans" (PhD diss., University of Arizona, 1964), 57n.

12. David Montejano argues that merchants served as "intermediaries" between the new and old economic order. They arrived early, often married women from the elite, and learned to speak Spanish, but despite acquiring a bicultural background, they "plant[ed] the foundation for a complete transformation." See Montejano, *Anglos and Mexicans in the Making of Texas, 1836–1986* (Austin: University of Texas Press, 1997), 25. For more information on one of Southern Arizona's most influential merchants, see Bettina O'Neil Lyons, *Zeckendorfs and Steinfelds: Merchant Princes of the American Southwest* (Tucson: Arizona Historical Society, 2009). I discuss the power of merchants in chapters 2 and 4.

13. Richard White and John M. Findley, in White and Findley, eds., *Power and Place in the North American West* (Seattle: Center for the Study of the Pacific Northwest; University of Washington Press, 1999), x, define place as "a spatial reality constructed by people." Linda McDowell, in *Gender, Identity and Place: Understanding Feminist Geographies* (Minneapolis: University of Minnesota Press, 1999), 2–6, goes into a lengthy discussion of how the various disciplines

use and define "place" and how their definitions have evolved. See also Dolores Hayden, *The Power of Place: Urban Landscapes as Public History* (Cambridge, Mass.: MIT Press, 1995); Paul C. Adams, Steven Hoelscher, and Karen E. Till, eds., *Textures of Place: Exploring Humanist Geographies* (Minneapolis: University of Minnesota Press, 2001); and Doreen Massey, *Space, Place, and Gender* (Minneapolis: University of Minnesota Press, 1994).

14. Albert Camarillo, *Chicanos in a Changing Society: From Mexican Pueblos to American Barrios in Santa Barbara and Southern California, 1848–1930* (Cambridge, Mass.: Harvard University Press, 1979). Most barrio histories have focused on the late nineteenth century, although a few have extended their coverage through the Great Depression. Other major historical works on the development of Mexican American barrios are George J. Sánchez, *Becoming Mexican American: Ethnicity, Culture, and Identity in Chicano Los Angeles, 1900–1945* (New York: Oxford University Press, 1993); Ricardo Romo, *East Los Angeles: History of a Barrio* (Austin: University of Texas Press, 1983); Richard Griswold del Castillo, *The Los Angeles Barrio, 1850–1890: A Social History* (Berkeley: University of California Press, 1979); Douglas Monroy, *Rebirth: Mexican Los Angeles from the Great Migration to the Great Depression* (Berkeley: University of California Press, 1999); Arnoldo De León, *The Tejano Community, 1836–1900* (Albuquerque: University of New Mexico Press, 1982); and Lisbeth Haas, *Conquests and Historical Identities in California, 1769–1936* (Berkeley: University of California Press, 1995).

15. This planning and zoning agenda applied to people of color in general. See Neil Kraus, *Race, Neighborhoods, and Community Power: Buffalo Politics, 1934–1997* (Albany: State University of New York Press, 2000); Christopher MacGregor Scribner, *Renewing Birmingham: Federal Funding and the Promise of Change, 1929–1979* (Athens: University of Georgia Press, 2002); Barbara Ferman, *Challenging the Growth Machine: Neighborhood Politics in Chicago and Pittsburgh* (Lawrence: University Press of Kansas, 1996). For postwar studies on Mexican American communities, see Rodolfo Acuña, *A Community under Siege: A Chronicle of Chicanos East of the Los Angeles River, 1945–1975* (Los Angeles: Chicano Studies Research Center, University of California at Los Angeles, 1984), and *Occupied America: A History of Chicanos* (New York: Longman, 2000). New works on urban Mexicans and Mexican Americans that have influenced my analysis include Gabriela F. Arredondo, *Mexican Chicago: Race, Identity, and Nation, 1916–39* (Chicago: University of Illinois Press, 2008); David R. Diaz, *Barrio Urbanism: Chicanos, Planning, and American Cities* (New York: Routledge, 2005); Laura Pulido, *Black, Brown, Yellow, and Left: Radical Activism in Los Angeles* (Berkeley: University of California Press, 2006); Daniel D. Arreola, ed., *Hispanic Spaces, Latino Places: Community and Cultural Diversity in Contemporary America* (Austin: University of Texas Press, 2004); and, of course, Matt García, *A World of Its Own: Race, Labor, and Citrus in the Making of*

Greater Los Angeles, 1900–1970 (Chapel Hill: University of North Carolina Press, 2001), one of the first books that made me consider the importance of claiming place. See also Irwin Altman and Setha M. Low, eds., *Place Attachment* (New York: Plenum Press, 1992).

16. On order, see Robert Lewis, "Frontier and Civilization in the Thought of Frederick Law Olmstead," *American Quarterly* 29, no. 4 (Autumn 1977), 385–403, and Robert H. Wiebe, *The Search for Order, 1877–1920* (New York: Hill and Wang, 1967); see also Walter Mignolo, *Local Histories/Global Designs* (Princeton, N.J.: Princeton University Press, 2000); Edward Soja, *Postmodern Geographies: The Reassertion of Space in Critical Social Theory* (London: Verso Press, 1989). Although valuable and insightful, Soja's work ignores the power of gender in spatial dynamics. As geographer Linda McDowell points out, in *Gender, Identity and Place*, 30, "both people and places are gendered and so social and spatial relations are mutually constituted."

17. McDowell, *Gender, Identity and Place*, 4.

18. In my attempt to "theorize the city," I follow urban anthropologist Setha M. Low, who views the "'urban' as a process rather than as a [essentialist] type of category." Low, "The Anthropology of Cities: Imagining and Theorizing the City," *Annual Review of Anthropology* 25 (1996), 384. This article provides an excellent evaluation of major works and trends in urban anthropology. See also Setha M. Low and Denise Lawrence-Zuñiga, eds., *The Anthropology of Space and Place: Locating Culture* (Malden, Mass.: Blackwell, 2006).

19. John H. Mollenkopf, *The Contested City* (Princeton, N.J.: Princeton University Press, 1983), 243. "In southwest cities," Mollenkopf also contends, "urban politics, federal programs, and economic development interacted in a different way [than in northern cities]." Ibid.

20. In addressing issues of the large-scale displacement of Mexican Americans, historian Eric Avila considers the expulsion of Mexican people from Chavez Ravine in Los Angeles to build Dodger Stadium as a form of urban renewal. See Avila, *Popular Culture in the Age of White Flight: Fear and Fantasy in Suburban Los Angeles* (Berkeley: University of California Press, 2004). Although civic leaders in both Los Angeles and Tucson considered Mexican American communities expendable in their designs to bring about "progress," a key word in the post–World War II era, as this book points out, Tucson authorities went two significant steps further. They invoked the federal housing commitment to "improve" the urban landscape to justify the forcible relocation of tucsonenses and the demolition of their neighborhoods in the city's core, and they enlisted federal aid to accomplish those ends.

21. Michel de Certeau, in *The Practice of Everyday Life* (Berkeley: University of California Press, 1984), xi, defines "everyday practices" as "'ways of operating' or doing things, [which] no longer appear as merely the obscure background of social activity" but instead provide "pathways for future research."

22. On "tactics," see ibid., xvii–xxii, 34–39. For more on the connection people have to their natural and built environments, see Keith H. Basso, *Wisdom Sits in Places: Landscape and Language among the Western Apache* (Albuquerque: University of New Mexico Press, 1996).

23. Michel-Rolph Trouillot, *Silencing the Past: Power and the Production of History* (Boston: Beacon Press, 1995), 99.

24. For an interesting discussion of the politics of memory, see John R. Gillis, "Memory and Identity: The History of a Relationship," in Gillis, ed., *Commemorations: The Politics of National Identity* (Princeton, N.J.: Princeton University Press, 1994), 3–24.

25. City-County Planning Department, *General Land Use Plan: Tucson and Environs* (City of Tucson, 1960).

26. "Editor's Urban Renewal Opinions Are Disputed: Architect Nelson Defends 'Center,'" *Star*, February 23, 1966. See also Robert M. Fogelson, *Downtown: Its Rise and Fall, 1880–1950* (New Haven, Conn.: Yale University Press, 2003).

27. See Roy P. Drachman and Vincent L. Lung, *The Pueblo Center Redevelopment Project*, Report presented to the Central City Council of the Urban Land Institute, April 23, 1965, by Roy Drachman, Chairman, Citizens Committee on Municipal Blight and Vincent L. Lung, Assistant City Manager and Coordinator of Community Development (Tucson: City of Tucson, 1965).

28. David M. P. Freund, *Colored Property: State Policy and White Racial Politics in Suburban America* (Chicago: University of Chicago Press, 2007), 39.

29. Drachman and Lung, *Pueblo Center*, ii, 7; see also Natalia Molina, *Fit to Be Citizens? Public Health and Race in Los Angeles, 1879–1939* (Berkeley and Los Angeles: University of California Press, 2006), for an analytical discussion of how phrases such as a "shot in the arm" can be construed as a response to "alien" or "foreign" influences in need of systematic interventions.

30. Freund, *Colored Property*, 216. For an assessment of racism in language in the Southwest, see Jane Hill, "Hasta la Vista, Baby: Anglo Spanish in the American Southwest," *Critique of Anthropology* 13, no. 2 (1993), 145–176.

31. Roy P. Drachman, Oral History, acc. no. 92-11, AV 0505-18, "Urbanization of Tucson: 1940–1990," 3, Arizona Historical Society/Tucson.

32. Lizabeth Cohen, *A Consumers' Republic: The Politics of Mass Consumption in Postwar America* (New York: Vintage, 2003), 195; see also chapter 5, "Residence: Inequality in Mass Suburbs" in ibid.; Cohen, "Buying into Downtown Revival: The Centrality of Retail to Postwar Urban Renewal in American Cities," *Annals of the American Academy of Political and Social Science* 611, no. 1 (2007), 94. See also Kenneth T. Jackson, *Crabgrass Frontier: The Suburbanization of the United States* (New York: Oxford University Press, 1985); Kevin M. Kruse, *White Flight: Atlanta and the Making of Modern Conservatism* (Princeton, N.J.: University, 2005); and Matthew D. Lassiter, *The Silent Majority: Suburban Politics in the Sunbelt South* (Princeton, N.J.: Princeton University Press, 2006).

33. Of the many postmodern works critical of modernity, see especially David Harvey, *The Condition of Postmodernity: An Enquiry into the Origins of Cultural Change* (Oxford: Blackwell, 1989), and Sharon Zukin, *The Cultures of Cities* (Cambridge, Mass.: Blackwell, 1995). See also Michael Peter Smith, "Postmodernity, Urban Ethnography, and the New Social Space of Ethnic Identity," *Theory and Society* 21, no. 4 (August 1992), 493–531; Janet Wolff, "The Real City, the Discursive City, the Disappearing City: Postmodernism and Urban Sociology," *Theory and Society* 21, no. 4 (August 1992), 553–560.

34. For more on "vanishing" Indians, see Peter Iverson, "American Indian History as a Continuing Story," *Historian* 66, no. 3 (2004), 524–531. See also Glen Gendzel, "Pioneers and Padres: Competing Mythologies in Northern and Southern California, 1850–1930," *Western Historical Quarterly* 32, no. 1 (Spring 2001), 55–79. I discuss the Anglo fantasy heritage in depth in chapter 3.

35. Richard White, *"It's Your Misfortune and None of My Own": A History of the American West* (Norman: University of Oklahoma Press, 1991), 617–626.

36. David Lowenthal, *The Past Is a Foreign Country* (Cambridge: Cambridge University Press, 1985), 348.

37. William Deverell, in *Whitewashed Adobe: The Rise of Los Angeles and the Remaking of Its Mexican Past* (Berkeley: University of California Press, 2004), 10, argues that these exclusions and boundaries served to solidify systems of social control that increased the visibility or "out of placeness" of Mexican people. On consigning Mexican people to the past in promotional campaigns designed to maintain social control, see also Phoebe S. Kropp, *California Vieja: Culture and Memory in a Modern American Place* (Berkeley: University of California Press, 2006). For insight into a city that consciously reinvented its historical narrative to shield itself from being perceived as a "Mexican city," see Harvey J. Graff, *The Dallas Myth: The Making and Unmaking of an American City* (Minneapolis: University of Minnesota Press, 2008). See also Chris Wilson, *The Myth of Santa Fe: Creating a Modern Regional Tradition* (Albuquerque: University of New Mexico Press, 1997).

38. Raúl Homero Villa, *Barrio-logos: Space and Place in Urban Chicano Literature and Culture* (Austin: University of Texas Press, 2000), 1.

39. On women and historic preservation, see Gail Lee Dubrow and Jennifer B. Goodman, eds., *Restoring Women's History through Historic Preservation* (Baltimore: Johns Hopkins University Press, 2003). On the often overlooked gender aspects of historic preservation and how these apply to space and communities, see Dolores Hayden, *The Grand Domestic Revolution: A History of Feminist Designs for American Homes, Neighborhoods, and Cities* (Cambridge, Mass.: MIT Press, 1981).

40. For more on the various forms of Chicana activism, see Vicki L. Ruíz, *From Out of the Shadows: Mexican Women in Twentieth-Century America* (New York: Oxford University Press, 1998).

41. See Lisa McGirr, *Suburban Warriors: The Origins of the New American Right* (Princeton, N.J.: Princeton University Press, 2001). For more examples of historic preservation movements based on idealized heritages, see Judy Mattivi Morley, *Historical Preservation and the Imagined West: Albuquerque, Denver, and Seattle* (Lawrence: University Press of Kansas, 2006).

Chapter 1. La Calle, the Tucsonense Downtown

1. Pedro Gonzales, videotaped interview, November 10, 2007, Tucson.

2. Sheridan, *Tucsonenses*, 79.

3. Edward W. Soja, *Thirdspace: Journeys to Los Angeles and Other Real-and Imagined Places* (Cambridge, Mass.: Blackwell, 1996), 98. Soja highlights "thirdspace" as an "evocative process of choosing marginality [that] reconceptualizes the problematic of subjection by deconstructing and disordering both margin and center." It is in those "restructured and recentered margins" that thirdspace is created. See also Homi K. Bhabha, *The Location of Culture* (London: Routledge, 1994); Emma Pérez, *The Decolonial Imaginary: Writing Chicanas into History* (Bloomington: Indiana University Press, 1999).

4. Tucsonenses have a rich history that merits further exploration, as do Mexican Americans in Arizona, who remain relatively underexplored in the United States historiography. See, for example, Sheridan, *Tucsonenses*; see also the following works of Patricia Preciado Martin, who specializes in oral tradition and concentrates on the social history of Mexican Americans from Southern Arizona: *Songs My Mother Sang to Me: An Oral History of Mexican American Women* (Tucson: University of Arizona Press, 1992); *Beloved Land: An Oral History of Mexican Americans in Southern Arizona*, photographs by José Galvez (Tucson: University of Arizona Press, 2004); and *Images and Conversations: Mexican Americans Recall a Southwestern Past*, photographs by Louis Carlos Bernal (Tucson: University of Arizona Press, 1983).

5. Undeniably, Anglo Americans benefited from these networks throughout the United States. Most considered themselves a superior race in the nineteenth century. According to historian Reginald Horsman, *Race and Manifest Destiny: The Origins of American Racial Anglo-Saxonism* (Cambridge, Mass.: Harvard University Press, 1981), 272, after the U.S.—Mexican War, "supreme confidence in the racial strength of white America was accompanied by the desire that this special race and its government should not be tainted and weakened by other peoples."

6. Sheridan, *Tucsonenses*, 37.

7. "80-Year-Old Map First of Tucson," *Tucson Daily Citizen* (hereafter *Citizen*), January 11, 1943, 9.

8. Thomas F. Saarinen, John Crawford, and Karen Thomas, "Street Patterns and Housing as Ethnic Indicators," in Saarinen and Lay J. Gibson, eds., *Territorial Tucson*, unpublished manuscript in possession of T. F. Saaringen, 6-4.

9. Jonathan Harris, "Changes in the Structure of Tucson during the First Decade of Anglo Infiltration," in Saaringen and Gibson, *Territorial Tucson*, 4-23. Harris suggests that tucsonenses moved southward to be closer to their *milpas*, or fields.

10. Nequette and Jeffery, *Tucson Architecture*, 17.

11. Ibid.,

12. For a history of New Spain's settlements in the Southwest, see Gilbert R. Cruz, *Let There Be Towns: Spanish Municipal Origins in the American Southwest, 1610–1810* (College Station: Texas A&M University Press, 1988).

13. Nequette and Jeffery, *Tucson Architecture*, 17.

14. Abigail A. Van Slyck, "What the Bishop Learned: The Importance of Claiming Space at Tucson's Church Plaza," *Journal of Arizona History* (Summer 1998), 127–128.

15. Ibid.

16. Sheridan, *Tucsonenses*, 82.

17. Ibid. The university did not officially open its doors until October 1891.

18. Ibid., 87.

19. Camarillo, *Chicanos in a Changing Society*, 117, 206–207; see also Raúl Homero Villa, *Barrio-logos*(Austin: University of Texas Press, 2000), 4–5.

20. Sheridan, *Tucsonenses*, 186.

21. Ibid., 184.

22. James E. Officer, "Power in the Old Pueblo: A Study of Decision Making in a Southwestern Community, 1961," p. 61, typescript photocopy, Special Collections, University of Arizona Library.

23. Roy Drachman, chap. 1, "The Family Page," II of III, http://parenteyes. Arizona.edu/drachman/0102.html/.

24. Information from the 1960 Census indicates that 212,892 people lived in Tucson and that 30,147 had "Spanish surnames." Of these, 5,575 were foreign-born. *U.S. Census of Population and Housing: 1960—Census Tracts—Final Report PHC(1)-161* (Washington, D.C: Government Printing Office, 1961), 13, table P-1: "General Characteristics of the Population, by Census Tracts: 1960." James E. Officer estimated in 1964 that 70 percent of tucsonenses had "been born in, or descended from persons born in, the Mexican State of Sonora." Officer, "Sodalities," 73.

25. Officer, "Sodalities," 76, map 1.

26. Mary Pat Brady, *Extinct Homelands, Temporal Geographies: Chicana Literature and the Urgency of Space* (Durham, N.C.: Duke University Press, 2002), 8.

27. For a more thorough discussion of internal geographical identity and barrio formations, see Homero Villa, *Barrio-logos*, 1–16.

28. On Barrio Tiburón, see Officer, "Sodalities," 77. Social characteristics also determined a barrio's name. The people I interviewed offered a variety of explanations as to how a West Side barrio became known as Barrio Hollywood. One explanation was that the "the women looked like movie stars"; another was that El Pasoans stayed there en route to Los Angeles (Hollywood). For more on this barrio's name, see Judy Donovan, "Bitterness, Pride Make 'Hollywood' More Than a Joke," *Arizona Daily Star* (hereafter *Star*), July 16, 1978, 27. I grew up in Barrio Kroeger Lane, which got its name from a prominent physician who played a key role in the barrio's development. For more on Tucson's barrios and their development, see Sheridan, *Tucsonenses*, 237–247; and "Tucson's Barrios: A View from the Inside," special report, *Star*, July 16, 1976, 1–27.

29. Guadalupe Castillo, videotaped interview, February 13, 2008, Tucson. I credit Guadalupe for motivating me to investigate further the complex associations and intimate connections that Mexican Americans felt toward their spaces.

30. G. W. Barter, *Directory of the City of Tucson for the Year 1881* (San Francisco: H. S. Crocker, 1881; reprint, Tucson: Arizona State Genealogical Society, 1988), 39–40. Deeply affected by descriptions of Barrio Libre that painted residents as "deviants," some tucsonenses may have consciously refused to refer to the area as "Libre."

31. "Arizona History from Newspaper Accounts: A Barrio Libre," *Arizona Weekly Journal* (Prescott), November 16, 1883, reprinted in the *Journal of Arizona History* (Summer 1962), 54.

32. A good source that illuminates Anglo American sentiments toward Mexicans and Mexican Americans is Cecil Robinson, *With the Ears of Strangers: The Mexican in American Literature* (Tucson: University of Arizona Press, 1963). Robinson looked at fiction and nonfiction publications of the late nineteenth century and uncovered numerous examples of Anglo American racist views and justifications for holding such views. For a more thorough discussion of race in the West, see Tomás Almaguer, *Racial Fault Lines: The Historical Origins of White Supremacy in California* (Berkeley: University of California Press, 1994).

33. Sheridan, *Tucsonenses*, 237.

34. "The original boundaries of Barrio Libre," writes James Officer, "were Broadway on the north, Stone on the east, 18th Street on the south, and Main (especially south of Simpson Street) on the west." By 1959, he noted, "Its boundaries had also extended into South Tucson." Officer, "Sodalities," 75.

35. Sheridan, *Tucsonenses*, 82. Caution must be exercised in referring to the barrio map in *Los Tucsonenses*, drawn in 1985. Although based on 1940 U.S. Census information, it incorporated the contemporary names of the barrios, most notably Barrio Histórico. For more on the U.S. Census and Mexican Americans, see José Hernandez, Leo Estrada, and David Alvarez, "Census Data

and the Problem of Conceptually Defining the Mexican American Population," *Social Science Quarterly* 53 (1973), 671–687. As part of gentrification after urban renewal, residents of a small section of the barrio that survived south of 14th Street appropriated the name Barrio Histórico around 1970.

36. Armando Durazo, "Barrio Libre: South Tucson Refuge," *Star*, July 16, 1978. Meanwhile, north of downtown, a smaller Mexican American community, aptly known as Barrio El Presidio, had established itself where the original presidio had once stood. The residents who settled around North Meyer Avenue were more affluent than their neighbors to the south. As early as the 1940s, speculators stepped in to buy properties. Many residents faced the same fate as the Perezes, who had owned and operated El Rapido Tortilla Factory since 1934. A developer purchased all the buildings on their block in the 1950s, and the family could not afford to relocate: "We had low overhead here, we couldn't set up new somewhere else." By 1975, Anglo Americans far outnumbered Mexican Americans. As part of the Old Pueblo Center Redevelopment Project, a new multilevel underground parking lot spelled the end to Barrio El Presidio. Judy Donovan, "El Presidio . . . Where It All Began," special report, *Star*, July 16, 1978, 13.

37. Dennis R. Bell et al., *Barrio Historico, Tucson* (Tucson: College of Architecture, University of Arizona, 1972), 1.

38. Ibid., 76. The story of gentrification in the older neighborhood spared by urban renewal is given more attention in the conclusion to *Barrio Histórico*. Architects Anne M. Nequette and R. Brooks Jeffery, in *A Guide to Tucson Architecture*, also refer to this area as Barrio Libre.

39. Bell et al., *Barrio Histórico*, 1.

40. Ibid., 2.

41. Griswold del Castillo, *Los Angeles Barrio*, 150.

42. *Tucson and Tombstone General and Business Directory for 1883 and 1884* (Tucson: Cobler and Company, 1883).

43. Daniel D. Arreola, "Urban Ethnic Landscape Identity," *Geographical Review* 85, no. 4 (October 1995), 518.

44. Castillo interview.

45. Adalberto Guerrero, a former Spanish professor at the University of Arizona who grew up in Bisbee, Arizona, recalls that Spanish speakers in other southwestern cities also used "la calle" to indicate their downtown area.

46. Lalo Guerrero and Sherilyn Mentes, *Lalo: My Life and Music* (Tucson: University of Arizona Press, 2002), 23, 26.

47. "A Few in Trouble: Business Nearly as Good Elsewhere but Old friends are Missing," *Citizen*, December 12, 1970, 7.

48. Enrique García, as quoted in Stephen Farley et al., eds., *Snapped on the Street: A Community Archive of Photos and Memories from Downtown Tucson, 1937–1963* (Tucson: Tucson Voices Press, 1999), 6. *Snapped on the Street* adds credence, in the form of photographs and oral histories, to tucsonenses' patronage

of and attachment to the city's commercial core (la calle). Concentrating on the three decades before urban renewal, it makes apparent the diverse ethnic environment that flourished on Tucson's downtown streets.

49. See City-County Planning Department, *General Land Use Plan: Tucson and Environs* (City of Tucson, 1960), iv, which outlines the idealized "progressive" plan designed "to guide development toward a balanced community" through "boldness and courage . . . and planning" (ellipsis in original).

50. Van Slyck, "What the Bishop Learned: The Importance of Claiming Space at Tucson's Church Plaza," *Journal of Arizona History* 39 (Summer 1998), 125.

51. María Isabel MacLaury, "La Placita: Vantages of Urban Change in Historic Tucson" (Master's thesis, University of Arizona, 1989), 37, 38.

52. "Living Yesterday" *Citizen*, January 21, 1963, 2.

53. Van Slyck, "What the Bishop Learned: The Importance of Claiming Space at Tucson's Church Plaza," *Journal of Arizona History* 39 (Summer 1998), 121–125.

54. See Bhabha, *Location of Culture.*

55. See Bernice Cosulich, "Chapel was Important Part of Presidio: Established by Spaniards Here in 1776," *Star*, n.d., found in Ephemera: Places—Tucson—Churches—Catholic—St. Augustine file, Arizona Historical Society/Tucson. John Baptist Salpointe, the Catholic vicar apostolic of Arizona, arrived in Tucson in 1866.

56. Ana María Comadurán Coenen, as interviewed by George Chambers and G. T. Urias, 1927, Tucson; Atanacia Santa Cruz, as quoted in "Sacrifice of Pioneers Recalled as Walls of Old Convent Tumble," *Citizen*, June 30, 1932, in Ephemera: Places—Tucson—Churches—Catholic—St. Augustine file, both the Coenen and Santa Cruz items are located in the same ephemera file at Arizona Historical Society/Tucson.

57. C. L. Sonnichsen, *Tucson: The Life and Times of an American City* (Norman: University of Oklahoma Press, 1987), 67–68. Note that Tucson has had a number of different churches named San Agustín at different times. The presidio's full name was Presidio de San Agustín del Tucsón. Tucsonenses also called the small military chapel once located within its walls San Agustín. Built in 1896, the current Saint Augustine's Cathedral (note the Anglicized spelling) still stands at 192 South Stone Avenue and is the only surviving church with this name. Tucsonenses unusually refer to it as "la catedral."

58. Alva Torres to Mayor Lew Murphy, October 14, 1973. MS 1134, Alva Torres Collection, box 2, f. 18, Plaza de la Mesilla—Correspondence, 1968–1974, Arizona Historical Society/Tucson.

59. Sheridan, *Tucsonenses*, 151, 163.

60. See Carlos Vélez-Ibáñez, *Border Visions: Mexican Cultures of the Southwest United States* (Tucson: University of Arizona Press, 1996).

61. My grandmother Rita Corrales Robles shared stories of the huge San Agustín festivals with my mother, who in turn related them to me. Efforts to revive the festivals are also discussed in chapter 3.

62. Ruben Moreno, as quoted in Farley et al., *Snapped on the Street*, 107, 122.

63. Mary Angel Pérez, as quoted in Farley et al., *Snapped on the Street*, 107.

64. Howard Simms, as quoted in Farley et al., *Snapped on the Street*, 68.

65. "Mexican Folk Song Idol Entertains Tucson Fans," *Citizen*, July 26, 1952, 6.

66. "It Pays to Be Funny, and Valdez Proves It," *Citizen*, January 4, 1963, 6.

67. "Spanish Singer to Appear Here," *Citizen*, October 23, 1965, 27. Itules and, later, the Imperial Furniture Store were located at 160 West Congress.

68. Don Jacinto "checked with hospitals, law enforcement agencies and mortuaries to find out about his people." He also heavily influenced their social consciousness through reporting and commentary regarding national and local news. In 1957 he received an award from the Mexican American business community in recognition of his aiding "the Mexican community extensively in various welfare and humanitarian projects." "Orozco Will Be Honored," *Citizen*, July 3, 1963, 16; see also "Don Jacinto Shares His Hearers' Joys, Sorrows," *Citizen*, May 11, 1957, 32; "Mexican-Americans had a 'Voice,'" *Citizen*, July 3, 1975, 3. As a child, I remember walking into neighbors' houses, and all of them had their radios tuned to Don Jacinto. Before 1975, the main Spanish-speaking radio stations were KVET and KXEW. On Sunday mornings, the KOLD television program *Mexican Theater* also provided local programming. Popular until the 1970s, the show made minor celebrities of the hosts, Tony and Henry Villegas. They interviewed Mexican Americans involved in various issues and provided coverage of local events. Music, of course, dominated their programming.

69. Alianza Papers in Control File, Special Collections, University of Arizona Library. These quotations are taken from the script of an Alianza film written to celebrate its fiftieth anniversary. I was unable to locate the actual film. My thanks to Veronica Reyes for guiding me through the Alianza files.

70. For more on the Alianza, see Kaye L. Briegel, "Alianza Hispano-Americana, 1894–1965: A Mexican-American Fraternal Insurance Society" (PhD diss., University of Southern California, 1974). In addition to its own internal activities, the Alianza participated in local and national events. During World War II, the organization bought and sold war bonds and worked closely with the Red Cross. It published its own magazine with articles on health and information on the general state of Mexican people.

71. "Huge 'Alianza' Begins Crumbling into History," *Citizen*, October 7, 1966, C-9.

72. Alicia Rodríguez García, as quoted in Farley et al., *Snapped on the Street*, 111.

73. "Mexican Independence Queen Hopefuls Parade Tonight," *Citizen*, July 20, 1951, 20.

74. "Huge 'Alianza' Begins Crumbling into History."

75. Works Progress Administration, *The WPA Guide to 1930s Arizona* (Tucson: University of Arizona Press, 1989), 254–255.

76. Howard Simms, as quoted in Farley et al., *Snapped on the Street*, 37.

77. Floyd Thompson, as quoted in Farley et al., *Snapped on the Street*, 102.

78. Margaret Jean Simms Price, as quoted in Farley et al., *Snapped on the Street*, 127.

79. Anna Don, as quoted in Farley et al., *Snapped on the Street*, 24, 86.

80. Henry García, as interviewed by Sharyn Wiley Yeoman, June 19, 1987, Tucson, transcript, p. 3, file AV 0605-3, Arizona Historical Society/Tucson.

81. Ibid., p. 56.

82. Anna Don, as quoted in Farley et al., *Snapped on the Street*, 25.

83. Suey Gee, as quoted in Sayre Auslander, "Chinese Stores Preserve Tradition," *Star*, special report, July 16, 1978," 12.

84. Joe Yee, as quoted in Edith Sayre Auslander, "Chinese Stores," 12.

85. John H. Denton and William S. King, "The Tucson Central Business District as a Changing Entity," *Arizona Review*, May 1960, 3.

86. Anna Don, as quoted in Farley et al., *Snapped on the Street*, 25. Despite all the evidence to the contrary, many Tucsonans were convinced that the malls had brought about the decline of downtown. See, for example, Herb Silverburg, as quoted in Farley et al., *Snapped on the Street*, 133.

87. Lydia Carranza Waer, as quoted in Farley et al., *Snapped on the Street*, 57.

88. "Downtown Pro and Con," *Citizen*, July 6, 1963, 14.

89. Robert E. Waugh, "Percentage of Mexican-American Pedestrians in the Downtown Tucson Shopping Area," *Arizona Business and Economic Review* 5, no. 5 (May 1956), 1–2.

90. Ibid., 1.

91. The Waugh survey area was demarcated "on the north by the Stone and Sixth Avenue underpass, on the south by the library, by the railroad tracks to the east and the Main Street on the west." Ibid.

92. Waugh, "Mexican-American Pedestrians," 2.

93. "Close Competition," *Time*, August 28, 1950, at http://www.time.com/time/.

94. Ibid., 1. Waugh cites the problem of using U.S. Census Bureau reports that relied only on "Spanish and Mexican surnames" to identify Mexican Americans. However, these statistics provide the only way to estimate the Mexican American population at mid-century. No survey exists that indicates how many tucsonenses drove automobiles to the downtown area. Waugh suggests that most walked.

95. Daniel W. Raaf, "Downtown Tucson and the Woman Shopper," *Arizona Business and Economic Review* 7, no. 4 (April 1958), 1–3.

96. Ibid., 3–4.

97. Denton and King, "Tucson Central Business District," 6.

98. Ibid.

99. Ashton Associates, *Second Re-Use Appraisal Pueblo Center Redevelopment Project* (Arizona R-8; Los Angeles, 1966), 13.

Chapter 2. Asserting Economic and Spatial Dominance

1. Sara Valencia, as quoted in Keith Carew, "Urban Renewal's Dispossessed," *Citizen*, December 12, 1970, 4. For more on the importance of kin and neighborhood networks to poor women, see Carol B. Stack, *All Our Kin: Strategies for Survival in a Black Community* (New York: Harper and Row, 1974).

2. Kieran McCarty, ed., *Selections from a Frontier Documentary: Mexican Tucson, 1821–1856* (Tucson: Mexican American Studies and Research Center, University of Arizona, 1994), 12.

3. Sonnichsen, *Tucson*, 37.

4. For more on intermarriage between Anglo and Mexican Americans, see Albert L. Hurtado, *Intimate Frontiers: Sex, Gender, and Culture in Old California* (Albuquerque: University of New Mexico Press, 1999).

5. James Officer's compilation of "wealthy Tucson Anglos" included only one farmer, who was worth $5,000.00. Officer's list of "well-to-do Mexican citizens of Tucson," on the other hand, included twenty-six farmers. Tucsonenses' attachment to outmoded economic pursuits served only to accelerate their collective decline. James Officer Papers, "Hispanics Tucson—Demographic Data," MS 1155, f. 582, Arizona Historical Society/Tucson.

6. Deena J. González, *Refusing the Favor: The Spanish-Mexican Women of Santa Fe, 1820–1880* (New York: Oxford University Press, 1999), 41.

7. For a more detailed account of the effects of the railroad on the city, see Sonnichsen, *Tucson*, 102–104.

8. Sheridan, *Tucsonenses*, 43.

9. Thomas E. Sheridan, *Arizona: A History* (Tucson: University of Arizona Press, 1995), 103–104.

10. Montejano, *Anglos and Mexicans*, 74.

11. Sheridan, *Tucsonenses*, 82.

12. Michael Omi and Howard Winant, *Racial Formation in the United States: From the 1960s to the 1980s* (New York: Routledge and Kegan Paul, 1986), 55.

13. Sheridan, *Tucsonenses*, 94–96.

14. For more about elite Mexican Americans' desire to distance themselves from lower classes and Anglo Americans' insistence on labeling all Mexican people "Mexicans," see David G. Gutiérrez, *Walls and Mirrors: Mexican Americans, Mexican Immigrants, and the Politics of Ethnicity* (Berkeley: University of California Press, 1995), 32, 33.

15. See Linda Gordon, *The Great Arizona Orphan Abduction* (Cambridge, Mass.: Harvard University Press, 1999). Gordon's analysis of how racially stigmatized Irish children—unwanted in New York City—became "whiter," more desirable, and more adoptable the farther west they moved on their way to Arizona provides insight into the power of "whiteness" in the West.

16. Matthew Frye Jacobson, *Whiteness of a Different Color: European Immigrants and the Alchemy of Race* (Cambridge, Mass.: Harvard University Press, 1998), 57.

17. Sheridan, *Arizona*, 106. Regarding Jewish American claims to "whiteness," see also Jacobson's discussion of "The White Other" in *Whiteness*, 52–68.

18. Achieving whiteness represented a complicated and changeable process in which inclusion, exclusion, and access to power were always negotiated and contested. For more on the dynamics of whiteness, see George Lipsitz, *The Possessive Investment in Whiteness: How White People Profit from Identity Politics* (Philadelphia: Temple University Press, 1998); David Roediger, *The Wages of Whiteness: Race and the Making of the American Working Class* (New York: Verso Press, 1991); Alexander Saxton, *The Rise and Fall of the White Republic: Class Politics and Mass Culture in Nineteenth-Century America* (London: Verso Press, 1990); and Omi and Winant, *Racial Formation*.

19. Howard R. Lamar, "The Reluctant Admission: The Struggle to Admit Arizona and New Mexico to the Union," in Robert Ferris, ed., *The American West: An Appraisal* (Santa Fe: Museum of New Mexico Press, 1963), 163–177; the quoted statements are from pp. 163 and 175. For a discussion of the Gadsden Purchase, see Officer, *Hispanic Arizona*, 391.

20. Lamar, "Reluctant Admission," 167.

21. Ibid.

22. Ibid., 169.

23. Karen Underhill Mangelsdorf, "The Beveridge Visit to Arizona in 1902," *Journal of Arizona History* 28 (Autumn 1987), 249.

24. For a discussion of discrimination against tucsonenses during the Great Depression, see Lydia R. Otero, "Refusing to be Undocumented: Chicanas/os in Tucson during the Depression Years," in Katherine Morrissey and Kirsten Jensen, eds., *Picturing Arizona: The Photographic Record of the 1930s* (Tucson: University of Arizona Press, 2005), 42–59.

25. Jacobson, *Whiteness*, 21.

26. "New Statehood Bill," *Senate Reports*, vol. 1, nos. 2127–2544, Miscellaneous, 57th Cong., 2d sess., 1902–1903, 4410, p. 7.

27. Nequette and Jeffery, *Tucson Architecture*, 22.

28. Sonnichsen, *Tucson*, 106, 107.

29. Ibid. Ironically, builders and architects have recently rediscovered the utility of adobe and rammed earth construction. See Rick Joy, *Desert Works* (New York: Princeton Architectural Press, 2002).

30. Bradford Luckingham, *The Urban Southwest: A Profile History of Albuquerque, El Paso, Phoenix and Tucson* (El Paso: Texas Western Press, 1982), 18.

31. Saarinen, Crawford, and Thomas, "Street Patterns."

32. Donald H. Bufkin, "The Broad Pattern of Land Use and Change in Tucson, 1862–1912," in Saaringen and Gibson, *Territorial Tucson*, 5-28.

33. "National Register of Historic Places—Nomination Form—Barrio Libre," Places—Arizona, Tucson—Barrios, and Districts—Barrio Libre file, Arizona Historical Society/Tucson.

34. García, Yeoman interview, 5.

35. Robert Giebner, "Tucson's 'Barrio Historico,'" *Arizona Architect* (August 1973), 9. Note that Giebner is writing about Barrio Histórico, a small section of the former barrio that was not destroyed by urban renewal, but presumably he would have expressed the same sentiments regarding the architecture of the larger barrio that *was* destroyed.

36. Fred D. Hughes, as quoted in Joseph Miller, *Arizona: The Last Frontier* (New York: Hastings House, 1956), 22.

37. Bufkin, "Land Use in Tucson," 5-3.

38. Ibid.

39. Ibid., 5-4.

40. These leaders contributed some $1,000 to the renewal effort. See Places—Arizona, Tucson—Barrios and Districts—The Wedge file, Arizona Historical Society/Tucson.

41. Although the city council passed an "ordinance setting aside Gay Alley as a restricted red-light district" in 1916, it made no move to destroy the area. *Star*, July 2, 1916, in Ephemera: Tucson—Streets—Gay Alley file, Arizona Historical Society/Tucson.

42. Alicia Cruz, as quoted in Sam Negri, "The Long Siesta: Sleepy Tucson Neighborhood Awakens to Dim of Progress," *Arizona Republic*, December 8, 1983, D-1.

43. Officer, *Hispanic Arizona*, 82.

44. Our neighbor Irma Nevarez Moreno, who lived across the street on Farmington, remembered her family going downtown to "pay a bill or something like that, because we paid bills in person in those days." Nevarez Moreno, as quoted in Farley et al., *Snapped on the Street*, 46.

45. "No Color Line Found in City: Lack of Restriction for Colored Residents Is Indicated," *Star*, May 5, 1938, 2.

46. Freund, *Colored Property*, 93.

47. John Kestner Goodman, "Race and Race Mixture as the Basis of Social Status in Tucson, Arizona" (Master's thesis, Yale University, 1942), 72.

48. Harry Thomas Getty, *Interethnic Relationships in the Community of Tucson* (New York: Arno Press, 1976), 141.

49. Officer, *Hispanic Arizona*, 82, 83.

50. For a general overview of suburbanization, see Jackson, *Crabgrass Frontier*; and Dolores Hayden, *Building Suburbia: Green Fields and Urban Growth, 1920–2000* (New York: Pantheon Books, 2003). Building or remodeling older structures to entice people to live downtown remains a much newer, post–urban renewal development. See, in this regard, Peter Katz, ed., *The New Urbanism: Toward an*

Architecture of Community (New York: McGraw-Hill, 1994); and Andres Duany, Elizabeth Plater-Zyberk, and Jeff Speck, *Suburban Nation: The Rise of Sprawl and the Decine of the American Dream* (New York: North Point Press, 2000).

51. Avila, *Popular Culture*, 4.

52. Lizabeth Cohen, in A *Consumers' Republic*, 255–256, argues that advances in automobile transportation (an integral factor in suburbanization) and the replacement of public meetings by radio and television resulted in the privatization of the "spread city."

53. Elaine Tyler May, *Homeward Bound: American Families in the Cold War Era* (New York: Basic Books, 1988), 10. May argues that Americans "felt intense need to feel liberated from the past and secure in the future."

54. See Jackson, *Crabgrass Frontier*, and Thomas J. Sugrue, *The Origins of the Urban Crisis: Race and Inequality in Postwar Detroit* (Princeton, N.J.: Princeton University Press, 1996).

55. Freund, *Colored Property*, 37.

56. "Retail Trade Bureau Keeps Downtown Busy," *Citizen*, October 22, 1958, 28. The bureau grew out of a Chamber of Commerce committee.

57. "Shoppers Favor Ride and Shop Plan," *Citizen*, October 22, 1958, 28.

58. "Downtown Expansion Continues," *Citizen*, October 22, 1958, National Downtown Week section.

59. Ibid.

60. Meyerson's Department Store, locally known as The White House, opened south of Congress in la calle in 1958; it was forced to close less than a decade later due to urban renewal.

61. Albert Steinfeld, a Zeckendorf nephew, bought out the Zeckendorfs' Tucson merchandising enterprises in the late nineteenth century, making Steinfeld's the "oldest firm in the city." See "Steinfeld Made Early Move North," *Citizen*, May 11, 1964, Dynamic Downtown section.

62. "Pioneer Family Controls Store," *Citizen*, October 22, 1958, National Downtown Week section. Although Alex Jácome, who built his large department store in the northern section of downtown, publicly supported urban renewal, he also supported the La Placita Committee, allowing committee members to set up their table and gather signatures in front of his downtown store. Jácome's Department Store courted wealthy Mexican customers from Sonora and from as far away as Mexico City. In 1960, business leaders estimated that Mexican shoppers constituted 20 to 25 percent of downtown patrons, spending more money on purchases than their American counterparts. See "Retail Trade Bureau Wins Merchant's Strong Backing," *Citizen*, March 18, 1960, 29.

63. "Found Fortune in West," *Citizen*, November 11, 1962, Levy's El Con section.

64. Advertisement announcing, "Opening Thursday: 9 New Stores on the Mall. . . , " *Citizen*, November 1, 1965, El Con section. The ad invited the public

to witness the Arizona Sky Divers parachute onto the parking lot. Local KTKT radio provided live coverage of the opening.

65. At its height, Sears provided employment for 385 Tucsonans. "'Chain Store' Growth Shows Close Ties in Tucson, *Citizen*, September 17, 1952, 15. The article highlighted the store's close ties with the larger Tucson community and praised its manager's civic involvement.

66. In 1974, with the addition of two more department stores, the 840,000 square foot site became Park Mall. The indoor mall has since expanded to 1.1 million square feet and now boasts 120 stores, 22 restaurants, and a 22-screen movie theater. Renamed Park Place Mall, it stands today as Tucson's premier mall. "Two Big Stores Near Opening," *Citizen*, July 19, 1974, 29. See Park Place Mall Web site, http://www.parkplacemall.com/html/mallinfo.asp/.

67. Richard Longstreth, "The Diffusion of the Community Shopping Center Concept in the Interwar Decades," *Journal of the Society of Architectural Historians* 56, no. 3 (September 1997), 268.

68. For insight into cases in which large department stores significantly affected the outcome of urban renewal, see Cohen, "Buying into Downtown Revival."

69. "New Name for New Downtown," *Citizen*, October 22, 1958, National Downtown Week section.

70. Harold Steinfeld, as quoted in "Retail Trade Bureau Wins Merchant's Strong Backing," *Citizen*, March 18, 1960, 29.

71. Jeff M. Hardwick, "A Downtown Utopia? Suburbanization, Urban Renewal and Consumption in New Haven," *Planning History Studies* 10 (Winter 1996), 47.

72. "Urban Renewal Project Moving," *Citizen*, October 22, 1958, National Downtown Week section.

73. Russell Hastings, AIA, "Pedestrian Mall Gives Suburban Look Downtown," *Citizen*, October 22, 1958, National Downtown Week section.

74. Avila, *Popular Culture*, 62.

75. "New Center Is Tucson's Largest," *Citizen*, April 6, 1960, Campbell Plaza section. On the same page, the article "Roy Drachman Is 'Man in Charge'" boasted that Drachman was "an authority on shopping centers" and that he and his partner had "developed seven shopping centers in Phoenix and Tucson." Drachman received the 1965 Realtor of the Year Award for his role in promoting the $23 million bond election that sanctioned urban renewal and for chairing the Committee on Municipal Blight. See "Roy Drachman Honored as 1965 Realtor of the Year," *Citizen*, January 22, 1966, 8.

Chapter 3. Selling Tucson

1. Henry García, as interviewed by Sharyn Wiley Yeoman, June 19, 1987, Tucson, transcript, 74, AV 0605-3, Arizona Historical Society/Tucson.

2. On the role of anti-Mexican sentiments in Arizona's development, see William E. Smythe, *The Conquest of Arid America* (New York: Harper, 1900), 238, 243; and Michael F. Logan, *Desert Cities: The Environmental History of Phoenix and Tucson* (Pittsburgh: University of Pittsburgh Press, 2006), 85. On the significance of and public opinion regarding desert environments in U.S. history, see Patricia Nelson Limerick, *Desert Passages: Encounters with the American Deserts* (Niwot: University Press of Colorado, 1989). See also Fannie A. Charles, *In the Country God Forgot: A Story of Today* (Boston: Little, Brown, 1902), a popular novel that highlights the "unbearable" living conditions the desert environment offered potential settlers.

3. Individuals and small companies often produced their own postcards and sometimes also their own promotional literature. For example, T. Roger Blythe edited, illustrated, and self-published the 38-page booklet *A Pictorial Souvenir of Tucson, Arizona: "The Old Pueblo"; The Sunshine City of America* (Tucson, 1945) as a way to disseminate his artwork. Despite the booklet's title and subtitles, I could find no relationship between Blythe and the Chamber of Commerce or the Sunshine Club, the main booster groups who collaborated with and received funding from local government. My analysis concentrates on tourist materials produced by these two groups, discussed later in the chapter. Blythe also published many other booklets, on the California missions, El Camino Real, and Tombstone, Arizona.

4. Chela Sandoval, *Methodology of the Oppressed* (Minneapolis: University of Minnesota Press, 2000), 4–5, claims that "cultural productions . . . can be scrutinized archaeologically just as any literary, filmic, or other cultural artifact can be examined to identify the meanings, hopes, aims, and desires contained within them." For more on "reading" cultural production, see Fredric Jameson, *Postmodernism, or the Cultural Logic of Late Capitalism* (Durham, N.C.: Duke University Press, 1991).

5. For more on the manipulation of collective memory, see Michael Kammen, *Mystic Chords of Memory: The Transformation of Tradition in American Culture* (New York: Knopf, 1991).

6. J. Ross Browne, *Adventures in the Apache Country: A Tour through Arizona and Sonora, with Notes on the Silver Regions of Nevada* (New York: Harper, 1869), 132–133. Sidney R. De Long decries disparaging characterizations of Arizona by a "class of writers" who, seeking national notoriety, had "misunderstood" and misrepresented Arizona. *The History of Arizona from the Earliest Times Known to the People of Europe to 1903* (San Francisco: Whitaker and Ray, 1905), 17–18.

7. C.M.K. Paulison, *Arizona, The Wonderful Country: Tucson Its Metropolis; A Comprehensive Review of the Past Progress, Present Condition and Future Prospects of the Territory of Arizona, Showing the Advantages Possessed by Tucson as the Commercial Metropolis* (Tucson: *Arizona Star*, 1881), 3.

8. Ibid., 13.

9. Logan, *Desert Cities*, 38.

10. Tucson remained the territorial capital until 1877, when Prescott again claimed the honor before yielding to Phoenix in 1889. Bradford Luckingham, in "The Old Pueblo and the Valley of the Sun: Notes on Urban Rivalry in Arizona," discusses other factors that influenced lawmakers to locate the state capital in Phoenix. This unpaginated 20-page article can be found in MS 1155, f. 635, Manuscript Tucson-Phoenix Rivalry, box 48, Arizona Historical Society/Tucson.

11. Luckingham, *Urban Southwest*, 14–15, 52.

12. See Logan, *Desert Cities*, which focuses on the evolution of these two cities. See also Don G. Campbell, "Tucson: Late Bloomer as Resort Destination: Southern Arizona City Emerges from Shadow of Phoenix in Attracting Industries, Housing," *Los Angles Times*, April 20, 1986, Real Estate section, 1.

13. Luckingham, *Urban Southwest*, 31.

14. The Phoenix Chamber of Commerce, 1891, as quoted in Logan, *Desert Cities*, 85.

15. Luckingham, *Urban Southwest*, x. As evidenced in the statehood debates, an underpopulation of Anglos became one of the main charges that national representatives held against Arizona.

16. Paulison, *Arizona*, 27.

17. Douglas D. Martin, "1896," in *An Arizona Chronology: The Territorial Years, 1846–1912* (Tucson, University of Arizona Press, 1963). A few references claim that the Chamber of Commerce was founded in 1902 or 1904. For more on these discrepancies, see Logan, Fighting Sprawl, p. 173, n. 2. Ultimately, Logan confirms that the Chamber of Commerce's founding date was 1896.

18. Alex Jay Kimmelman, "Luring the Tourists to Tucson: Civic Promotion during the 1920s," *Journal of Arizona History* 28, no. 2 (Summer 1987), 136. By World War II, the merits of climatotherapy had been medically refuted.

19. Sonnichsen, *Tucson*, 148.

20. Kimmelman, "Luring Tourists," 136.

21. Drachman, *Desert Metropolis*, 187.

22. Bonnie Henry, *Another Tucson* (Tucson: *Arizona Daily Star*, 1992), 219.

23. Drachman, *Desert Metropolis*, 188.

24. "Club Organized 1922, Tucson Metropolitan District," Tucson Sunshine-Climate Club folder, Arizona Historical Society/Tucson. Soon after its founding, the club came to be called simply the Sunshine Club. In 1963, it was formally incorporated into the Tucson Chamber of Commerce. "Luncheon Set by Corona de Tucson," *Citizen*, March 12, 1963, 8.

25. Kammen, *Mystic Chords*, 401.

26. Tucson Sunshine-Climate Club, *Tucson Arizona: Man-Building in the Sunshine Climate* (Tucson: 1925?), Special Collections, University of Arizona Library.

27. Luckingham, *Urban Southwest*, 60.

28. Roy Drachman, Oral History, acc. no. 92-11, AV 0505-18, "Urbanization of Tucson: 1940–1990," 2, Arizona Historical Society/Tucson. Drachman also became director of the Sunshine Club in the 1940s and served on its board of directors. See also Kimmelman, "Luring Tourists," 135.

29. *Tucson, the World's Sunshine Center* (Tucson: Consolidated National Bank, 1925?), Special Collections, University of Arizona Library. See also Tucson Chamber of Commerce, "The Tucson Story," in *Welcome Visitor*, published circa 1956, in "Miscellaneous Publications," MS 1079, 52, f. 101, Arizona Historical Society/Tucson, for a similar narrative. This publication dedicated two entire pages to various Square Dance Club events held on each day of the week and in multiple locations and times in Tucson.

30. See De Long, *History of Arizona*, which largely glorifies Anglo Americans despite the author's pledge to "write the truth regardless of whom it may please or displease." The invisibility of Mexican people and culture is evident in one of Tucson's premier museums, the Arizona State Museum at the University of Arizona. Established by the territorial legislature in 1893, its focus is the "archaeology and anthropology of the southwestern United States and northern Mexico." No displays speak to or educate the public about Mexican American history.

31. University of Arizona, *Twenty-First Arizona Town Hall on Arizona's Heritage—Today and Tomorrow: Research Report, Recommendations, and List of Participants*, October 15–18, 1972 (Phoenix: Arizona Academy, 1972), 7, 8–175. I chose to review this text because of the large number of influential leaders who monitored and approved the final project. Three male participants involved in this project had Spanish surnames.

32. Officer, *Hispanic Arizona*, 101–103, 120.

33. For more on Tucson's role as a resupply station during the Gold Rush of 1849, see James E. Officer, "Yanqui Forty-Niners in Hispanic Arizona: Interethnic Relations on the Sonoran Frontier," *Journal of Arizona History* 28, no. 2 (Summer 1987), 101–134.

34. Officer, *Hispanic Arizona*, 103, 120, 122; see also chap.7, note 7.

35. "Records Relating to the Publication *Arizona's Heritage—Today and Tomorrow*," October 1972, Special Collections, University of Arizona Library.

36. Tucson Chamber of Commerce, *Tucson: Arizona's Playground, Home of Health and Sunshine* (Tucson, 1906), Special Collections, University of Arizona Library.

37. David J. Weber, *The Mexican Frontier, 1821–1846: The American Southwest under Mexico* (Albuquerque: University of New Mexico Press, 1982), xvi.

38. Officer, *Hispanic Arizona*, 1. Officer refutes references to Tucson as teetering and precarious during the Mexican era and contends that, contrary to previous portrayals, the Mexican settlers never "abandoned [the presidio] because of Apache raids." Tucson did face a sharp decline in population in the mid-

nineteenth century when Mexicans left to go south, or north to follow the Gold Rush. An outbreak of cholera took the lives of more than a quarter of Tucson's population. See ibid., 24. See Hubert Howe Bancroft, *History of Arizona and New Mexico, 1530–1888* (San Francisco: History, 1889). See also Genaro M. Padilla, *My History, Not Yours: The Formation of Mexican American Autobiography* (Madison: University of Wisconsin Press, 1993); Deena J. González, *Refusing the Favor*; and Andrés Reséndez, *Changing National Identities at the Frontier: Texas and New Mexico, 1800–1850* (Cambridge: Cambridge University Press, 2005), all of which challenge Bancroft's version of history.

39. Officer, *Hispanic Arizona*, 2.

40. Drachman and Lung, *Pueblo Center*, 2.

41. Tucson Chamber of Commerce, *Arizona's Playground*.

42. Carey McWilliams, *North from Mexico: The Spanish-Speaking Peoples of the United States* (Philadelphia: Lippincott, 1949), 43–53. Anthropologist Renato Rosaldo, *Culture and Truth: The Remaking of Social Analysis* (Boston: Beacon Press, 1989), 69, notes that the idealization of a more meaningful and unrecoverable past is typical of "'agents of colonialism' who . . . often display nostalgia for the colonized culture as it was 'traditional' (that is, when they first encountered it). The peculiarity of their yearning, of course, is that agents of colonialism long for the very forms of life they intentionally altered or destroyed . . . people mourn the passing of what they themselves have transformed."

43. Kropp, *California Vieja*, 89. For Mexican Americans' perceptions of these types of myths, see also David G. Gutiérrez, "Significant to Whom? Mexican Americans and the History of the American West," *Western Historical Quarterly* 24, no. 4 (November 1993), 519–539.

44. Charles Montgomery, *The Spanish Redemption: Heritage, Power, and Loss on New Mexico's Upper Rio Grande* (Berkeley: University of California Press, 2002), 104.

45. *Tucson, the World's Sunshine Center* (Tucson: Consolidated National Bank, 1925?) Special Collections, University of Arizona Library.

46. Phoebe S. Kropp, "'All Our Yesterdays': The Spanish Fantasy Past and the Politics of Public Memory in Southern California, 1884–1939" (PhD diss., University of California, San Diego, 1999), 3.

47. "The Birth of the Historical Sites Committee: An Editorial," *Arizoniana* 1, no. 3 (November 13, 1960), 2–3.

48. Ibid., 2. Cottonwood Lane, where army officers' quarters were located, was their second choice. In 1945, the Chamber of Commerce had intervened to ensure the preservation of Fort Lowell. They succeeded in turning the area over to the Catalina Council of Boy Scouts of America, who used it as a campsite. See "Scouts to Take over Ft. Lowell," *Citizen*, May 12, 1945, 5.

49. Logan, *Desert Cities*, 105. Luckingham makes a similar observation in *Urban Southwest*, 66.

50. *Merriam-Webster's Collegiate Dictionary*, 11th edition (2003), defines *pueblo* as "an American Indian village of the southwestern United States." See http://www.merriam-webster.com/dictionary/pueblo/.

51. This same article promised that visitors would find a "New Pueblo, new as a bright, polished penny, gleaming in the sun, building and growing in every direction." "Tucson the O̶l̶d̶ New Pueblo" in *Tucson: The New Pueblo* (Tucson: Sunshine-Climate Club, 1950?), 2.

52. Robert E. Waugh, "What Does Your Vacationer *Really Want*—and How You Can Find Out," *Arizona Business and Economic Review* 7, no. 8 (August 1958), 2–5. All statements and information cited here are taken from page 3.

53. Gilbert G. González, *Culture of Empire: American Writers, Mexico, and Mexican Immigrants, 1880–1930* (Austin: University of Texas Press, 2004), 8–10.

54. Ibid., 10.

55. Tucson Chamber of Commerce, *Welcome Visitor: Official Guide to Tucson* (Tucson: Tucson Chamber of Commerce, 1935–1936), 12.

56. For a more thorough discussion of tourism and the imagery associated with "Old Mexico," see Daniel D. Arreola and James R. Curtis, *The Mexican Border Cities: Landscape Anatomy and Place Personality* (Tucson: University of Arizona Press, 1993), 90–96. El Paso also used "Old Mexico" to lure tourists, especially during Prohibition, inviting visitors to cross the border to consume alcohol. See Luckingham, *Urban Southwest*, 57–58.

57. Tucson Chamber of Commerce, *Welcome Visitor* (1935–36), 12.

58. See Mark Cronlund Anderson, *Pancho Villa's Revolution by Headlines* (Norman: University of Oklahoma Press, 2000), which examines mass media and public opinion in the United States regarding the Mexican Revolution.

59. Goodman, "Race in Tucson," 81. Goodman confirms Historian Grace Elizabeth Hale's observations that both the North and the South of the United States had became accustomed to African American servitude. See Hale, *Making Whiteness: The Culture of Segregation in the South, 1890–1940* (New York: Pantheon Books, 1998), 160–165.

60. Goodman, "Race in Tucson," 81. In his unpaginated chapter "Negros in Tucson," Goodman recalled hearing "over and over again [that] in Tucson, that there just 'doesn't seem to be enough good colored help to go around.'"

61. Ibid., 82. Interestingly, a limited command of English did not rank as a complaint.

62. Officer, "Sodalities," 177. In 1978, a federal judge confirmed Officer's findings in a desegregation lawsuit against the local school district when he declared that there was "a history of discrimination against Mexican Americans in Tucson." *Star*, July 16, 1978.

63. Sugrue, *Race in Postwar Detroit*, 9.

64. Goodman, "Race in Tucson," 108.

65. In the late 1920s, the Desert Sanatorium produced its own advertisements that dispelled national misconceptions of Tucson as an "unclean and dusty" town by claiming that "scrumptious cleanliness is observed in connection with the preparation and serving of meals, and all the dishes and utensils are washed, rinsed and sterilized mechanically." See *The Desert Sanatorium* (Tucson, 1928), Desert Sanatorium folder, Arizona Historical Society/Tucson.

66. Chamber of Commerce, *Tucson: A City, an Opportunity, a Way of Life* (Tucson: Chamber of Commerce, 1958).

67. See http://www.dimenovels.com/. This Web site allows visitors to purchase and review the covers and sample text of a variety of dime novels. The home page offers that they follow "the tradition of the dime novel, carried in the back pocket of every fan of the West for more than two hundred years."

68. John Mack Faragher, "The Myth of the Frontier: Progress or Lost Freedom." *History Now* 9 (September 2006): http://www.historynow.org/09_2006/historian3.html.

69. Harold Bell Wright, *The Mine with the Iron Door: A Romance* (New York: D. Appleton, 1923).

70. Logan, *Desert Cities*, 100.

71. Wright, *Iron Door.*

72. "Sunshine-Climate Club Correspondence, 1940–1945," George Chambers Collection, MS 1079, sec. 2, box 6, f. 90, Arizona Historical Society/Tucson. The correspondence file also contains letters from tourists who wrote to complain about accommodations, food, and travel.

73. Luckingham, *Urban Southwest*, 66.

74. See Gail Bederman, *Manliness and Civilization: A Cultural History of Gender and Race in the United States, 1880–1917* (Chicago: University of Chicago Press, 1995).

75. "Did You Know?" *Tucson Magazine*, May 1938. The Tucson Chamber of Commerce produced this magazine.

76. Jack Williams, "Tucson Was Dude Ranch Capital for Ranching Experience," *Nogales International*, July 22, 1987. For a summary of dude and guest ranches, see Frank Blaine Norris, "The Southern Arizona Guest Ranch as a Symbol of the West" (Master's thesis, University of Arizona, 1976). Interestingly, by the 1980s many of the old dude and guest ranches had evolved into substance-abuse treatment centers. See "Dudes and Saddles," in Henry, *Another Tucson.* Henry discloses that ethnic restrictions led to the creation of dude ranches that catered only to Jewish Americans. See also Levi J. Long, "Dude, Where's My Ranch?" *Star*, January 29, 2006, D-1; and Gabriela Rico, "Signature Tucson Attraction Is Fading," *Star*, January 3, 2008, A-1.

77. "Treat 'Em Tenderly Succeeds Old Policy of Rough Initiation: Comfort and Luxury in Accommodations and Food Keynote of Success of Many

Guest Ranches—'Wooliness' Now Taboo," *Citizen*, not dated, "Ranches, Guest—Arizona," Arizona Historical Society/Tucson.

78. On traditions, which are created to serve a variety of social purposes, see Eric Hobsbawm and Terence Ranger, eds., *The Invention of Tradition* (Cambridge: Cambridge University Press, 1983), a classic work on the subject.

79. For more on the manipulation of public heritage, see David Lowenthal, "Identity, Heritage, and History," in John Gillis, ed., *Commemorations: The Politics of National Identity* (Princeton, N.J.: Princeton University Press, 1994), 41–60. See also Lowenthal, *Possessed by the Past: The Heritage Crusade and the Spoils of History* (New York: Free Press, 1996); Kammen, *Mystic Chords*.

80. The Polo Association hoped that the rodeo would "get national publicity for Arizona" and make Tucson the "winter capital of Polo." Comprising the business elite, the Polo Association convinced "sixty Tucsonans [to] contribute $250.00 each for rodeo prize money." Local merchants also chipped in donations for the first rodeo. The $250 donation also bought a membership to the Polo Association. Kimmelman, "Luring Tourists," 142. See also "Rodeo," in Henry, *Another Tucson*, 209–210.

81. Tucson Chamber of Commerce, *Welcome Visitor* (1935–36), 23.

82. As quoted in Kimmelman, "Luring the Tourists to Tucson," 143.

83. Logan and Molotch, *Urban Fortunes*, 61–62. The editor of the *Citizen* also said, "It is the civic duty of every loyal Tucsonan to contribute his bit to the success of the rodeo by attending." "Attend the Rodeo," *Citizen*, February 2, 1925, 4. For more on the first rodeo, see "Great Parade Today Starts Off Initial Fiesta of Cowboys," *Citizen*, February 21, 1925, 2; "Large Crown Sees Rodeo Get in Action," *Citizen*, February 22, 1925, 1; and "Huge Crowd on Hand for Rodeo Opening," *Citizen*, February 22, 1925, 3.

84. Sheridan, *Tucsonenses*, 18. As used in rodeos, "dally" means to wrap a lasso around a saddle horn after roping a calf or steer. See also Carey McWilliams, "The Heritage of the Southwest," in Renato Rosaldo, Robert A. Calvert, and Gustav L. Seligmann, eds., *Chicano: The Evolution of a People* (Minneapolis: Winston Press, 1973); and Doris K. Seibold, "Cattle Raising and Spanish Speech in Southern Arizona," *Arizona Quarterly* 2, no. 2 (1946): 24–34. See also Officer, *Hispanic Arizona*, 14.

85. Historian Ricardo Romo asserts that by 1930 the majority of Mexican people in the United States lived in cities. Romo, "The Urbanization of Southwestern Chicanos in the Early Twentieth Century," in Manuel G. Gonzales and Cynthia M. Gonzales, eds., *En Aquel Entonces: Readings in Mexican-American History* (Bloomington: Indiana University Press, 2000), 32.

86. Jack N. Young to Mr. Roger L. Nichols, February 2, 1972, in "Records Relating to the Publication, Arizona's Heritage," f. 3, Special Collections, University of Arizona Library.

87. Ibid. See also Louis De Mayo, *Old Tucson: The Classic West* (Phoenix: De Mayo, 1972).

Chapter 4. The Politics of Belonging and Exclusion

1. Pedro Gonzales, videotaped interview, Tucson, November 10, 2007.

2. Officer, *Hispanic Arizona*, 404n92.

3. For election statistics, see "The Bond Election: March 1, 1966" in chapter 5.

4. The Sunshine Club took endless photographs of the filming of *Gay Desperado*, possibly for future promotional campaigns. The surviving contact sheets indicate that the club's photographer ignored the scenes filmed in la calle and concentrated his efforts on shots of Ida Lupino and other cast members wearing bathing suits and frolicking in pools. See Robert Riddell Collection, Arizona Historical Society/Tucson.

5. "Romance of Old, 'City within City' Revealed by Strolling Down Meyer: Quaint Atmosphere of Old Mexico to Be Found a Few Steps from Bustling East Congress Street and Unusual American Sights," *Citizen*, July 4, 1931, 3.

6. Edward H. Wilson, as quoted in "Editor's Urban Renewal Opinions Are Disputed: Architect Nelson Defends 'Center,'" *Star*, February 23, 1966, A-5.

7. Although Raymond Williams does not focus on the word "slums," his book *Keywords: A Vocabulary of Culture and Society* (London: Fontana, 1976) is an excellent source for understanding the subjective nature of "keywords" and how their meanings change over time.

8. Jan Lin, "Ethnic Places, Postmodernism, and Urban Change in Houston," *Sociological Quarterly* 36, no. 4 (Autumn 1995), 629.

9. John Gourley, "The Pueblo and the Public: Urban Realities in Counterpoint" (PhD diss., University of Arizona, 1992), 226, 228. The same silence that permeated the racial environment in mid-century Tucson resembled that described in William H. Chafe's, *Civilities and Civil Rights: Greensboro, North Carolina, and the Black Struggle for Freedom* (New York: Oxford University Press, 1980). As in Tucson, a coalition of business leaders in Greensboro ran the city. These leaders took pride in their city's "better class" of colored citizens, just as Tucson's business leaders took pride in their assimilationist-minded and elite Mexican American population. Business leaders in both cities saw themselves as "forward-looking" people and ignored the racial discrimination that prevailed. They preferred the illusions they had created about their city being progressive and free of racial disharmony.

10. Goodman, "Race in Tucson," 107.

11. Kimmelman, "Luring Tourists," 138–139.

12. Tucson Sunshine-Climate Club and G. Curiel, *Tucson, the World's Sunshine Center* (Tucson: Consolidated National Bank, Acme Print, 1925).

13. Cuco Fusco urges an awareness of racial dynamics that are often institutionalized and therefore go unnoticed: "Racial identities are not only Black, Latino, Asian and Native American and so on; they are also white. To ignore ethnicity is to redouble its hegemony by naturalizing it." Fusco, as quoted in David Roediger, *Towards an Abolition of Whiteness* (New York: Verso Press, 1994), 12.

14. Jacobson, *Whiteness*, 11.

15. An unnamed source quoted in Roy Kenneth Fleagle, "Politics and Planning: Tucson Metropolitan Area" (Master's thesis, University of Arizona, 1966), 19–21.

16. Roy P. Drachman, "Whither Goest Tucson?" *Realty Digest* (Tucson: Roy Drachman Realty) 17, no. 4 (December 1964), unpaginated.

17. Hal K. Rothman, *Devil's Bargains: Tourism in the Twentieth-Century American West* (Lawrence: University Press of Kansas, 1998), 10–11.

18. Ibid., 11–12.

19. "The Rodeo, a Permanent Tucson Attraction," *Star*, February 26, 1931, 10.

20. Logan and Molotch, *Urban Fortunes*, 3, 32–34.

21. George Chambers of the Sunshine Club to A. A. Sundin, September 21, 1940, "Sunshine-Climate Club Correspondence, 1940–1945," MS 1079, section 2, f. 90, box 6, Arizona Historical Society/Tucson.

22. City and county governments often reported on the increase in electricity and telephone customers because such data substantiated population growth in the city. Within the city limits, electricity customers grew from 8,715 in 1940 to 17,741 in 1955. Telephone customers similarly increased, from 16,736 in 1943 to 62,191 at the end of 1955. See "City-County Planning Department," *Tucson-Pima County Fact Book* (most likely published in 1956), MS 1173, f. 29, box 3, Arizona Historical Society/Tucson.

23. In 1946–47, the Sunshine Club received $8,400 and the Chamber of Commerce $7,200 for advertising from the City of Tucson. Places—Arizona—Tucson—Organizations—Sunshine Climate folder, Arizona Historical Society/Tucson. In 1946–47, they also shared the same treasurer.

24. Logan and Molotch, *Urban Fortunes*, 62.

25. "Tucson Regional Plan, Minutes, Board of Director's Meeting, Pioneer Hotel, May 15, 1959," MS 1173, f. 3, box 1, Arizona Historical Society/Tucson. See also Fleagle, "Politics and Planning"; Donald Wayne Richards, "Economic Development Efforts of the City Government: Tucson, Arizona—1963 to 1973" (Master's thesis, University of Arizona, 1973); and "'Merchant Control' Cited as Barrier to Industry," *Citizen*, December 8, 1964, 9.

26. Chamber of Commerce, *Tucson: Arizona's Playground, Home of Health and Sunshine,* unpaginated.

27. A survey by the *Nirenstein's National Realty Map*, Business section, City of Tucson, Arizona (Springfield, Mass., 1950?), ranked as Tucson's principal businesses the Arizona Portland Cement Company, the Boeing Aircraft Corporation,

Grand Central Aircraft, Hughes Aircraft (electronics), Infilco (water filtering manufacturing), and the Rainbo Bakery. Map Collection, University of Arizona Library. Its list did not include examples from "soft" industries such as higher education (the University of Arizona), the military (Davis-Monthan Air Force Base), real estate, agriculture, and tourism.

28. See J. J. Wagoner, "History of the Cattle Industry in Southern Arizona, 1540–1940," *University of Arizona Social Science Bulletin* 23, no. 2 (April 1952), 1–132.

29. Goodman, "Race in Tucson," 10. See also "Early Cattle Ranching in Anglo Arizona," MS 1155, f. 4.22; "Arizona Cattle Industry—Research," box 31, Arizona Historical Society/Tucson. Big cattle drives that predated the railroads often bypassed Southern Arizona for fear of attack by the Apaches.

30. Fleagle, "Politics and Planning," 21–23. See also "City C of C Role? Mayor Promises Study of Industry Issue," *Citizen*, January 6, 1965, 9.

31. See William A. Small Jr., editorial, "Voters Don't Want 'Another Phoenix,'" *Citizen*, September 18, 1975, 28. The mayoral primary election of 1975 marked a turning point: local voters nominated candidates who advocated controlled growth. The *Citizen* conducted an unofficial "straw poll" survey of its readers in response to the city's growth agenda in 1975. Out of the 326 readers surveyed, 134 (41 percent) voted for "no growth," 160 (49 percent) for "controlled growth," and 32 (10 percent) for "unrestrained growth." "Not Much Enthusiasm for Growth," *Citizen*, August 15, 1975, 35.

32. Fleagle, "Politics and Planning," 100.

33. Harold Steinfeld, as quoted in "San Diego Newsman 'Twisted' Hughes Remarks, Says Steinfeld," *Citizen*, February 28, 1964, 13.

34. Drachman, "Whither Tucson?"

35. Andrew Wilson, as quoted in "'Merchant Control,'" 9. "Aggressive selling of industry is very different from merchandizing necessities and luxuries," Wilson explained in a *Star* article that appeared the following day. Industry would create a more competitive economic environment, he said, resulting in higher wages for most Tucsonans, something clearly not in the interests of Tucson merchants, "who have a captive market. They compete among themselves . . . [and] can always hire someone else willing to work for less, in a town that has no challenging industry." See Marilyn Johnson, "Merchants, Editor Control City, University Professor Asserts," *Star*, December 9, 1964, B-9.

36. "'Merchant Control,'" 9.

37. James E. Officer, "Power in the Old Pueblo: A Study of Decision Making in a Southwestern Community," 1961, unpublished manuscript, AZ 395, Special Collections, University of Arizona Library. See also "Citizen Matthews: The Man Who Led the *Arizona Daily Star* for 39 Years Used His Paper as a Bully Pulpit, Setting a Community Agenda," *Citizen*, January 19, 2001, 16.

38. Andrew Wilson, as quoted in "'Merchant Control,'" 9.

39. "The City and Industrial Recruiting," *Star*, January 12, 1965, B-12, and editorial, "What Can Be Done to Push Industrial Development," *Citizen*, January 15, 1965, 12.

40. "Davis, Council Agree on C of C Industry Role," *Citizen*, January 19, 1965, 1.

41. Editorial, "What Can Be Done to Push Industrial Development," *Citizen*, January 15, 1965, 12.

42. Board of Directors meeting of the Tucson Chamber of Commerce, February 6, 1939, as quoted in Rachel Gragg, "Tucson: The Formation and Legitimation of an Urban Renewal Program" (Master's thesis, University of Arizona, 1969), 27, 28.

43. Roy Drachman, Oral History, Arizona Historical Society/Tucson. J. C. Nichols, a successful Kansas City developer, was one of the founders of the Urban Land Institute.

44. "Roy Drachman Dies: City's Prime Mover Helped Define Us over 9 Decades," *Citizen*, January 10, 2002, A-1.

45. For more on the history and effects of zoning, see Freund, *Colored Property*, chap. 2, 45–98.

46. Ellsworth A. Moe to unnamed recipients, December 1958?, MS 1173, box 1, f. 3, Arizona Historical Society/Tucson. Moe addressed this letter, which began simply "Dear Sir," "to each person invited to participate in this reorganizing effort." See also "Tucson Regional Plan Reactivated: Would be Watchdog of Area Growth," *Citizen*, March 21, 1960, 3. Director Donald F. Hill explained that his committee had come back to "guard the community against the threat of losing its beauty and charm. . . . If we don't plan we can have another Los Angeles." Its members included Terry Atkinson, Fred Busby, Harry Cameron, Hamilton Catlin, Harry Chambers, Walter Clapp, Tom Clark, Marion Donaldson, Roy Drachman, William S. Dunipace, Sam Goddard, Donald F. Hill, Porter Homer, Mundey Johnston, Sidney Little, Jack B. O'Dowd, R. B. O'Rielly, Gordon Paris, Prior Pray, Fred Rhodes, Carlos Ronstadt, Harold Steinfeld, and J. Thomas Via. Fred Busby was the president of the Home Builders Association.

47. Logan and Molotch, *Urban Fortunes*, 36.

48. Moe to unnamed recipients, December 1958?

49. Roy Drachman, Oral History, 3–4, Arizona Historical Society/Tucson. In a 1940 letter to the mayor and City Council, Harold Steinfeld, chairman of the Tucson Regional Plan, claims that private citizens paid only $8,000 and that the city and county each paid Segoe $2,000. Steinfeld, as quoted in Fleagle, "Politics and Planning," 100.

50. Fleagle, "Politics and Planning," 100.

51. Ladislas Segoe and Associates, *The Rehabilitation of Blighted Areas: Conservation of Sound Neighborhoods* (Cincinnati, 1942), 20. Segoe's assistant, Andre Faure, stayed on in Tucson to become the city's, and later Pima County's, planning director.

52. Sugrue, *Urban Crisis*, 43–44.

53. S. L. Schorr and the Citizens' Advisory Redevelopment Committee, *Urban Renewal: A Teamwork of Private Enterprise and Government for Slum Clearance and Redevelopment of the Old Pueblo District, Tucson, Arizona* (Tucson: City of Tucson, 1961), 6.

54. Sugrue, *Urban Crisis*, 43.

55. Segoe and Associates, *Rehabilitation*, 20. Assisting residents to install indoor plumbing in some South and West Side neighborhoods became a priority in the 1970s during the city's Model Cities Program.

56. Ibid.

57. Ibid.

58. Ibid. 59. Henry García, as interviewed by Sharyn Wiley Yeoman, June 19, 1987, Tucson, transcript, p. 56, file AV 0605-3, Arizona Historical Society/Tucson.

60. *Citizen*, March 1, 1966, 6.

61. Haas, *Conquests and Identities*, 192.

62. See Suzanne Mettler, *Dividing Citizens: Gender and Federalism in New Deal Public Policy* (Ithaca, N.Y.: Cornell University Press, 1998).

63. Sugrue, *Urban Crisis*, 59–63. See also Mettler, *Dividing Citizens*.

64. Sugrue, *Urban Crisis*, 59.

65. Carole Pateman, "The Patriarchal State," in Amy Gutmann, ed., *Democracy and the Welfare State* (Princeton, N.J.: Princeton University Press, 1988), 231–260.

66. Don Robinson, "Voters Decide on Urban Renewal Fate Tuesday," *Star*, February 27, 1966, A-1.

67. "The History of the Bond Election Law," *Star*, January 22, 1966, B-14.

68. Segoe and Associates, *Rehabilitation*, 20.

69. Don Robinson, "Urban Plan Given OK by Voters," *Star*, March 2, 1966, A-1. See also "The History of the Bond Election Law," *Star*, January 22, 1966, B-14.

70. Gragg, "Tucson," 27.

71. Donald Laidlaw, audiotaped interview, February 10, 2003, Tucson. See also Tucson Department of Community Development, *Tucson's New Opportunity: Model Cities Program* (Tucson, 1970).

72. Vincent L. Lung, "The City Tells Its Story: COMB Untangles Tucson," *American City*, November 1966, 144–145.

73. Steve Emerine, "City Bond Election Slated for May," *Citizen*, December 7, 1964, 1.

74. Roy P. Drachman, "The Community Center's Hotel Situation," *Realty Digest* (Tucson: Roy P. Drachman Realty), January 1972, unpaginated.

Chapter 5. Reaffirming Order

1. Guadalupe Castillo, audiotaped interview, February 13, 2008, Tucson.

2. "Community Center Has Been Years in the Making," *Citizen*, November 5, 1971, Tucson Community Center section, 5.

3. Board of Directors meeting of the Tucson Chamber of Commerce, February 6, 1939, as quoted in Gragg, "Tucson," 27, 28. The federal government's Housing Act of 1937 persuaded Arizona to pass enabling legislation that allowed its cities to participate in federal public housing programs in 1939. See Municipal Housing Law, 1939, State of Arizona, *Session Laws*, chap. 82, p. 240. The original 160 public housing units, called La Reforma and located south of downtown and near Santa Rosa Park, were built under this act.

4. Don Robinson, "Financing of Urban Renewal Is Prime Interest of Voter," *Star*, February 26, 1966, A-6. Though one of the nation's largest cities, Phoenix never applied for federal urban renewal dollars. For an extensive discussion of Phoenix housing policy and the political discourse that prevented the city from implementing urban renewal, see Robert B. Fairbanks, "The Failure of Urban Renewal in the Southwest: From City Needs to Individual Rights," *Western Historical Quarterly* 37 (Autumn 2006): 303–325. Phoenix voters rejected a bond proposal in April 1966 that would have supported the city's urban renewal agenda.

5. "Years in Making," 5, claims that Ladislas Segoe introduced the idea of a large outside community-convention center that included a stage and an auditorium in the downtown area as early as 1938, which seems too early since he arrived around 1940. See Mark Adams, "City Growth Plan of '40s Recalled," *Citizen*, March 13, 1975, 31, in which Segoe reminisces about his arrival in Tucson. William A. Small, the editor of the *Tucson Daily Citizen*, chaired a short-lived group of individuals interested in promoting such a center in 1952. Future governor Samuel P. Goddard, involved in this early project, offered to donate twenty acres on the far east side of Tucson near 22d Street and Swan. This offer of free land to build a community-convention center did not garner much interest in terms of acreage and location, as indicated by the Chamber of Commerce's formation of another new group the next year. See Tucson Civic Center Planning Group, "History of Organized Efforts for a Tucson Community-Convention Center," in *A Community-Convention Center for Tucson* (Tucson: Arizona Mimeographing Service, 1960), 3, Arizona Historical Society/Tucson.

6. "Arthur Pack Elected President of Chamber," *Citizen*, December 13, 1958, 2.

7. Tucson Civic Center Planning Group, "History," 3.

8. Ibid., 66–69.

9. "Civic Square Federal Aid Questioned," *Citizen*, January 31, 1953, 1. Roy P. Drachman chaired the five-member tax study committee, which included Harold Steinfeld, Jack B. O'Dowd, J. M. Sakrison (president of the Southern Arizona Bank), and planner Andre Faure. Drachman appeared confident that

he could qualify the project for federal aid. In "Civic Center Studied," *Citizen*, February 4, 1953, 1, Drachman reported that he "had worked on the same type of program in Detroit and St. Louis" and that he "had conferred by long-distance telephone with N. S. Keith, director of slum clearance, and been assured of aid in the proposed project." There can be little doubt that his national contacts helped expedite his urban planning projects and real estate transactions in Tucson. It should also be noted that the above-mentioned men remained active members of the Tucson Regional Plan, Inc., which also envisioned a civic center as early as 1945. "Modern Auditorium Urged for One of City's Civic Centers," *Star*, January 26, 1945, 8.

10. Arthur Pack, "Auditorium Ideas," *Citizen*, August 23, 1954, 8.

11. "Slum Clearance Act Passed," *Citizen*, April 7, 1954, 6, and "City Slum Bill Backed," *Citizen*, January 28, 1954, 6. See also Slum Clearance and Urban Redevelopment Law, 1954, State of Arizona, *Session Laws*, chap. 128, p. 217.

12. Tucson Civic Center Planning Group, "History," 68.

13. Ibid., 1, 65, 57. Donations for *A Community-Convention Center for Tucson* came from American and Trans World Airlines, local architects, banks, auto dealers, and veterinarians, the Arizona Inn, the Santa Rita Hotel, Lions Clubs, Hughes Aircraft, the Schmidt Construction Company, arts organizations, and a few moneyed individuals. The Tucson Civic Center Planning Group, which included most members of the Chamber of Commerce's tax study group, studied some 100 auditoriums across the nation. See "Years in Making," 5.

14. James E. Ayres, "The Tucson Urban Renewal Archaeology Project," July 6, 1994, unpublished presentation in mthe author's files.

15. Barbara A. Anderson, "From Family Home to Slum Apartment: Archaeological Analysis within the Urban Renewal Area, Tucson, Arizona" (Master's thesis, University of Arizona, 1970), 20–25.

16. Ibid., 26–27.

17. Ladislas Segoe and C. W. Matthews, *Tentative Report on Survey of Low-Rent Housing Needs: Tucson, Arizona* (Tucson Housing Authority: Tucson, 1941), MS 1173, box 4, f. 48, Arizona Historical Society/Tucson. Segoe and Matthews's survey indicates that almost 23 percent of the houses in the entire city of Tucson did not meet municipal housing standards.

18. Schorr et al., *Urban Renewal*, 6.

19. "People Removed from 'The Hole' Bear Most Bitterness," *¡olé! Tucson Daily Citizen Magazine*, December 12, 1970, 4.

20. Anna Montaño, audiotaped interview, March 3, 2007, Tucson.

21. Margaret Regan, "There Goes the Neighborhood: The Downfall of Downtown," *Tucson Weekly*, March 6–12, 1997, at http://www.tucsonweekly.com/tw/03-06-97/cover.htm/.

22. Steve Emerine, "Mayor and Councilmen Take Look at Tucson Slums," *Citizen*, December 10, 1964, 21.

23. Ronald F. Ferguson and William T. Dickens, *Urban Problems and Community Development* (Washington, D.C.: Brookings Institution Press, 1999), 96. See also see Housing Act of 1949, 63 *United States Statutes at Large*, 81st Cong., 1st sess., July 15, 1949, 413.

24. John J. Riling Jr. and Bertha O. Whitterson, Office of Urban Renewal, City of Tucson, "Workable Program for Urban Renewal, 1958–1959," *Arizona Architect*, May 1959, 8. The Housing Act of 1954 mandated that cities develop a "workable program" for redevelopment.

25. Don Schellie, editorial, *Citizen*, August 1, 1961, reprinted in Citizens' Advisory Redevelopment Committee, *Urban Renewal*.

26. See William Deverell, *Whitewashed Adobe: The Rise of Los Angeles and the Remaking of Its Mexican Past* (Berkeley: University of California Press, 2004), 4–5. See also ibid., 3, for an assessment regarding Los Angeles as the "metropolis that would inherit the future." For more on California urbanism, see Kevin Starr, *Golden Dreams: California in an Age of Abundance, 1950–1963* (New York: Oxford Press, 2009).

27. Steve Emerine, "Mayor and Councilmen Take Look at Tucson Slums," *Citizen*, December 10, 1964, 21.

28. Ibid.

29. Gourley, "Pueblo and Public," 164.

30. "Federal Approval Given for Urban Renewal: Allocation of $151,00 for Survey First Step in Tucson Redevelopment Project," *Star*, May 1, 1958, A-1.

31. "Urban Renewal Has Lengthy History," *Citizen*, September 16, 1959, Downtown Tucson section, 1. See also Riling and Whitterson, "Workable Program."

32. "Tucson's Slum Clearance Program Is Most Ambitious in the Nation," *Citizen*, August 26, 1958, 19.

33. "City Argues Slums Place Unfair Load on Taxpayers," *Citizen*, August 27, 1958, 4.

34. "Noted Architect Expresses Views on Downtown Area," *Citizen*, September 16, 1959, Downtown Tucson section, 1.

35. Schorr et al., *Urban Renewal*, 1, 13. See also "City Argues Slums Place Unfair Load on Taxpayers," *Citizen*, August 27, 1958, 4.

36. Schorr et al., *Urban Renewal*, 13–18.

37. Ibid., 2, 33.

38. The council applied the designation of "slum" according to *Arizona Revised Statutes*, secs. 36-1473 and 36-1479. See also City of Tucson, "Redevelopment Plan: Southwestern Section Central District Development Plan" (Old Pueblo Project, Arizona R-6; City of Tucson: March 22, 1962; unpaginated).

39. Schorr et al., *Urban Renewal*, 19.

40. Ibid., 9.

41. Steve Emerine, "Socialism? Humanitarianism? Public Housing Bid under Advisement," *Citizen*, January 3, 1963, 1.

42. William Mathews, "Some Facts about Urban Renewal," *Star*, October 22, 1961, D-16.

43. "New Group Backs Modified Urban Renewal Proposal," *Citizen*, February 23, 1962, 3.

44. Lester N. Inskeep and Pete Cowgill, "800 at Public Hearing: Urban Renewal Foes, Friends Give Views," *Star*, April 25, 1962, A-1.

45. "City Council Kills Urban Plan" and "Renewal Department Employees Will be Dismissed," *Star*, May 8, 1962, A-1, B-1. Peter Starrett, "Hard Core Slum Area Was First Target in Housing Cleanup Drive," *Citizen*, September 10, 1963, 21.

46. "City Council Kills Urban Plan," *Star*, May 8, 1962, B-1.

47. Starrett, "Hard Core Slum," 21.

48. Ibid.

49. Peter Starrett, "Progress Comes Slowly in Fight against the Slums," *Citizen*, September 9, 1963, 1, 8.

50. "Group May Be Invited to Study Housing Here," *Citizen*, March 1, 1963, 3. Members of the Tucson Board of Realtors included a number of planners such as Sydney Little and Dennis O'Harrow, ex-director of the American Society of Planning Officials. The Build America Better Advisory Committee had also been assigned the task of "checking the planning and zoning machinery of the city." The advance team arrived in Tucson in June 1963. The city's realtor organization paid $4,000 to underwrite the expense of their advisory team's advice and report. See "Strong City Housing Code Said 'A Must,'" *Citizen*, July 17, 1963, 11.

51. Build America Better Committee, *An Action Plan for Tucson* (Tucson: National Association of Real Estate Boards, 1963), 1.

52. Ibid., 4, 12, 7, 9. For more on the Cincinnati influence, see Robert B. Fairbanks, *Making Better Citizens: Housing Reform and the Community Development Strategy in Cincinnati, 1890–1960* (Urbana: University of Illinois Press, 1988).

53. Build America Better Committee, *Action Plan*, 3.

54. Ibid., 22, 32. The committee also called for rehabilitation of El Rio and South Park areas.

55. Ibid., 35, 37. See also "South Meyer Tabbed No. 1 Challenge," *Citizen*, July 18, 1963, 45, and "Clear, Rebuild Meyer Avenue Slum, Private Group Urges, *Citizen*, September 23, 1963, 15.

56. "Committee Hopes for Intensive Urban Renewal Here," *Citizen*, July 15, 1963, 11. Although most local newspaper reports pronounced the Build America Better Committee as pushing federally funded urban renewal, Mechlin D. Moore, the director, is quoted in the July 15 *Citizen* article as saying, "Urban renewal doesn't necessarily mean federal aid. Adding a bathroom to your home is a form of urban renewal." His stance is typical of most conservative national realtor groups.

57. Cecil James, "B.A.B. Report: Build for 750,000, City Advised," *Citizen*, July 19, 1963, 9.

58. Drachman and Lung, *Pueblo Center*, 6; see also "Public Invited: Urban Renewal Hearing Slated for Monday," *Citizen*, November 5, 1968, 6.

59. "Old Pueblo Section Called One of the Worst in All U.S.," *Citizen*, October 16, 1964, 13.

60. Drachman and Lung, *Pueblo Center*, ii, 7.

61. Ibid., iii.

62. "Leadership Need Seen, Ex-Mayor Hummel," *Star*, January 22, 1965, C-10.

63. Donald H. Bufkin, Oral History, acc. no. 91-42, AV 0505-4, "Urbanization of Tucson: 1940–1990," 8, Arizona Historical Society/Tucson. See also "Hughes to Lay Off 1,000 Workers Here" *Citizen*, August 7, 1963, 1.

64. Richards, "Economic Development Efforts," 19.

65. "1,100 Take City's Labor Test," *Star*, February 27, 1964, B-1. The newspaper calculated the odds at 1 in 220 that an applicant would obtain one of the 5 jobs available for the City of Tucson. Only men were allowed to take the written and physical exam, which required applicants to lift and carry 80 pounds for a "short" distance.

66. Donald Laidlaw, audiotaped interview, February 10, 2003, Tucson. See also Drachman and Lung, *Pueblo Center*, ii, 7.

67. U.S. Department of Housing and Urban Development, *Annual Report* (Washington D.C., 1965), 6.

68. Drachman and Lung, *Pueblo Center*, 10.

69. HUD, *Annual Report*, 6.

70. For more on the unbalanced implementation of federal housing policies, see Sugrue, *Urban Crisis*, 60. See also Kenneth W. Goings and Raymond A. Mohl, eds., *The New African American Urban History* (Thousand Oaks, Calif.: Sage, 1996).

71. "Waiting List for La Reforma Long," *Citizen*, February 8, 1963, 12. In 1970, Philip B. Whitmore, urban renewal administrator, explained, "An anticipated influx of people into Tucson beginning in 1966–67 grabbed up the hundreds of apartments and houses left vacant after the speculative overbuilding of houses in the 1960s." See "The City's Side: Mistakes but Future Better, ¡olé! *Tucson Daily Citizen Magazine*, December 12, 1970, 17.

72. Peter Starrett, "Urban Renewal Plan Adopted," *Citizen*, November 9, 1965, 1, 2.

73. Jay Hall, "Standing Room Only Crowd Backs Plan," *Citizen*, November 9, 1965, 2.

74. Ibid.

75. "$8.1 Million Would Go for New Buildings," *Citizen*, November 11, 1966, 15.

76. "Financing of Urban Renewal Is Prime Interest of Voter, *Star*, February 26, 1966, A-6, and "Urban Plan Given OK By Voters: 80 Acres Involved in City's Project," *Star*, March 2, 1966, A-1.

77. "City Readies First Step for Help in Redevelopment of Old Pueblo District, "*Star*, January 21, 1965, B-1.

78. Don Robinson, "Project Hinges on Outcome," *Star*, March 1, 1966, A-1. See also "Financing of Urban Renewal Is Prime Interest of Voter," *Star*, February 26, 1966, A-6.

79. City officials intended to pay back most of the $15 million in borrowed funds from reselling the properties they had acquired from the project area and from federal grants, together totaling an anticipated $11.5 million. They assured voters that parking fees from a new underground garage to be built near the proposed nine-story city hall and government complex would cover at least some of the $3.5 million deficit. See Don Robinson, "Voters Decide on Urban Renewal Fate Tuesday," *Star*, February 27, 1966, A-1. City planners and management had already used the power of eminent domain to displace mostly people of Mexican descent to make way for the new interstate highway in the 1950s. See also "Community Center Ruled Off March 1 Urban Renewal Ballot," *Star*, January 21, 1966, A-1.

80. Roy P. Drachman, as quoted in "Ruled Off Ballot," A-1.

81. William R. Mathews, editorial, "The Urban Renewal Election," *Star*, February 22, 1966, D-10.

82. Edward H. Nelson, as quoted in "Editor's Urban Renewal Opinions Are Disputed: Architect Nelson Defends 'Center,'" *Star*, February 23, 1966, A-5. Nelson became cochairman of the Civic Center Planning Group in 1958. See Tucson Civic Center Planning Group, "History," 69.

83. Editorial, "A Positive Look at City Renewal," *Citizen*, February 23, 1966, 30.

84. See Don Mosher and Jerry Cohen, *The Pied Piper of Tucson* (New York: New American Library, 1967).

85. Lew Davis, as quoted in "Laidlaw Named Director," *Citizen*, March 2, 1966, 1.

86. Robinson, "Plan Given OK," A-1.

87. Ibid.; Drachman and Lung, *Pueblo Center*, 1.

88. Don Robinson, "Barren Land Near City Hall to Mark Progress: Cultural Center to Spring Up," *Star*, January 2, 1969, A-1.

89. Bonnie Newlon, *Pueblo Center Redevelopment Project, 1967–1969* (Tucson: City of Tucson, Department of Community Development, Urban Renewal Division, 1969), 7–8.

90. "The Boxscore," *¡olé! Tucson Daily Citizen Magazine*, December 12, 1970, 10. In 1965, the City of Tucson had amended its housing code to make it easier to evict building occupants, whether tenants or owners. See "City Urged to

OK New Housing Code," *Citizen*, August 4, 1965, 28; and "New Housing Code Passed by Council," *Citizen*, November 23, 1965, 9.

91. Urban Renewal Commissioner William Slayton, as quoted in "Nelson Defends 'Center,'" A-5.

92. Gonzales, videotaped interview, November 10, 2007, Tucson.

93. Patricia J. Clark and Martha M. Fimbres, "A Study to Identify and Access the Psychological Ramifications Inherent in the Process of Relocation Regarding Census Tract I in Downtown Tucson, Arizona" (Master's thesis, Arizona State University, 1978), 24–25.

94. Ernest C. Heltsley, "Tucson Is Sued in Bar Eviction," *Star*, October 9, 1968, B-3.

95. "The Saga of the Old State Bar," ¡olé! *Tucson Daily Citizen Magazine*, December 12, 1970, 9.

96. Keith Carew, "City Tried to Find 'Decent Home' in Relocating Woman," *Citizen*, December 12, 1970, 1; and George McEvoy, "Neighborhoods Called Very Important: Planners Weigh 'Human Factors,'" *Star*, December 11, 1970, A-10. The city found a home for Wall in a public housing project. She was relocated in 1967 and died in 1969.

97. "City Sued for Damages in El Charro Land Sale," *Star*, December 3, 1970, A-5.

98. Ron Radcliff, "Renewal Area Owners Entitled to Reappraisal, Judge Rules," *Star*, October 22, 1969, A-1.

99. Donald Laidlaw, as quoted in Charles Turbyville, "Not Every Urban Renewal Story Will End Happily," *Citizen*, October 5, 1967, 1. City officials like Don Laidlaw and his administrative assistant, Philip Whitmore, faced many logistical and administrative challenges in implementing the city's urban renewal plans. Laidlaw eventually quit his position. See "Laidlaw Quits Planning Post, Sharply Criticizes City Hall," *Citizen*, September 30, 1970, 1.

100. Turbyville, "Not Every Story," 9.

101. Charles Turbyville, "Urban Renewers Turn Pitchmen," *Citizen*, September 28, 1968, 3.

102. Renters had no legal recourse in condemnation proceedings even though they paid hidden property taxes with their rents.

103. "People Removed from 'Hole,'" 4.

104. Alva Torres, audiotaped interview, December 6, 2002, Tucson.

105. Carew, "'Decent Home,'" 1.

106. "People Removed from 'Hole,'" 4.

107. Diocese of Tucson to Donald Laidlaw, December 21, 1967, in box 2, M/C History file, binder 5, Report on Planning Proposals, Code no. R-214, City of Tucson Archives, City Clerk. The Church bought 77,000 square feet of land made vacant by the demolition of structures adjacent to Saint Augustine Cathedral to locate a "diocesan structure" between Corral, Stone, McCormick, and Convent.

108. Robinson, "Barren Land," A-1.

109. C of C Again Attempts to Get Center Bill," *Star*, January 22, 1965, A-4.

110. Jim Corbett, Mayor, to Alva B. Torres, Chairwoman, Society for the Preservation of Tucson's Plaza de la Mesilla," May 5, 1969, in Plaza de la Mesilla—Correspondence, 1968–1974, MS 1134, Alva Torres Collection, box 2, f. 18, Arizona Historical Society/Tucson.

111. Jay Hall, "Name Goes Unchanged: Commission Thinks 'Civic' Sounds 'Cold' for the Center," *Citizen*, December 10, 1970, 2.

112. Valley National Bank Research Department, "Spotlight on Tucson—New Community Center Opens," *Arizona Progress*, November 1971.

113. Schorr et al., *Urban Renewal*, 21.

114. "Community Center Dedication Today," *Star*, November 6, 1971, A-1.

115. "First Concert in New Music Hall Draws Glittering, Admiring Crowd," *Citizen*, November 9, 1971, 13.

116. Gordon R. Brown, "Fiedler's Downbeat Opens Music Hall," *Citizen*, November 9, 1971, 38.

117. Dan Pavillard, "'First-Nighters' Hear Exceptional Dedicatory Concert," *Citizen*, November 9, 1971, 27.

118. "Ice Capades Inaugurates Arena Tonight" *Star*, November 9, 1971, 1.

119. Micheline Keating, "Ice Capades Show Opens Area as Tucson Finds a 'Family Room,'" *Citizen*, November 10, 1971, 27, and Jon Kamman, "Tucson's Future . . . or Fantasy . . . amid All the Glitter?" *Citizen*, November 10, 1971, 33.

120. Micheline Keating, "Ice Capades Show Opens Area as Tucson Finds a 'Family Room,'" *Citizen*, November 10, 1971, 27.

121. "Center Pays Rent to Local Authority," *Citizen*, November 5, 1971, TCC section, 19.

122. Jane Jacobs, *The Death and Life of Great American Cities* (New York: Random House, 1961), 1. "This book," reads Jacobs's opening line, "is an attack on current city planning and rebuilding." See also Martin Anderson, *The Federal Bulldozer: A Critical Analysis of Urban Renewal, 1949–1962* (Cambridge, Mass.: MIT Press, 1964).

123. "From Right and Left: What Urban Renewal Critics Have to Say," *Citizen*, February 23, 1966, 29.

124. Drachman and Lung, *Pueblo Center*, 7.

125. The activist efforts of Alva Torres and the La Placita Committee inspired the drafting, adoption, and implementation of a new city ordinance requiring preservation of historic structures, an ordinance that remains in effect to this day.

Chapter 6. The La Placita Committee

An earlier version of this chapter appeared in *Memories and Migrations: Mapping Boricua and Chicana Histories,* edited by Vicki L. Ruiz and John R. Chávez (University of Illinois Press, 2008).

1. Alva Torres, audiotaped interview, December 6, 2002, Tucson.

2. Ibid.

3. This inscribed place, which Michel Foucault would call "disciplinary space," encompasses the discursive processes that differentiate in order to regulate and maintain societal norms. See Foucault, *Discipline and Punish: The Birth of the Prison,* trans. Alan Sheridan (New York: Pantheon Books, 1977).

4. Allegedly, in the 1880s, a disgruntled gambler, who also happened to be a state legislator, had lost money at one of the San Agustín fiesta's infamous games. In retaliation, he had a law passed that prohibited women and children from being present in sites where gambling took place. "Whirling Roulette Wheels Once Part of Holidays Here," *Citizen,* August 29, 1949, 1, 11.

5. Sheridan, *Tucsonenses,* 162–163.

6. George W. Chambers and C. L. Sonnichsen, *San Agustín: First Cathedral Church in Arizona* (Tucson: Arizona Historical Society, 1974), 26. For more detailed information regarding the history of the Catholic Diocese of Tucson, see John Baptist Salpointe, *Soldiers of the Cross: Notes on the Ecclesiastical History of New Mexico, Arizona, and Colorado* (Banning, Calif.: Saint Boniface's Industrial School, 1898).

7. Chambers and Sonnichsen, *San Agustín,* 26.

8. "Early Church Lost: Preservation Effort Failed 40 Years Ago," *Citizen,* March 16, 1967, 8.

9. Ronni Neufeld, "Santa Cruz River Project May Be Last Chance to Preserve Tucson's Birthplace," *Changing Tucson,* October 1974, in MS 1134, Alva Torres Collection, box 2, f. 15, Historic Preservation: Tucson, 1969–1980, Arizona Historical Society/Tucson. *Changing Tucson* magazine was published by the Citizen Participation Division of the Department of Urban Resource Coordination.

10. MacLaury, "La Placita," 52.

11. Pedro Gonzales, videotaped interview, November 10, 2007, Tucson.

12. "Alianza Will Open Fiesta with Parade: Defense Bond Sale, Parleys Are on Program for Day; Dance Is Scheduled," *Citizen,* April 24, 1942, 5.

13. "Old Pueblo Fiesta Is to Be Revived: La Plazita to Come to Life Again in Heart of Old Adobe City," *Citizen,* December 15, 1943, 2. The Good Neighbor policy encouraged pan-Americanism. See Steven R. Niblo, *War, Democracy, and Development: United States–Mexican Relations, 1918–1945* (Wilmington, Del.: Scholarly Resources, 1995).

14. "Old Pueblo Fiesta," 2.

15. Ibid. "Plazita" was a common misspelling in Tucson's newspapers and promotional literature.

16. The Mexican government, along with private businesses, published maps and guides for U.S. tourists. Alex Saragoza, "The Selling of Mexico: Tourism and the State, 1929–1952," in Gilbert M. Joseph, Anne Rubenstein, and Eric Zolov, eds., *Fragments of a Golden Age: The Politics of Culture in Mexico since 1940* (Durham, N.C.: Duke University, 2001), 102; see also note 31.

17. "Old Pueblo Fiesta," 2.

18. Ibid.

19. William A. Small, editorial, "A Tucson Tanglewood," *Citizen*, October 2, 1950, 16.

20. Between 1951 and 1954, the Tucson Festival Society's "Mexican Fiestas" sometimes took place in Armory Park. They were moved to La Placita in 1955. "Historical Information on Mexican Fiesta," in MS 921, f. 1, T. F. Collection: Festival History, Arizona Historical Society/Tucson. Alva Torres's Club Mavis always had a booth at this festival. Olga Otero Litel, mentioned in chapter 7, also worked to raise money for her social group, Club Esmeralda. See also "A Bit of Old Mexico Comes North for Annual Fiesta at La Placita, *Star*, May 6, 1962, A-6.

21. Torres interview.

22. Josephina Lizárraga, videotaped interview, March 9, 2005, Tucson.

23. "Historic Sites Committee Named," *Citizen*, September 9, 1964, 12.

24. The Historical Sites Committee also recommended saving these other sites in la calle. Most were recognized for their distinctiveness during the territorial period, such as McCoy's Inn, at 329 South Main Avenue, the first customhouse, known as the "William F. Scott Home," at 202 South Main Avenue, and the entire block along the east side of South Meyer between McCormick and 14th Streets, which the committee considered the best complete commercial area reflecting the territorial period. The Estevan Ochoa House at 32–44 West McCormick Street was built before the Civil War. The Wishing Shrine, in the 300 block of South Main Avenue, is recognized as a "legendary" historical spot. Offices at 18–34 South Convent Street had already been restored and were being used for commercial purposes in 1964. Note that the Samaniego House, which survived urban renewal, did not make the list at this time—or the newspaper did not feel it merited mentioning. "Sites Listed as Worth Saving," *Citizen*, March 16, 1967, 3 [8?]. Research by the Historic Sites Committee found its way into a valuable book by a coalition of preservationists, the Historic Areas Committee, which provides detailed historical and architectural background on sixty-nine buildings that, it concluded, merited restoration. See Historic Areas Committee, *Historical Sites* (Tucson, 1969).

25. Dan Pavillard, "In Urban Renewal Planning, Historic Buildings Will Be Saved," *Citizen*, February 23, 1966, 29. See also John Bret Harte, "Tucson's

Historic Sites: Once They're Gone, You Can't Go Back," *Citizen*, February 13, 1978, 3-C.

26. City of Tucson Department of Community Development and Candeub, Fleissig, Adley and Associates, *Pueblo Center Project, Tucson, Arizona: Concept Plan* (Tucson: Candeub, Fleissig, Adley and Associates, 1965), 3–6. The last quotation is from page 5.

27. Ibid., 4.

28. "The City Tells Its Story: COMB Untangles Tucson," *American City*, November 1966, 144–145.

29. "Placita Groups Meet: Dramatic Plaza Plans Called For," *Citizen*, September 29, 1967, 39. When built, La Placita village covered almost 3 acres.

30. Torres interview.

31. Torres's activism conforms to sociologist Mary S. Pardo's observations that grassroots activism "happens at the juncture between larger institutional politics and people's daily experiences. Women play a central role in the often unrecorded politics at this level." Pardo, *Chicana/o Women Activists: Identity and Resistance in Two Los Angeles Communities* (Philadelphia: Temple University Press, 1998), 5.

32. Torres interview. It is also probable that Torres turned to Mathews because of his stance on the city's failed 1962 urban renewal plan.

33. Donald H. Laidlaw to COMB, undated memo, in MS 1134, Alva Torres Collection, box 2, f. 17, Plaza de la Mesilla—Correspondence, 1967, Arizona Historical Society/Tucson. Written on City of Tucson stationery, Laidlaw's memo dates his meeting with Torres as October 4, 1967.

34. Torres interview.

35. Ibid. and "La Placita Restoration Plans Told: Group Seeking Historical Link," *Citizen*, September 14, 1967, in MS 1134, Alva Torres Collection, box 3, f. 20, Plaza de la Mesilla—Newspaper Clippings, 1967–1986, Arizona Historical Society/Tucson.

36. Diocese of Tucson to Donald Laidlaw, December 21, 1967, in City of Tucson Archives, City Clerk, box 2, M/C History file, binder 5, Report on Planning Proposals, Code no. R-214. As noted in chapter 5, note 107, the Church bought 77,000 square feet of land to locate a "diocesan structure" between Corral, Stone, McCormick and Convent Streets.

37. Despite an extensive search of City of Tucson and other local archives, I have not been able to locate information regarding the origins of the San Agustín Committee, how and whether its members were formally appointed, and how they became the recognized spokespersons for the area. Don Laidalaw informed COMB that, "in January 1966, Mr. Vincent Lung and the undersigned met with members of the new committee called the Placita de San Augustin [*sic*] Committee for purpose of discussing the proposed commercial development and to determine how it would affect the annual Fiesta in Tucson. Many

members of this committee were associated with the Tucson Festival Society and were concerned that the redevelopment would make it impossible to continue their festival." Laidlaw to COMB, [undated] memo, p. 2.

38. "La Placita Restoration Plans Told," *Citizen*, September 14, 1967, in MS 1134, Alva Torres Collection, box 3, f. 20, Plaza de la Mesilla—Newspaper Clippings, 1967–1986, Arizona Historical Society/Tucson.

39. Ibid.

40. Torres interview. Although Torres had been brought up Catholic, her Methodist minister grandfather strongly influenced her. In her interview with me, she referred to herself as "Christian," preferring a more inclusive religious identification. Born in 1932, she is a fourth-generation tucsonense. Her maternal and paternal ancestors arrived in Tucson in the early nineteenth century; her father's family traces its origins, not to Mexico, but to South America. After living in Tucson for many generations and intermarrying into a Mexican community with whom they shared a similar ethnic background, the members of Alva's family considered themselves tucsonenses.

41. Ibid.

42. "Rosequist Galleries Moves to New Home," *Citizen*, October 11, 1969, 32. The gallery was razed in 1969.

43. See Don Robinson, "Landmark Relocation Advocated," *Star*, November 11, 1966, A-1.

44. Torres interview.

45. Ibid. According to Alva Torres and committee documents, the following people were core members of the La Placita Committee: Arturo Torres (Alva's husband), Ana Montaño, Viola Terrazas, Grace Esperon (acting chairman when Torres was unavailable), Carlitos Vasquez, Alberto Elias, Ruben Villaseñor, Alene and Paul Smith, Julieta and Ernest Portillo (Alva's sister and brother-in-law), Miguel Bustamante (Alva's brother), Arturo Soto, Rodolfo Soto, Alberto Torres (Arturo Torres's brother), and Felizardo Valencia. Those involved to a lesser degree were David Herrera, Edward Jacobs, Natalia Nieto Slana, Alberto Montiel, Mr. Illeano, Tito Carrillo, Sybil Ellenwood, Louis Barassi, Cheto Valencia, Lorraine Aguilar, John Gabusi, Clarence Garrett, Basilio Morrillo, Dr. and Mrs. Marrow, Dr. Floyd Thompson, Kieran McCarty, and María Urquidez.

46. Ibid. Their personal correspondence indicates that Alene Smith recognized Alva Torres's leadership qualities. As Alene wrote to Alva, "Both Paul [Smith's husband] and I want to you to know how proud we were of you Friday night—and how grateful we are to you for including us in your awesome endeavor." Alene Smith to Alva Torres, August 12, 1967, in MS 1134, Alva Torres Collection, box 2, f. 17, Plaza de la Mesilla—Correspondence, 1967; see also "Tucson Historical Buff Dies of Cancer at Age 59," *Citizen*, April 12, 1980, in Alene Dunlap Smith Clipbook file, both at Arizona Historical Society/Tucson.

47. Alva B. Torres to Mr. Jim Corbett, Mayor of Tucson, December 6, 1968, in MS 1134, Alva Torres Collection, box 2, f. 17, Plaza de la Mesilla—Correspondence, 1967, Arizona Historical Society/Tucson.

48. Hayden, *Power of Place*, 9.

49. Within the context of the Civil Rights and anti–Vietnam War movements, which often seemed revolutionary, Torres formed the La Placita Committee in 1967. Despite the passage of a series of civil rights acts in the 1960s, however, Mexican Americans were not officially considered an identifiable minority or a disadvantaged group. They had to wait until the *Cisneros v. Corpus Christi Independent School District* decision in 1970 for the judicial system to classify them as an "identifiable ethnic minority with a pattern of discrimination." This ruling officially made segregation and discrimination against Mexican Americans unconstitutional. Acuña, *Occupied America*, 319. See also Allen J. Matusow, *The Unraveling of America: A History of Liberalism in the 1960s* (New York: Harper and Row, 1984).

50. La Placita Committee to Robert B. Pitts, Regional Administrator, HUD, October 14, 1967, in MS 1134, Alva Torres Collection, box 2, f. 17, Plaza de la Mesilla—Correspondence, 1967, Arizona Historical Society/Tucson.

51. Alva B. Torres to Mrs. L[yndon B.] Johnson, September 27, 1967, in MS 1134, Alva Torres Collection, box 2, f. 17, Plaza de la Mesilla—Correspondence, 1967, Arizona Historical Society/Tucson.

52. Alva Torres to Congressman Morris Udall, undated, in MS 1134, Alva Torres Collection, box 2, f. 17, Plaza de la Mesilla—Correspondence, 1967, Arizona Historical Society/Tucson.

53. Irma Villa to Society for the Preservation of Tucson's Plaza de la Mesilla, October 18, 1967, in MS 1134, Alva Torres Collection, box 2, f. 17, Plaza de la Mesilla—Correspondence, 1967, Arizona Historical Society/Tucson.

54. Hayden, *Power of Place*, 9.

55. The letters read: "Members of the Society for the Preservation of Tucson's Plaza de la Mesilla would like to extend a cordial invitation to you, and hopefully to several members of your group to attend a meeting." Ann Montaño to Mrs. Walter [Isabel] Fathauer, August 30, 1967, in MS 1134, Alva Torres Collection, box 2, f. 17, Plaza de la Mesilla—Correspondence, 1967, Arizona Historical Society/Tucson.

56. Minutes, June 15, 1967, in MS 1134, Alva Torres Collection, box 2, f. 16, Plaza de la Mesilla—Minutes, 1967–1968, Arizona Historical Society/Tucson. The June 15 minutes indicate that five Mexican American women and ten Mexican American men, many of them spouses of the women present, were in attendance, among them Alva Torres, Alene and Paul Smith, and Soto's son Arturo.

57. Estimated attendance is based on the number of signatures on the sign-in sheet. Preservations—La Placita Committee—Guests—Formal Presentation of Plan, El Charro Restaurant, August 11, 1967, and from Master Sheet Reservations

in Alphabetical Order for the same event, in MS 1134, Alva Torres Collection, box 2, f. 16, Plaza de la Mesilla—Minutes, 1967–1968, Arizona Historical Society/Tucson.

58. Regan, "There Goes the Neighborhood."

59. James C. Scott, *Domination and the Arts of Resistance: Hidden Transcripts* (New Haven, Conn.: Yale University Press, 1990), xii, 4.

60. Laidlaw to COMB, undated memo; and Torres interview.

61. Torres interview.

62. Society for the Preservation of Tucson's Plaza de la Mesilla to the Honorable Mayor and [City] Council of Tucson, Arizona, undated. The petitions were presented to the mayor and City Council in September 1967. MS 1134, Alva Torres Collection, box 2, f. 17, Plaza de la Mesilla—Correspondence, 1967, Arizona Historical Society/Tucson. La Placita Committee documents make many references to the La Plaza Theatre, which had been targeted for demolition by urban renewal. It is likely that the committee proposed building the new 750-seat theater as an updated version of La Plaza.

63. Ibid.

64. Ibid.

65. The territorial governor's connection with the Frémont House continues to be a matter of debate. It was renamed the Sosa-Carrillo-Frémont House in 1992.

66. Torres to Udall, undated.

67. "La Placita Restoration Plans Told," *Citizen*, September 14, 1967, in MS 1134, Alva Torres Collection, box 3, f. 20, Plaza de la Mesilla—Newspaper Clippings, 1967–1986, Arizona Historical Society/Tucson.

68. Donald L. Woods to Mrs. Alva Torres, September 28, 1967, in MS 1134, Alva Torres Collection, box 2, f. 17, Plaza de la Mesilla—Correspondence, 1967, Arizona Historical Society/Tucson.

69. Robert E. McCabe, Deputy Assistant Secretary for Renewal Assistance, to Alva Torres, October 9, 1967, in MS 1134, Alva Torres Collection, box 2, f. 18, Plaza de la Mesilla—Correspondence, 1968–1974, Arizona Historical Society/Tucson. The McCabe letter begins, "This is a further reply to your letters to President Johnson of July 11 and August 27, 1967, both of which the President has asked this Department to answer."

70. Ibid.

71. Dan Pavillard, "Laidlaw Charts La Placita Peace," *Citizen*, September 12, 1967, 17. Present for the San Agustín Committee were Dorothy Haas (chair), Blair Glennie, Cele Peterson, William Blenman, Steve Ochoa, Tom Price, and Gilbert Ronstadt. Minutes, Combined Meeting, December 13, 1967, in MS 1134, Alva Torres Collection, box 2, f. 16, Plaza de la Mesilla—Minutes, 1967–1968, Arizona Historical Society/Tucson, and Torres interview.

72. Pavillard, "La Placita Peace," 17.

73. Ibid.

74. Donald H. Laidlaw, Urban Renewal Administrator, to Alva B. Torres, August 10, 1967, in MS 1134, Alva Torres Collection, box 2, f. 17, Plaza de la Mesilla—Correspondence, 1967, Arizona Historical Society/Tucson.

75. Ibid.

76. Minutes, Combined Meeting, December 13, 1967; Torres interview.

77. Ibid.

78. "Tucson's Identity Should Be Retained," *Citizen*, April 2, 1968, in MS 1134, Alva Torres Collection, box 3, f. 20, Plaza de la Mesilla—Newspaper Clippings, 1967–1986, Arizona Historical Society/Tucson.

79. Torres interview.

80. Ibid.

81. Ibid.

82. City officials rebuilt the Samaniego House so that it could be integrated into the new La Placita Village. The structure never stood in the way of any proposed urban renewal changes. It has housed a series of restaurant and bars.

83. Alva Torres to Mr. [Robert?] Royal, February 20, 1970, in MS 1134, Alva Torres Collection, box 2, f. 18, Plaza de la Mesilla—Correspondence, 1968–1974, Arizona Historical Society/Tucson.

84. Bob Albano, "Downtown Site Developers to Be Sought," *Citizen*, February 19, 1971, 29.

85. "Festive Opening at La Placita," *Citizen*, May 4, 1974, in MS 1134, Alva Torres Collection, box 3, f. 20, Plaza de la Mesilla—Newspaper Clippings, 1967–1986, Arizona Historical Society/Tucson.

86. "La Placita Dedicated May 3 with a Fiesta Spirit," *Noticias de La Placita* 1, no. 1 (June 1974), in MS 1134, Alva Torres Collection, box 2, f. 21, Plaza de la Mesilla—Miscellaneous, 1969–1974, Arizona Historical Society/Tucson.

87. Tucson City Council, Minutes, September 7, 1971, City of Tucson Archives; and Torres interview.

88. Historic Zone Ordinance (1972), in MS 1076, box 1, Ordinances, T.H.C., 1971–1973, Arizona Historical Society/Tucson.

89. The La Placita Committee disbanded in 1974, but its members remained friends and potential allies on historic preservation issues. When it became known that El Tiradito (Tucson's old wishing shrine) stood in the path of the proposed freeway, Torres received a telephone call asking for help. Committee members joined the protests and helped guarantee the site's survival. Some individual committee members also worked to save the Samaniego House. The Tucson Advertising Club selected Torres as their Woman of the Year in 1976. She was the first Mexican American woman to receive the award. Torres eventually became a journalist and wrote a popular weekly column for the *Tucson Daily Citizen* in the 1980s, raising community concerns and issues. She also worked as director of the Legalization and Amnesty Program for the Catholic Community Services of Southern Arizona and served on various charities and community

boards. In 2002, Torres received the YWCA's Lifetime Achievement Award for Women Who Make Tucson Better, and she remains a committed activist to this day. Romano Cedillos, "YWCA Recognizes Women Who Make Tucson Better," *Citizen*, December 27, 2002; and Torres interview.

90. In analyzing Chicana/o social movements, political scientist Benjamin Márquez argues that "identities provide a frame of reference through which political actors can initiate, maintain and structure relationships with other groups and individuals." Márquez, "Choosing Issues, Choosing Sides: Constructing Identities in Chicana/o Social Movement Organizations," *Ethnic and Racial Studies* 24, no. 2 (March 2001), 220.

91. Although Alva Torres and other members of the La Placita Committee never identified themselves as "Chicanas/os," they formed an important and unrecognized component of the early development and ideology of the unfolding Chicana/o movement. Historian Rodolfo Acuña claims that heterogeneity best describes the Chicano movement. Acuña, *Occupied America*, 357–358. Using Acuña's standard of Chicana/o "pride of identity and self-determination," the La Placita Committee's historic preservation efforts embodied Chicanismo.

92. See "Greyhound Bus Depot Planned," *Citizen*, December 4, 1947, 2. See also David Glassberg, *Sense of History: The Place of the Past in American Life* (Amherst: University of Massachusetts Press, 2001), 7, 20.

93. See Barbara J. Howe, "Women in the Nineteenth-Century Preservation Movement," in Gail Lee Dubrow and Jennifer B. Goodman, eds., *Restoring Women's History through Historic Preservation* (Baltimore: Johns Hopkins University Press, 2003), 17–36.

Chapter 7. The Politics of Memory

1. Leticia Jacobs Fuentes, interview, May 5, 1987, Tucson, transcript, p. 21, AV 0605-02, Arizona Historical Society/Tucson.

2. The Arizona Historical Society renamed it the Sosa-Carrillo-Frémont House in 1992.

3. Countless other towns throughout the West rightly considered the arrival of the railroad to be a momentous event. See Richard White, *"It's Your Misfortune and None of My Own": A History of the American West* (Norman: University of Oklahoma Press, 1991), 257–263.

4. Charles D. Poston, as quoted in Sonnichsen, *Pioneer Heritage*, 7.

5. Alexandra Harmon, *Indians in the Making: Ethnic Relations and Indian Identities around Puget Sound* (Berkeley: University of California Press, 1999), 146.

6. Gordon, *Orphan Abduction*, 163.

7. Since the eighteenth century, battling the Apache Indians had been the primary focus of Spanish and later Mexican military endeavors, and those of their Indian allies. Apaches posed an unremitting threat to Mexicans, Pimas, Tohono O'odham, and later Anglos who had inhabited Sonora and later Southern Arizona. The fear of Apaches ensured and strengthened mutually dependent interethnic alliances: Tohono O'odham, tucsonenses, and Anglo settlers often collaborated to defend the presidio and later the town. They also came together to seek retribution. Far from heroic, one raid by vigilantes on the Apaches, the Camp Grant Massacre, which is notable for its atrocities, took place near Tucson. Sonnichsen, *Tucson*, 48–49, 80–81. See also Karl Jacoby, *Shadows at Dawn: A Borderlands Massacre and the Violence of History* (New York: Penguin Press, 2008); Chip Colwell-Chanthaphonh, *Massacre at Camp Grant: Forgetting and Remembering Apache History* (Tucson: University of Arizona Press, 2007). For more on military campaigns against the Apaches, see Bancroft, *Arizona and New Mexico*; Farish, *History of Arizona*.

8. Sonnichsen, *Pioneer Heritage*, 27.

9. Gordon, *Orphan Abduction*, 165 (emphasis in original).

10. Sonnichsen, *Pioneer Heritage*, 5, 15.

11. "The Birth of the Historical Sites Committee," *Arizoniana* 1 (Fall 1960): 1.

12. Ibid.

13. George M. Lubick, "Forging Ties with the Past: Historic Preservation in Arizona," *Journal of the West* 24 (April 1985): 98.

14. John C. Frémont, *Narratives of Exploration* (New York: Longmans, Green, 1956), 432. Despite his French ancestry, John C. Frémont's Americanness and heroic status were never suspect.

15. Ibid., 434. The meeting with Webster took place after Frémont's second expedition. Webster's statement stands in sharp contrast to his later position, when he publicly denounced the war as one of aggression staged by the Democrats.

16. Horsman, *Race and Manifest Destiny*, 210.

17. For more on Frémont's attempts to incite the locals to declare their independence from Mexico, see Allan Nevins, *Frémont: Pathmarker of the West* (New York: Longmans, Green, 1955), 228, 270–271.

18. Having served as one of first two senators from California (1850–51), the Pathfinder ran as the first presidential candidate of the newly established Republican Party in 1856. As an indication of his popularity, Frémont garnered 1,341,264 votes, against Democrat James Buchanan's 1,927,995. See Don C. Sietz, *The "Also Rans": Great Men Who Missed Making the Presidential Goal* (Freeport: Books for Libraries Press, 1968), 148–157.

19. Harold C. Richardson, "John C. Frémont: Territorial Governor," *Journal of Arizona History* 3 (Summer 1962): 41–46.

20. Sidney Brinckerhoff to Irene Spuhler, August 6, 1971, in MS 1155, Jim E. Officer Collection, box 47, f. 627, Research—Tucson—Frémont Home, box 2, Arizona Historical Society/Tucson.

21. Officer, *Hispanic Arizona*, 66; Sheridan, *Arizona*, 52–53.

22. In 1966, the chief administrator of Saint Mary's Hospital wrote, "Each time the priest raises the golden monstrance during the Benediction of the Blessed Sacrament, Sabino's name is literally carried in benediction. 'In memory of the Otero Family' is inscribed on the base of the consecrated vessel." Letter from Sister Mary, Administrator, Saint Mary's Hospital to Mrs. J. K. Litel, November 22, 1966, in possession of Olga Otero Litel.

23. Eleazar Diaz Herraras interview, 1982, transcript, p. 41, Special Collections, University of Arizona Library.

24. De Long, *History of Arizona*, 197.

25. City of Tucson, Exhibit 1 to Resolution 7282, May 20, 1968, in microfilm, Resolutions no. 7076–7380, City of Tucson, City Clerk's Office.

26. Olga Otero Litel, audiotaped interview, November 28, 2002, Tucson. Litel is not clear on the date of her meeting with Corbett and Laidlaw, but her husband, James, confirmed the conversation and the promises made because he, too, was at this meeting.

27. "Home Removal Draws Criticism," *Star*, October 28, 1966, A-7. Two years later, the mayor and council affirmed that the Otero home would be "dismantled and reconstructed in the center of the Pueblo Center Plaza, surrounded . . . by the Cathedral, the theater, and the auditorium." They even allocated $40,000 for landscaping and restoration. City of Tucson, Exhibit 1 to Resolution 7282, May 20, 1968 in microfilm, Resolutions no. 7076–7380, City of Tucson, City Clerk's Office.

28. "Home Removal Draws Criticism," *Star*, October 28, 1966, A-7.

29. Ibid.

30. Robinson, "Landmark Relocation," A-1.

31. Litel interview, October 25, 1998.

32. *Citizen*, May 9, 1969, 29.

33. "Otero Home Demolition Puts Focus on Samaniego Home," *Citizen*, May 9, 1969, 29.

34. Don Schellie, "Arizona's OTHER Frémont House," *Citizen*, September 8, 1971, in MS 1155, f. 742 Organizations—AHS—Sosa-Carrillo-Frémont House, 1992–1993, Arizona Historical Society/Tucson.

35. *1881 Tucson City Directory*, as quoted in "A Busman's Holiday: Newsman Re-Locates General Frémont's Old Tucson Home," *Star*, August 31, 1958, A-7.

36. "A Busman's Holiday: Newsman Re-Locates General Frémont's Old Tucson Home," *Star*, August 31, 1958, A-7. Parker underscored that as an "American explorer," Frémont "is ranked by historians" as being on an equal plane with Lewis and Clark.

37. Edith Sayre Auslander, "Pioneer Family: 'Panchanga' Will Pay Tribute to Carrillos," *Star*, October 16, 1977, H-2.

38. The Sosa family name is often spelled "Soza." Descendants of this family acknowledge both spellings by writing "Sos/za" in their newsletters. For the sake of simplicity, I will use "Sosa."

39. Fuentes interview, transcript, p. 21, and James Officer, "Sequence of Events: Preserving and Naming the 'Frémont House,'" "1968" MS, p. 3, f. 626, Arizona Historical Society/Tucson.

40. See James Officer, "Sequence of Events: Preserving and Naming the 'Frémont House,'" MS, p. 1, f. 626, Tucson—Frémont Home, box 1; "The Historic Sites Committee of the Arizona Pioneers' Historical Society, 1960" in MS 1155, James E. Officer Collection, box 47, f. 626, Tucson—Frémont Home, both at Arizona Historical Society/Tucson.

41. "Group Forms to Preserve Historic Sites: Heritage Foundation Non-Profit," *Citizen*, September 13, 1965, 35. In a distinct merging of political influences, the *Citizen* characterized the new organization as an "outgrowth" of the City of Tucson's Committee on Historical Sites.

42. Ibid. Ronstadt also served as director of the Southern Arizona Bank & Trust Company and Tucson Gas and Electric. "Ronstadt Noted for Civic Work," *Citizen*, May 11, 1960, 3. Although Mayor Don Hummel claimed that "Ronstadt was working in association with the city" as he coordinated the sale of some 1,300 acres of land to the city in 1960, Ronstadt had in fact formed a trust, of which he was the only public member. Having secured the land the city desired for $75 an acre, he then turned around and sold it to the city for $300 an acre, making a gross profit of $292,875. See Peter Starrett, "Hummel Asks City to Cancel San Pedro Land Purchase: Says Trust Made 'Exorbitant Profit,'" *Citizen*, May 11, 1960, 1. See also Peter Starrett, "Kirk Based His Charges on Disputed Statements: Ronstadt Named as Source," *Citizen*, June 1, 1961, 1.

43. Ralph Ellinwood and William Mathews together purchased the *Arizona Daily Star* in 1924. After Ellinwood's death, his widow, Clare, took over. "Local Newspaper Growth Related," *Citizen*, July 30, 1946, 2. See also "Former *Star* Co-publisher Clare R. Ellinwood Dies at 92," Clare R. Ellinwood Clip book, Arizona Historical Society/Tucson.

44. "First Effort: Group Seeks to Save General Frémont Home," *Citizen*, October 16, 1965, 7. In 1976, in recognition of her role as the "most active promoter of the Frémont House," the Heritage Foundation appointed Ann-Eve Johnson as Doña de la Casa. See "Frémont House 'Builder' Acclaimed 'Dona de la Casa,'" *Citizen*, May 11, 1976, 11.

45. "'Dona de la Casa,'" 11.

46. "Ann-Eve Johnson: Joy of Service," *Star*, June 9, 1974, and "Ann-Eve Johnson Dead at 73: Longtime Civic, Cultural Leader," *Star*, March 13, 1981, in Johnson, Ann-Eve M., file, in Clip books, Arizona Historical Society/Tucson.

47. "Kitchel Gets Top Position in Campaign," *Star*, January 4, 1964, in "Johnson, Ann-Eve M." file, Clip books, Arizona Historical Society/Tucson.

48. "The Historic Sites Committee of the Arizona Pioneers' Historical Society, 1960," in MS 1155, James E. Officer Collection, box 47, f. 626, Tucson—Frémont Home, Arizona Historical Society/Tucson. The Heritage Foundation never discussed Leopoldo Carrillo's political affiliation as a Republican.

49. By this time, the Heritage Foundation was describing itself as a "non-profit corporation whose purpose is to preserve historical artifacts and encourage the preservation, promotion, and restoration of the Southwestern heritage of Tucson and Southern Arizona." "New President: Heritage Group Elects Haury," *Citizen*, November 24, 1966, 47.

50. Emil W. Haury, University of Arizona, Arizona State Museum, to Alva Torres, September 20, 1967, in MS 1134, Alva Torres Collection, box 2, f. 17, Plaza de la Mesilla—Correspondence, 1967, Arizona Historical Society/Tucson.

51. Sidney B. Brinckerhoff to Alva Torres, October 13, 1967, in MS 1134, Alva Torres Collection, box 2, f. 17, Plaza de la Mesilla—Correspondence, 1967, Arizona Historical Society/Tucson.

52. Isabel Fathauer, Chairman Historic Sites Committee of Tucson, letter to the editor, *Citizen*, November 10, 1966, 32.

53. "Heritage Foundation Wants to Buy Historic Frémont House," *Citizen*, May 28, 1970, 43. According to James Officer, the Tucson Historical Sites Committee disbanded in July 1971; "Sequence of Events: Preserving and Naming the 'Frémont House,'" July 17, 1971, MS, p. 7, f. 626, Tucson—Frémont Home, box 1, Arizona Historical Society/Tucson.

54. Tucson City Documents dated October 28, 1970, quoted from James Officer, "Sequence of Events: Preserving and Naming the 'Frémont House,'" MS, p. 5, f. 626, Tucson—Frémont Home, box 1, Arizona Historical Society/Tucson.

55. Letters of support for the "Frémont House" came from the Catalina Junior Women's Club, the Junior League of Women, and Alpha Phi Mothers' Club. James Officer, "Sequence of Events: Preserving and Naming the 'Frémont House,'" MS, pp. 4–5, f. 626, Tucson—Frémont Home, box 1, Arizona Historical Society/Tucson. La Noche Plateada had an annual ball that raised funds for Mexican American scholarships and local arts projects. "Una Noche Plateada Elects Mrs. Acosta," *Star*, May 24, 1971, in "Acosta, Mrs. Ruben" file, in Clip Books, Arizona Historical Society/Tucson.

56. "Frémont House Funds Goal of D.C. Lobbyist," *Citizen*, February 23, 1971, 2.

57. "Foundation Has Funds, Restoration Work Due," *Citizen*, March 20, 1971, 6.

58. L. E. Woodhall, Director of Community Development, to the City Manager, March 24, [1971], Tucson City Archives, quoted from James Officer, "Sequence of Events: Preserving and Naming the 'Frémont House,'" MS, p. 6, f. 626, Tucson—Frémont Home, box 1, Arizona Historical Society/Tucson.

59. "For Frémont House: Foundation Has Funds, Restoration Work Due," *Citizen*, March 20, 1971, 6. Reporter Adolfo Quezada mentions that the society bought the house from the city for a "nominal sum." Quezada, "Name of Historical House: Chicanos Want to Keep it 'Frémont-Carrillo,'" *Citizen*, July 17, 1971, 17.

60. "Frémont House Sale to Historical Group OK'd," *Citizen*, April 5, 1971, 21. Despite the headline, the article makes no mention of any actual exchange of money or land. Reporter Adolfo Quezada mentions that the Society bought the house from the city for a "nominal sum." Quezada, "Name of Historical House: Chicanos Want to Keep it 'Frémont-Carrillo,'" *Citizen*, July 17, 1971, 17.

61. "Restorations Already Begun: Frémont-Carrillo House Given For Historical Site," *Star*, April 6, 1971, A-15. The Arizona Historical Society intervened to save the Charles O. Brown home, built in the 1860s, known as the "Old Adobe Patio" at 40 West Broadway, east of La Placita. It was listed in the National Register of Historical Places in 1971. To preserve the house, the owners and Brown descendants directly deeded it to the Arizona Historical Society, even though the society had made the preservation of historic sites a major part of its agenda only since June 1970. See Sonnichsen, *Pioneer Heritage*, 180.

62. Al Bradshaw Jr., "Work to Begin Soon on Frémont House," *Star*, March 2, 1971, B-1.

63. Robert Fink, Historic Sites Preservation Officer for the State of Arizona, had started preparing an application that would go to the National Park Service responsible for the register. James Officer, "Sequence of Events: Preserving and Naming the 'Frémont House,'" MS, p. 4, f. 626, Tucson—Frémont Home, box 1, Arizona Historical Society/Tucson.

64. Helen Mehrhoff to Sidney Brinckerhoff, August 11, 1971, in MS 1155, Jim E. Officer Collection, box 47, f. 627, Research—Tucson—Frémont House, box 2, Arizona Historical Society/Tucson. This letter from Brinckerhoff's secretary states that "Dennis McCarthy called from Phoenix this morning and he wanted me to let you know and to reassure you that . . . in their application . . . they will de-emphasize the Carrillo aspect and highlight the Frémont name." See also correspondence in MS 1155, Jim Officer Collection, box 47, f. 627, Research—Tucson—Frémont Home, box 2, Arizona Historical Society/Tucson.

65. "Frémont Arizona Chronology," in FM 1076, Tucson-Pima County Historical Commission, Arizona Historical Society/Tucson. For more on the listing of the Frémont House in the National Register, see James Officer, "Sequence of Events: Preserving and Naming the 'Frémont House,'" MS, p. 4, f. 626, Tucson—Frémont Home, box 1, Arizona Historical Society.

66. Mike Goodkind, "Councilmen Suggest Moving Old Carrillo-Frémont House," *Citizen*, February 27, 1971, 4.

67. "Agreement Expected on Frémont House," *Citizen*, December 4, 1970, 31.

68. "Historical Cover-Up," *Citizen*, January 8, 1971, 8.

69. Michel-Rolph Trouillot, *Silencing the Past: Power and the Production of History* (Boston: Beacon Press, 1995), xix.

70. Peter Johnson and Arthur C. Hall, Tucson Heritage Foundation, to Members of the Board of Directors, Arizona Historical Society, September 11, 1992, in MS 1155, Jim E. Officer Collection, f. 742, Organizations—Arizona Historical Society—Sosa-Carrillo-Frémont House, 1992–1993, Arizona Historical Society/Tucson. See also "Foundation Has Funds, Restoration Work Due," *Citizen*, March 20, 1971, 6.

71. Charles C. Colley to Carlos E. Ronstadt, August 21, 1971, in MS 1155, Jim E. Officer Collection, box 47, f. 627, Research—Tucson—Frémont House, box 2, Arizona Historical Society/Tucson.

72. In a letter to the mayor dated June 29, [1971], Mary Acosta expressed her opposition to the listing of the Frémont House in the National Registry of Historic Places and the removal of the Carrillo name. She also complained to Arizona Historical Society president Harry Montgomery. In a letter to Sidney Brinckerhoff of the Heritage Foundation, Isabel Fathauer also went on record to state her opposition: "I believe the Carrillo name should be retained to recognize the Mexican-American history of the house." Alene Smith and Irene Carrillo Spuhler also wrote Brinckerhoff to protest the name change. James Officer, "Sequence of Events: Preserving and Naming the 'Frémont House,'" MS, p. 4, f. 626, Tucson—Frémont Home, box 1, Arizona Historical Society/Tucson.

73. "Name of Historic House Protested by New Group," *Star*, August 3, 1971, 17; see also Adolfo Quezada, "Tucsonians Form Group to Keep Carrillo Name for Restored Home," *Citizen*, August 3, 1971, 37.

74. "Name of Historic House," 17.

75. Alva Torres, audiotaped interview, December 6, 2002, Tucson. Mary Acosta died in April 1975.

76. "Name of Historic House Protested by New Group," *Star*, August 3, 1971, 17.

77. "It's Frémont Residence; Carrillo Out; Historical Society Board Votes Continuation as Is," *Citizen*, August 5, 1971, 29; James Officer, "Sequence of Events: Preserving and Naming the 'Frémont House,'" August 4, 1971, MS, p. 8, f. 626, Tucson—Frémont Home, box 1, Arizona Historical Society/Tucson. Brinckerhoff also mentions that ten out of twenty-five directors were present at that meeting, one more than the number needed for a quorum. A few directors, like Bert M. Fireman, later voiced their disagreement with the vote. Influential Alex Jácome Jr., then vice president of the Tucson Trade Bureau, pleaded at the bureau's August 5, 1971, meeting that members rally to oppose "dropping the Carrillo name." *Star*, August 6, 1971, in MS 1155, Jim E. Officer Collection, box 47, f. 627, Research—Tucson—Frémont Home, box 2, Arizona Historical Society/Tucson.

78. "It's Frémont Residence; Carrillo Out; Historical Society Board Votes Continuation As Is," *Citizen*, August 5, 1971, 29.

79. Harry Montgomery to Mrs. Ruben Acosta, August 12, 1971, in MS 1155, Jim E. Officer Collection, box 47, f. 627, Research—Tucson—Frémont Home, box 2, Arizona Historical Society/Tucson.

80. "Carrillo Left Out: Society OK's Changing Frémont House Name," *Star*, August 5, 1971, in MS 1155, Jim E. Officer Collection, box 47, f. 627, Research— Tucson—Frémont Home, box 2, Arizona Historical Society/Tucson.

81. Sidney Brinckerhoff to Kieran McCarty, August 9, 1971, in MS 1155, Jim Officer Collection, box 47, f. 627, Research—Tucson—Frémont Home, box 2, Arizona Historical Society/Tucson.

82. Director, Arizona Historical Society, to staff, memo regarding the Frémont House situation, August 9, 1971, in MS 1155, Jim E. Officer Collection, box 47, f. 627, Research—Tucson—Frémont Home, box 2, Arizona Historical Society/ Tucson.

83. Editorial, "The Frémont House," *Citizen*, August 5, 1971, 30.

84. "End A Foolish Quarrel," *Star*, August 25, 1971.

85. "Carrillo Family Has Lived 5 Generations in Tucson," *Star*, March 31, 1972, in Jacobs, Edward C., file, in Clip books, Arizona Historical Society/Tucson. Active in the Democratic Party, Jacobs encouraged the Democrats of Greater Tucson to resist efforts to rename the house and to continue calling it the Carrillo House. They passed a resolution on August 30, 1971, and appealed to the Arizona Historical Society to keep the "original" name. James Officer, "Sequence of Events: Preserving and Naming the 'Frémont House,'" MS 1971, p. 10, f. 626, Tucson—Frémont Home, box 1. Edward Carrillo Jacobs died in 1975.

86. See "Statement of the Historic Tucson Committee," *Citizen*, August 30, 1971, 19.

87. McCarty's plea mirrors his statements made in Kieran McCarty's editorial, "Frémont House Furor," *Citizen*, August 13, 1971. It must be noted that the City of Tucson had established a Historical Sites Committee in 1965 to recommend structures worthy of preservation; it was disbanded in July 1971.

88. Kieran McCarty, audiotaped conversation, Tucson, February 17, 1999.

89. Tucson City Council, Minutes, September 7, 1971, City of Tucson Archives.

90. Ibid. Appointed as founding members of the Tucson Historic Committee were Kieran McCarty (chairman), Mary Acosta, Alva Torres, Arparo Carrillo-Covarrubias, Edward Carrillo Jacobs, Ernesto Portillo (Torres's brother-in-law), Alene Smith, Hector Morales, Arnufo Trejo, Irene Spuhler, Eugene Benton, and Adalberto Guerrero.

91. Alva Torres, as quoted in Quezada, "Name of Historical House," 17. The mayor and city council initially objected to the inclusion of Torres, Jacobs, and Morales on the Historic Committee. Torres recalls that they were perceived as the main troublemakers. In a private, off-the-record huddle during a recess,

Jacobs apparently flew into a tirade. Torres concluded that whatever Jacobs said forced the mayor and council to reconsider and include them. Torres interview.

92. In a letter to the mayor and city council, the committee affirmed as one of its goals "to acknowledge the renewed interest in history, both nationally and locally, and the necessity to furnish not only the new voices in Tucson an outlet for recognition and acceptance, but also the concerns of the older voices whose awareness of and pride in the past have been retained though long unheeded." The Tucson Historic Committee to the Honorable Mayor James N. Corbett and members of the Council, September 7, 1971, in MS 1155, Jim E. Officer Collection, box 47, f. 627, Research—Tucson—Frémont House, box 2, Arizona Historical Society/Tucson; "Tucson Historical Sites" dated September 1969 in MS 1155, James E. Officer, box 47, f. 626, Tucson—Frémont Home, Arizona Historical Society/Tucson.

93. James Officer, "Sequence of Events: Preserving and Naming the 'Frémont House,'" December 1, 1971, MS, p. 11, f. 626, Tucson—Frémont Home, box 1, Arizona Historical Society/Tucson.

94. Ibid., March 14, 1972, MS, p. 12.

95. "First Lady Dedicates Frémont House in Colorful Ceremony," *La Realta: The Arizona Historical Society Newsletter*, no. 1 (1972), 1.

96. "Frémont 'Anglo' House," *News-Gazette* (Tucson), April 13, 1972, and "Tucson's Historic Names," September 2, 1971, in MS 1155, Jim E. Officer Collection, box 47, f. 627, Research—Tucson—Frémont Home, box 2, Arizona Historical Society/Tucson.

97. Charles C. Colley, "The Old Otero Home," Sabino Otero file, Arizona Historical Society/Tucson.

98. Olga Otero Litel, audiotaped interview, November 28, 2002, Tucson.

99. The stated purpose of Ordinance 3815 is "to promote the educational, cultural, economic, and general welfare of the community, and to ensure the harmonious growth of the municipality, by encouraging the preservation of historic sites and structures located within historic zones." Tucson City Council, Minutes, April 3, 1972, City of Tucson Archives.

100. Mrs. Emery C. (Ann-Eve) Johnson to the Honorable James Corbett Jr., October 31, 1969, in MS 1155, James E. Officer Collection, box 47, f. 626, Tucson—Frémont Home, Arizona Historical Society/Tucson.

101. Alene Smith to Sidney Brinckerhoff, July 31, 1971, in MS 1155, Jim E. Officer Collection, box 47, f. 627, Research—Tucson—Frémont Home, box 2, Arizona Historical Society/Tucson.

102. Sarah Dillard Pope, "Hispanic History in the National Register of Historic Places," at the National Registry Web site: http://crm.cr.nps.gov/archive/20-11/20-11-5.pdf/.

Chapter 8. Conclusion

1. James N. Corbett, as quoted in Regan, "There Goes the Neighborhood."

2. Ibid.

3. Pedro Gonzales, videotaped interview, November 10, 2007, Tucson.

4. Ayres, "Archaeology Project."

5. On city planners who had hoped the project would proceed unencumbered, see Bill Kimmey, "Community Favors Butterfield Route," *Citizen*, September 27, 1968, A-25. For more on protests, see Edwin S. Finkelstein, "Singing Marchers Protest Proposed Butterfield Route," *Citizen*, September 25, 1971, 2.

6. John Neary, "One Man's Fight to Save the Barrio: A Tucson Auto Dealer Brings New Life to the Barrio after High-Rise Developers and Highway Planners Nearly Tore It All Down," *Americana* 6, no. 6 (January–February 1979): 54–57.

7. Carmen Duarte, "Bad Feelings in the Barrio: Development Stirs Up Old Animosities," *Star*, October 11, 1988, A-2.

8. Lourdes Medrano Leslie, "Vandals' Graffiti Mar First Tour of Barrio Libre," *Star*, October 10, 1988, A-3.

9. Ibid.

10. Attributed to David Carter, one of the new barrio's major preservationists and owner of Barrio Development, in Jordan Gruener, "In the Old Ways," *Star*, October 2, 1988, J-1. In a subsequent article, Carter insisted that the quotation came from the 1881 directory and "is fact." See Duarte, "Bad Feelings in the Barrio," A-2.

11. Evangelina Cota, as quoted in Duarte, "Bad Feelings in the Barrio," A-2.

12. Judy Bernal, as quoted Duarte, "Bad Feelings in the Barrio," A-2.

13. John Bret Harte, "Constant Battle to Preserve the City's Past: Tucson's Historic Sites," *Citizen*, February 13, 1978, C-3.

14. Mrs. [Belen] Herman Camacho, as quoted in "Never a Brothel," *Citizen*, March 24, 1978, in MS 1155, Jim E. Officer Collection, box 48, f. 629. Tucson—Frémont Home, box 4, Arizona Historical Society/Tucson.

15. "Editor's Note" in ibid.

16. Joana D. Diamos, Tucson–Pima County Historical Commission, to William C. Porter, President, Board of Directors, Arizona Historical Society, December 6, 1991, in MS 1155, Jim E. Officer Collection, f. 628, Tucson—Frémont Home, box 3, Arizona Historical Society/Tucson.

17. Peter Johnson and Arthur C. Hall, Tucson Heritage Foundation, to Members of the Board of Directors, Arizona Historical Society, September 11, 1992, in MS 1155, Jim E. Officer Collection, f. 742, Organizations—Arizona Historical Society—Sosa-Carrillo-Frémont House, 1992–1993, Arizona Historical Society/Tucson. The date of this letter indicates that it was probably read the same day the Arizona Historical Society met to discuss the name change. Although both

Johnson and Hall signed the letter, only Johnson addressed the society at the September 11 meeting.

18. Emil W. Haury, "Re-naming in the National Registry," in MS 1155, Jim E. Officer Collection, f. 742, Organizations—Arizona Historical Society—Sosa-Carrillo-Frémont House, 1992–1993, Arizona Historical Society/Tucson.

19. Despite the official name change, the original plaque continued to recognize the structure as the "Frémont House" until it was updated in 2007. Diamos to Porter, December 6, 1971.

20. Abe Campillo, as quoted in Bonnie Henry, "Plaza Part of West Congress," *Star*, May 30, 1990, C-3. As a side note, Ted DeGrazia managed La Plaza Theatre around 1935. He went on to become a renowned painter. Thirty years later, he credited his exposure to Mexican culture at La Plaza for influencing the themes that made him famous. "The movies at the Plaza," he recalled, "sparked my visit to Mexico City and no doubt later influenced my paintings."

21. "Theatre Relocation Site Sought," *Citizen*, February 17, 1969, 25. In 1971, businessman Edward C. Jacobs had purchased a block on Congress Street that included the old Paramount movie house. It had been built in 1919 as the Rialto Theatre that featured the first talkie in 1929. (It still stands today and is now called the Rialto.) Jacobs attempted to "revive" the La Plaza Theater and bring people back to downtown. See "Revitalization of Downtown Area Seen," *Citizen*, March 24, 1971, A-31. His attempt failed. In less than a year, the La Plaza management turned to adult films.

22. Abe Campillo, as quoted in "Theatre Relocation," 25.

23. Editorial, "Community Center Faces Long Pull," *Citizen*, September 10, 1971, A-32. Less than a year after its opening, Roy P. Drachman had determined that "the Community Center may never pay its way and will cost local taxpayers yearly, but so what? It will enrich the cultural life of our town." "The Community Center's Hotel Situation," *Realty Digest* 31 (January 1972), unpaginated.

24. Rob O'Dell, "Council Expected to OK $300 Million Hotels Deal," *Star*, November 18, 2007, B-1.

25. Rhonda Bodfield, "La Placita, a Dreary Landmark, to Get a Lively, Colorful Face Lift," *Star*, March 15, 1999, A-1.

26. "Forget about Taking Gazebo Out of La Placita," *Star*, November 20, 2006, A-6.

27. Cohen, "Buying into Downtown Revival," 93–94.

28. Roy P. Drachman, "National Trend Predicts: Downtown Tucson Dying Now . . . but New Life Is in Sight" ("Perspective"), *Citizen*, March 20, 1975, A-31.

29. Bernard J. Friedman, as quoted in Lawrence Wippman, "A Popular Place, But in the Red: Should Community Center Show a Profit?" ("Perspective"), *Citizen*, July 26, 1976, A-33.

30. Philip Whitmore, as quoted in Christina Collins, "Can Tucson Keep Its Heart Pumping," *Citizen*, January 18, 1977, A-2. Around this time, Don Robinson,

one of the *Citizen's* most ardent urban renewal advocates, who only nine years before had boasted that a 40-acre hole downtown represented "progress," declared: "Downtown Is Dead; Forget It!" *Citizen*, October 8, 1978, F-1.

31. Voters had rejected a $41.3 million bond issue in 1984 to pay for the expansion of the center, but city officials still found another way to pay for these costs. Bob Christman, "City Hopes to Draw Bigger Conventions with Larger Center," *Star*, April 10, 1988, F-1.

32. For more on the persistence of memories that associate people with places that no longer exist, see Michael Mayerfeld Bell, "The Ghosts of Place," *Theory and Society* 26, no. 6 (December 1997): 813–836. Bell contends that "ghosts" are "ubiquitous in the places in which we live, and they give a life to those places. Ghosts are much of what makes a space a place. Yet as well, ghosts are terrifically specific. 'George Washington slept here,' says many (probably too many) a historical marker, not somewhere else" (828).

33. Panchita Leon, as quoted in Jane Kay, "El Hoyo: Home Is Disappearing," *Star*, Special Report, July 16, 1970, A-6.

34. Gonzales interview.

35. Leon and Rosendo Pérez, as quoted in Kay, "El Hoyo," A-6.

36. Salamón Baldenegro, as quoted in "People's Coalition Takes Plea for El Rio to Tourists," *Citizen*, October 12, 1970, A-1.

37. In 1967, generally younger, more militant college students started to organize in what would later be recognized as the start of the Chicana/o movement in Tucson. Salomón "Sal" Baldenegro had just founded the Chicana/o Student Association (MASA) at the University of Arizona. Guadalupe Castillo, Raúl Grijalva, and he became the city's most visible self-identified Chicana/os. They formed the Chicana/o Liberation Committee, which organized walkouts at local high schools and demanded Chicano history and Chicano studies courses in the high schools and at the University of Arizona. The committee used more confrontational tactics to force the city to convert the El Rio Golf Course, located in the heart of a Chicana/o neighborhood, into a community center in the early 1970s. See Francisco A. Rosales, *Chicano! The History of the Chicana/o Civil Rights Movement* (Houston: Arte Público Press, 1996), 211, and "Militants at El Rio Stone Police Cars," *Sunday Star-Citizen*, September 6, 1970, 1.

38. See Bonnie Henry, "Old Barrio, Its Way of Life All but Vanished," *Star*, August 23, 1992, B-1.

39. Angie Quiroz, as quoted in Ernesto Portillo Jr., "To Get the OK for Rio Nuevo, Go to the Barrios, Planners Learn," *Star*, January 7, 2001, B-1.

40. Raúl Rodríguez, as quoted in ibid. Fernando Galvan, who has "painful memories" of urban renewal, stated, "I don't like any of it and I don't believe them. They tell you we are going to do one thing and then they do another—just like the TCC." Carmen Duarte, "Reaction: Rio Nuevo—Some Barrio Residents Are Wary of How Project Will Affect Them," *Star*, January 5, 2001, A-1.

41. Daniel Gamez García, as recorded on tape 1, Mayor and Council Strategic Focus Area Subcommittee, Rio Nuevo, Thursday, February 21, 2008, Tucson City Archives.

42. Nina Trasoff, as recorded on tape 1, Mayor and Council Strategic Focus Area Subcommittee, Rio Nuevo, Thursday, February 21, 2008, Tucson City Archives. Having arrived in Tucson only in 1976, Trasoff did not personally witness and experience urban renewal. The Rio Nuevo Project has had its own share of problems. See "77 Million Has Been Spent on Rio Nuevo, and This Is What We Have So Far . . . " (part of the ongoing series "*Star* Investigation: Rio Nuevo Audit"), *Star*, July 27, 2008, A-1. See also Rob O'Dell, "Where Your Rio Nuevo Taxes Went," *Star*, October 26, 2008, A-1.

43. Regina Romero, as recorded on tape 1, Mayor and Council Strategic Focus Area Subcommittee, Rio Nuevo, Thursday, February 21, 2008, Tucson City Archives.

44. David Glassberg, *Sense of History: The Place of the Past in American Life* (Amherst: University of Massachusetts Press, 2001) 7, 20.

Selected Bibliography

Newspapers Consulted

Arizona Daily Star (Tucson)
News-Gazette (Tucson)
Tucson Daily Citizen
Arizona Republic (Phoenix)
Los Angeles Times

Interviews with the Author

Castillo, Guadalupe. Tucson, February 13, 2008.
Gonzales, Pedro. Tucson, November 10, 2007.
Laidlaw, Donald. Tucson, February 10, 2003.
Lizárraga, Josephina. Tucson, March 9, 2005.
Montaño, Anna. Tucson, March 3, 2007.
Torres, Alva. Tucson, December 6, 2002.

Unpublished Sources

Ayres, James E. "The Tucson Urban Renewal Archaeology Project." July 6, 1994. Unpublished presentation in author's files.

Bufkin, Donald H. "The Broad Pattern of Land Use and Change in Tucson, 1862–1912." In Thomas F. Saarinen and Lay J. Gibson, eds., "Territorial Tucson." Tucson, n.d., 5–28. Unpublished manuscript in possession of Thomas F. Saarinen.

———. "Urbanization of Tucson: 1940–1990." Arizona Historical Society/Tucson, oral history, acc. no. 91–42, AV 0505-4.

Colley, Charles C. "The Old Otero Home." Sabino Otero file, Arizona Historical Society/Tucson.

Diocese of Tucson to Donald Laidlaw. December 21, 1967 City of Tucson Archives, City Clerk's Office, box 2, M/C History file, binder 5, Report on Planning Proposals, Code no. R-214.

Drachman, Roy P. "The Family," n.d. http://www.parentseyes.arizona.edu/drachman/0102.html/.

———. "Urbanization of Tucson: 1940–1990." Arizona Historical Society/Tucson, oral history, acc. no. 92–11, AV 0505-18.

García, Henry. Interview by Sharyn Wiley Yeoman. June 19, 1987, Tucson. Arizona Historical Society/Tucson, AV 0605-3.

Goodman, John Kestner. "Arizona Cattle Industry—Research," Arizona Historical Society/Tucson, box 31.

Historic Zone Ordinance (1972). Arizona Historical Society/Tucson, MS 1076, box 1, Ordinances, T.H.C., 1971–1973.

Luckingham, Bradford. "The Old Pueblo and the Valley of the Sun: Notes on Urban Rivalry in Arizona." Arizona Historical Society/Tucson, MS 1155, file 635, Manuscript Tucson-Phoenix Rivalry, box 48.

Saarinen, Thomas F., and Lay J. Gibson, eds. "Territorial Tucson." Tucson, n.d. Unpublished manuscript in possession of Thomas F. Saarinen.

Tucson Sunshine-Climate Club. "Club Organized 1922, Tucson Metropolitan District." Arizona Historical Society/Tucson.

Published Sources

Acuña, Rodolfo. *A Community under Siege: A Chronicle of Chicanos East of the Los Angeles River, 1945–1975.* Los Angeles: Chicano Studies Research Center, University of California at Los Angeles, 1984.

———. *Occupied America: A History of Chicanos.* New York: Longman, 2000.

Adams, Paul C., Steven Hoelscher, and Karen E. Till, eds. *Textures of Place: Exploring Humanist Geographies.* Minneapolis: University of Minnesota Press, 2001.

Almaguer, Tomás. *Racial Fault Lines: The Historical Origins of White Supremacy in California.* Berkeley: University of California Press, 1994.

Altman, Irwin, and Setha M. Low, eds. *Place Attachment.* New York: Plenum Press, 1992.

Anderson, Barbara A. "From Family Home to Slum Apartment: Archaeological Analysis within the Urban Renewal Area, Tucson, Arizona." Master's thesis, University of Arizona, 1970.

Anderson, Mark Cronlund. *Pancho Villa's Revolution by Headlines.* Norman: University of Oklahoma Press, 2000.

Anderson, Martin. *The Federal Bulldozer: A Critical Analysis of Urban Renewal, 1949–1962.* Cambridge, Mass.: MIT Press, 1964.

Arredondo, Gabriela F. *Mexican Chicago: Race, Identity, and Nation, 1916–39.* Chicago: University of Illinois Press, 2008.

Arreola, Daniel D. "Urban Ethnic Landscape Identity." *Geographical Review* 85, no. 4 (October 1995): 518–534.

———, ed. *Hispanic Spaces, Latino Places: Community and Cultural Diversity in Contemporary America*. Austin: University of Texas Press, 2004.

Arreola, Daniel D., and James R. Curtis. *The Mexican Border Cities: Landscape Anatomy and Place Personality*. Tucson: University of Arizona Press, 1993.

Ashton Associates. *Second Re-Use Appraisal Pueblo Center Redevelopment Project (Arizona R-8)*. Los Angeles, 1966.

Avila, Eric. *Popular Culture in the Age of White Flight: Fear and Fantasy in Suburban Los Angeles*. Berkeley: University of California Press, 2004.

Bancroft, Hubert Howe. *History of Arizona and New Mexico, 1530–1888*. San Francisco: The History Company, 1889.

Barter, G. W. *Directory of the City of Tucson for the Year 1881*. San Francisco: H. S. Crocker, 1881. Reprint, Tucson: Arizona State Genealogical Society, 1988.

Basso, Keith H. *Wisdom Sits in Places: Landscape and Language among the Western Apache*. Albuquerque: University of New Mexico Press, 1996.

Bauman, John F. *Public Housing, Race, and Renewal: Urban Planning in Philadelphia, 1920–1974*. Philadelphia: Temple University Press, 1986.

Bederman, Gail. *Manliness and Civilization: A Cultural History of Gender and Race in the United States, 1880–1917*. Chicago: University of Chicago Press, 1995.

Bell, Dennis R., et al. *Barrio Historico, Tucson*. Tucson: College of Architecture, University of Arizona, 1972.

Bell, Michael Mayerfeld. "The Ghosts of Place." *Theory and Society* 26, no. 6 (December 1997): 813–836.

Bhabha, Homi K. *The Location of Culture*. London: Routledge, 1994.

Blackhawk, Ned. *Violence over the Land: Indians and Empires in the Early American West*. Cambridge: Harvard University Press, 2006.

Blythe, T. Roger, ed. *A Pictorial Souvenir of Tucson, Arizona: "The Old Pueblo"; The Sunshine City of America*. Tucson, 1945.

Brady, Mary Pat. *Extinct Homelands, Temporal Geographies: Chicana Literature and the Urgency of Space*. Durham, N.C.: Duke University Press, 2002.

Briegel, Kaye L. "Alianza Hispano-Americana, 1894–1965: A Mexican-American Fraternal Insurance Society." Ph.D. diss., University of Southern California, 1974.

Browne, J. Ross. *Adventures in the Apache Country: A Tour through Arizona and Sonora, with Notes on the Silver Regions of Nevada*. New York: Harper, 1869.

Bufkin, Donald H. "From Mud Village to Modern Metropolis: The Urbanization of Tucson." *Journal of Arizona History* 22 (Spring 1981): 63–81.

Build a Better America Committee. *An Action Plan for Tucson*. Tucson: National Association of Real Estate Boards, 1963.

Camarillo, Albert. *Chicanos in a Changing Society: From Mexican Pueblos to American Barrios in Santa Barbara and Southern California, 1848–1930*. Cambridge, Mass.: Harvard University Press, 1979.

Certeau, Michel de. *The Practice of Everyday Life*. Berkeley: University of California Press, 1984.

Chafe, William. *Civilities and Civil Rights: Greensboro, North Carolina, and the Black Struggle for Freedom*. New York: Oxford University Press, 1980.

Chambers, George W., and C. L. Sonnichsen. *San Agustín: First Cathedral Church in Arizona*. Tucson: Arizona Historical Society, 1974.

Charles, Fannie A. *In the Country God Forgot: A Story of Today*. Boston: Little, Brown, 1902.

City-County Planning Department. *General Land Use Plan: Tucson and Environs*. City of Tucson, 1960.

City of Tucson. *Redevelopment Plan: Southwestern Section Central District Development Plan (Old Pueblo Project, Arizona R-6)*. Tucson, March 22, 1962.

City of Tucson, Department of Community Development, and Candeub, Fleissig, Adley and Associates. *Pueblo Center Project, Tucson, Arizona: Concept Plan*. Tucson: Candeub, Fleissig, Adley and Associates, 1965.

Clark, Patricia J., and Martha M. Fimbres. "A Study to Identify and Access the Psychological Ramifications Inherent in the Process of Relocation Regarding Census Tract I in Downtown Tucson, Arizona." Master's thesis, Arizona State University, 1978.

Cohen, Lizabeth. "Buying into Downtown Revival: The Centrality of Retail to Postwar Urban Renewal in American Cities." *Annals of the American Academy of Political and Social Science* 611, no. 1 (2007): 82–95.

———. *A Consumers' Republic: The Politics of Mass Consumption in Postwar America*. New York: Vintage, 2003.

Colwell-Chanthaphonh, Chip. *Massacre at Camp Grant: Forgetting and Remembering Apache History*. Tucson: University of Arizona Press, 2007.

Crane, Susan A. "Writing the Individual Back into Collective Memory." *American Historical Review* 102, no. 5 (December 1997): 1372–1385.

Cruz, Gilbert R. *Let There Be Towns: Spanish Municipal Origins in the American Southwest, 1610–1810*. College Station: Texas A&M University Press, 1988.

De León, Arnoldo. *The Tejano Community, 1836–1900*. Albuquerque: University of New Mexico Press, 1982.

De Long, Sidney R. *The History of Arizona from the Earliest Times Known to the People of Europe to 1903*. San Francisco: Whitaker and Ray, 1905.

De Mayo, Louis. *Old Tucson: The Classic West*. Phoenix: De Mayo, 1972.

Denton, John H., and William S. King. "The Tucson Central Business District as a Changing Entity." *Arizona Review*, May 1960: 3.

Deverell, William. *Whitewashed Adobe: The Rise of Los Angeles and the Remaking of Its Mexican Past*. Berkeley: University of California Press, 2004.

Diaz, David R. *Barrio Urbanism: Chicanos, Planning, and American Cities*. New York: Routledge, 2005.

Drachman, Roy P. "The Community Center's Hotel Situation." *Realty Digest* 31 (January 1972): unpaginated.

———. *From Cowtown to Desert Metropolis: Ninety Years of Arizona Memories*. Tucson: Whitewing Press, 1999.

———. "Whither Goest Tucson?" *Realty Digest* (Roy Drachman Realty, Tucson) 17, no. 4 (December 1964): unpaginated.

Drachman, Roy P., and Vincent L. Lung. *The Pueblo Center Redevelopment Project*. Report presented to the Central City Council of the Urban Land Institute, April 23, 1965, by Roy Drachman, Chairman, Citizens' Committee on Municipal Blight, and Vincent L. Lung, Assistant City Manager and Coordinator of Community Development. Tucson: City of Tucson, 1965.

Duany, Andres, Elizabeth Plater-Zyberk, and Jeff Speck. *Suburban Nation: The Rise of Sprawl and the Decine of the American Dream*. New York: North Point Press, 2000.

Dubrow, Lee, and Jennifer B. Goodman, eds. *Restoring Women's History through Historic Preservation*. Baltimore: Johns Hopkins University Press, 2003.

Fairbanks, Robert B. "The Failure of Urban Renewal in the Southwest: From City Needs to Individual Rights." *Western Historical Quarterly* 37 (Autumn 2006): 303–325.

———. *Making Better Citizens: Housing Reform and the Community Development Strategy in Cincinnati, 1890–1960*. Urbana: University of Illinois Press, 1988.

Faragher, John Mack. "The Myth of the Frontier: Progress or Lost Freedom." *History Now* 9 (September 2006), http://www.historynow.org/09_2006/historian3.html.

Farish, Thomas Edwin. *History of Arizona*. 8 vols. San Francisco: Filmer Brothers Electrotype, 1915–18.

Farley, Stephen, Regina Kelly, and the Ward VI Youth History Team, eds. *Snapped on the Street: A Community Archive of Photos and Memories from Downtown Tucson, 1937–1963*. Tucson: Tucson Voices Press, 1999.

Ferguson, Ronald F., and William T. Dickens. *Urban Problems and Community Development*. Washington, D.C.: Brookings Institution Press, 1999.

Ferman, Barbara. *Challenging the Growth Machine: Neighborhood Politics in Chicago and Pittsburgh*. Lawrence: University Press of Kansas, 1996.

Ferris, Robert, ed. *The American West: An Appraisal*. Santa Fe: Museum of New Mexico Press, 1963.

Fleagle, Roy Kenneth. "Politics and Planning: Tucson Metropolitan Area." Master's thesis, University of Arizona, 1966.

Fogelson, Robert M. *Downtown: Its Rise and Fall, 1880–1950*. New Haven, Conn.: Yale University Press, 2003.

Foucault, Michel. *Discipline and Punish: The Birth of the Prison*. Trans. Alan Sheridan. New York: Pantheon Books, 1977.

Frémont, John C. *Narratives of Exploration*. New York: Longmans, Green, 1956.

Freund, David M. P. *Colored Property: State Policy and White Racial Politics in Suburban America*. Chicago: University of Chicago Press, 2007.

Gans, Herbert J. *The Urban Villagers: Group and Class in the Life of Italian-Americans*. New York: Free Press of Glencoe, 1962.

García, Matt. *A World of Its Own: Race, Labor, and Citrus in the Making of Greater Los Angeles, 1900–1970*. Chapel Hill: University of North Carolina Press, 2001.

Gendzel, Glen. "Pioneers and Padres: Competing Mythologies in Northern and Southern California, 1850–1930." *Western Historical Quarterly* 32, no. 1 (Spring 2001): 55–79.

Getty, Harry Thomas. *Interethnic Relationships in the Community of Tucson*. New York: Arno Press, 1976.

Giebner, Robert. "Tucson's 'Barrio Historico.'" *Arizona Architect*, August 1973 , 9–10.

Gillis, John R., ed. *Commemorations: The Politics of National Identity*. Princeton, N.J.: Princeton University Press, 1994.

Glassberg, David. *Sense of History: The Place of the Past in American Life*. Amherst: University of Massachusetts Press, 2001.

Goering, John M., Maynard Robison, and Knight Hoover. *The Best Eight Blocks in Harlem: The Last Decade of Urban Reform*. Washington, D.C.: University Press of America, 1977.

Goings, Kenneth W., and Raymond A. Mohl, eds. *The New African American Urban History*. Thousand Oaks, Calif.: Sage, 1996.

Gonzales, Manuel G., and Cynthia M. Gonzales, eds. *En Aquel Entonces: Readings in Mexican-American History*. Bloomington: Indiana University Press, 2000.

González, Deena J. *Refusing the Favor: The Spanish-Mexican Women of Santa Fe, 1820–1880*. New York: Oxford University Press, 1999.

González, Gilbert G. *Culture of Empire: American Writers, Mexico, and Mexican Immigrants, 1880–1930*. Austin: University of Texas Press, 2004.

Goodman, John Kestner. "Race and Race Mixture as the Basis of Social Status in Tucson, Arizona." Master's thesis, Yale University, 1942.

Gordon, Linda. *The Great Arizona Orphan Abduction*. Cambridge, Mass.: Harvard University Press, 1999.

Gourley, John. "The Pueblo and the Public: Urban Realities in Counterpoint." Ph.D. diss., University of Arizona, 1992.

Graff, Harvey J. *The Dallas Myth: The Making and Unmaking of an American City*. Minneapolis: University of Minnesota Press, 2008.

Gragg, Rachel. "Tucson: The Formation and Legitimation of an Urban Renewal Program." Master's thesis, University of Arizona, 1969.

Griswold del Castillo, Richard. *The Los Angeles Barrio, 1850–1890: A Social History*. Berkeley: University of California Press, 1979.

Guerrero, Lalo, and Sherilyn Mentes. *Lalo: My Life and Music.* Tucson: University of Arizona Press, 2002.

Gutiérrez, David G. "Significant to Whom? Mexican Americans and the History of the American West." *Western Historical Quarterly* 24, no. 4 (November 1993): 519–539.

———. *Walls and Mirrors: Mexican Americans, Mexican Immigrants, and the Politics of Ethnicity.* Berkeley: University of California Press, 1995.

Gutmann, Amy. *Democracy and the Welfare State.* Princeton, N.J.: Princeton University Press, 1988.

Haas, Lisbeth. *Conquests and Historical Identities in California, 1769–1936.* Berkeley: University of California Press, 1995.

Hale, Grace Elizabeth. *Making Whiteness: The Culture of Segregation in the South, 1890–1940.* New York: Pantheon Books, 1998.

Hardwick, Jeff M. "A Downtown Utopia? Suburbanization, Urban Renewal and Consumption in New Haven." *Planning History Studies: A Journal of the Society for American City and Regional Planning History* 10 (Winter 1996): 41–54.

Harmon, Alexandra. *Indians in the Making: Ethnic Relations and Indian Identities around Puget Sound.* Berkeley: University of California Press, 1999.

Harvey, David. *The Condition of Postmodernity: An Enquiry into the Origins of Cultural Change.* Oxford: Blackwell, 1989.

Hayden, Dolores. *Building Suburbia: Green Fields and Urban Growth, 1920–2000.* New York: Pantheon Books, 2003.

———. *The Grand Domestic Revolution: A History of Feminist Designs for American Homes, Neighborhoods, and Cities.* Cambridge, Mass.: MIT Press, 1981.

———. *The Power of Place: Urban Landscapes as Public History.* Cambridge, Mass.: MIT Press, 1995.

Hernández, José, Leo Estrada, and David Alvírez. "Census Data and the Problem of Conceptually Defining the Mexican American Population." *Social Science Quarterly* 53 (1973): 671–687.

Hill, Jane. "Hasta la Vista, Baby: Anglo Spanish in the American Southwest." *Critique of Anthropology* 13, no. 2 (1993): 145–176.

Historic Areas Committee. *Historical Sites* (Tucson, 1969).

Hobsbawm, Eric, and Terence Ranger, eds. *The Invention of Tradition.* Cambridge: Cambridge University Press, 1983.

Homero Villa, Raúl. *Barrio-logos: Space and Place in Urban Chicano Literature and Culture.* Austin: University of Texas Press, 2000.

Horsman, Reginald. *Race and Manifest Destiny: The Origins of American Racial Anglo-Saxonism.* Cambridge, Mass.: Harvard University Press, 1981.

Howe, Barbara J. "Women in Nineteenth-Century Preservation Movement." In Gail Lee Dubrow and Jennifer B. Goodman, eds., *Restoring Women's History through Historic Preservation*, 17–36. Baltimore: Johns Hopkins University Press, 2003.

Hurtado, Albert L. *Intimate Frontiers: Sex, Gender, and Culture in Old California.* Albuquerque: University of New Mexico Press, 1999.

Iverson, Peter. "American Indian History as a Continuing Story." *Historian* 66, no. 3 (2004): 524–531.

Jackson, Kenneth T. *Crabgrass Frontier: The Suburbanization of the United States.* New York: Oxford University Press, 1985.

Jackson Smith, Fay, John L. Kessell, and Francis F. Fox, *Father Kino in Arizona.* Phoenix: Arizona Historical Foundation, 1966.

Jacobs, Jane. *The Death and Life of Great American Cities.* New York: Random House, 1961.

Jacobson, Matthew Frye. *Whiteness of a Different Color: European Immigrants and the Alchemy of Race.* Cambridge, Mass.: Harvard University Press, 1998.

Jacoby, Karl. *Shadows at Dawn: A Borderlands Massacre and the Violence of History.* New York: Penguin Press, 2008.

Jameson, Fredric. *Postmodernism, or the Cultural Logic of Late Capitalism.* Durham, N.C.: Duke University Press, 1991.

Jones, E. Michael. *The Slaughter of Cities : Urban Renewal as Ethnic Cleansing.* South Bend, Ind.: St. Augustine's Press, 2004.

Joy, Rick. *Desert Works.* New York: Princeton Architectural Press, 2002.

Kammen, Michael. *Mystic Chords of Memory: The Transformation of Tradition in American Culture.* New York: Knopf, 1991.

Katz, Peter, ed. *The New Urbanism: Toward an Architecture of Community.* New York: McGraw-Hill, 1994.

Kelly, William. *Indians of the Southwest: A Survey of Indian tribes and Indian Administration in Arizona.* Tucson: University of Arizona Press, 1953.

Kimmelman, Alex Jay. "Luring the Tourists to Tucson: Civic Promotion during the 1920s." *Journal of Arizona History* 28, no. 2 (Summer 1987): 135–154.

Kraus, Neil. *Race, Neighborhoods, and Community Power: Buffalo Politics, 1934–1997.* Albany: State University of New York Press, 2000.

Kropp, Phoebe S. "'All Our Yesterdays': The Spanish Fantasy Past and the Politics of Public Memory in Southern California, 1884–1939." Ph.D. diss., University of California, San Diego, 1999.

——. *California Vieja: Culture and Memory in a Modern American Place.* Berkeley: University of California Press, 2006.

Kruse, Kevin M. *White Flight: Atlanta and the Making of Modern Conservatism.* Princeton, N.J.: Princeton University Press, 2005.

Lamar, Howard R. "The Reluctant Admission: The Struggle to Admit Arizona and New Mexico to the Union." In Robert Ferris, ed., *The American West: An Appraisal,* 163–177. Santa Fe: Museum of New Mexico Press, 1963.

Lassiter, Matthew D. *The Silent Majority: Suburban Politics in the Sunbelt South.* Princeton, N.J.: Princeton University Press, 2006.

Lewis, Robert. "Frontier and Civilization in the Thought of Frederick Law Olmstead." *American Quarterly* 29, no. 4 (Autumn 1977): 385–403.

Limerick, Patricia Nelson. *Desert Passages: Encounters with the American Deserts*. Niwot: University Press of Colorado, 1989.

Lin, Jan. "Ethnic Places, Postmodernism, and Urban Change in Houston." *Sociological Quarterly* 36, no. 4 (Autumn 1995): 629–647.

Lipsitz, George. *The Possessive Investment in Whiteness: How White People Profit from Identity Politics*. Philadelphia: Temple University Press, 1998.

Logan, John R., and Harvey L. Molotch. *Urban Fortunes: The Political Economy of Place*. Berkeley: University of California Press, 1987.

Logan, Michael F. *Desert Cities: The Environmental History of Phoenix and Tucson*. Pittsburgh: University of Pittsburgh Press, 2006.

———. *Fighting Sprawl and City Hall: Resistance to Urban Growth in the Southwest*. Tucson: University of Arizona Press, 1995.

Longstreth, Richard. "The Diffusion of the Community Shopping Center Concept in the Interwar Decades." *Journal of the Society of Architectural Historians* 56, no.3 (September 1997): 268–293.

Low, Setha M. "The Anthropology of Cities: Imagining and Theorizing the City." *Annual Review of Anthropology* 25 (1996): 383–409.

Low, Setha M., and Denise Lawrence-Zuñga, eds. *The Anthropology of Space and Place: Locating Culture*. Malden, Mass.: Blackwell, 2006.

Lowenthal, David. "Identity, Heritage, and History." In John Gillis, ed., *Commemorations: The Politics of National Identity*, 41–60. Princeton, N.J.: Princeton University Press, 1994.

———. *The Past Is a Foreign Country*. Cambridge: Cambridge University Press, 1985.

———. *Possessed by the Past: The Heritage Crusade and the Spoils of History*. New York: Free Press, 1996.

Lubick, George M. "Forging Ties with the Past: Historic Preservation in Arizona." *Journal of the West* 25 (April 1985): 96–107.

Luckingham, Bradford. *The Urban Southwest: A Profile History of Albuquerque, El Paso, Phoenix, Tucson*. El Paso: Texas Western Press, 1982.

Lung, Vincent L. "The City Tells Its Story: COMB Untangles Tucson." *American City*, November 1966, 144–145.

MacLaury, María Isabel. "La Placita: Vantages of Urban Change in Historic Tucson." Master's thesis, University of Arizona, 1989.

Mangelsdorf, Karen Underhill. "The Beveridge Visit to Arizona in 1902." *Journal of Arizona History* 28 (Autumn 1987): 243–260.

Márquez, Benjamin. "Choosing Issues, Choosing Sides: Constructing Identities in Chicana/o Social Movement Organizations." *Ethnic and Racial Studies* 24, no. 2 (March 2001): 218–235.

Martin, Douglas D. "1896." In *An Arizona Chronology: The Territorial Years, 1846–1912*. Tucson, University of Arizona Press, 1963.

Martin, Patricia Preciado. *Beloved Land: An Oral History of Mexican Americans in Southern Arizona*. Photographs by José Galvez. Tucson: University of Arizona Press, 2004

————. *Images and Conversations: Mexican Americans Recall a Southwestern Past*. Photographs by Louis Carlos Bernal. Tucson: University of Arizona Press, 1983.

————. *Songs My Mother Sang to Me: An Oral History of Mexican American Women*. Tucson: University of Arizona Press, 1992.

Massey, Doreen. *Space, Place, and Gender*. Minneapolis: University of Minnesota Press, 1994.

Matusow, Allen J. *The Unraveling of America: A History of Liberalism in the 1960s*. New York: Harper and Row, 1984.

May, Elaine Tyler *Homeward Bound: American Families in the Cold War Era*. New York: Basic Books, 1988.

McCarty, Kieran, ed. *Selections from a Frontier Documentary: Mexican Tucson, 1821–1856*. MASRC Working Paper, no. 22 Tucson: Mexican American Studies and Research Center, University of Arizona, 1994.

McCleneghan, Thomas J. "Population Trends in Arizona, 1910–1960." *Arizona Business and Economic Review* 10, no. 5 (May 1961).

McDowell, Linda. *Gender, Identity and Place: Understanding Feminist Geographies*. Minneapolis: University of Minnesota Press, 1999.

McGirr, Lisa. *Suburban Warriors: The Origins of the New American Right*. Princeton, N.J.: Princeton University Press, 2001.

McKanna, Clare V., Jr. *White Justice in Arizona: Apache Murder Trials in the Nineteenth Century*. Lubbock: Texas Tech University Press, 2005.

McWilliams, Carey. "The Heritage of the Southwest." In Renato Rosaldo, Robert A. Calvert, and Gustav L. Seligmann, eds., *Chicano: The Evolution of a People*, 3–14. Minneapolis: Winston Press, 1973.

————. *North from Mexico: The Spanish-Speaking People of the United States*. Philadelphia: Lippincott, 1949.

Meeks, Eric V. *Border Citizens: The Making of Indians, Mexicans, and Anglos in Arizona*. Austin : University of Texas Press, 2007.

Mettler, Suzanne. *Dividing Citizens: Gender and Federalism in New Deal Public Policy*. Ithaca, N.Y.: Cornell University Press, 1998.

Mignolo, Walter. *Local Histories/Global Designs*. Princeton, N.J.: Princeton University Press, 2000.

Miller, Joseph. *Arizona: The Last Frontier*. New York: Hastings House, 1956.

Mitchell, Janet. "Vanished Tucson." *City Magazine*, May 1989, 44–48.

Molina, Natalia. *Fit to Be Citizens? Public Health and Race in Los Angeles, 1879–1939*. Berkeley and Los Angeles: University of California Press, 2006.

Mollenkopf, John H. *The Contested City*. Princeton, N.J.: Princeton University Press, 1983.

Monroy, Douglas. *Rebirth: Mexican Los Angeles from the Great Migration to the Great Depression*. Berkeley: University of California Press, 1999.

Montejano, David. *Anglos and Mexicans in the Making of Texas, 1836–1986*. Austin: University of Texas Press, 1997.

Montgomery, Charles. *The Spanish Redemption: Heritage, Power, and Loss on New Mexico's Upper Rio Grande*. Berkeley: University of California Press, 2002.

Morley, Judy Mattivi. *Historical Preservation and the Imagined West: Albuquerque, Denver, and Seattle*. Lawrence: University Press of Kansas, 2006.

Morrissey, Katherine, and Kirsten Jensen, eds. *Picturing Arizona: The Photographic Record of the 1930s*. Tucson: University of Arizona Press, 2005.

Mosher, Don, and Jerry Cohen. *The Pied Piper of Tucson*. New York: New American Library, 1967.

Neary, John. "One Man's Fight to Save the Barrio: A Tucson Auto Dealer Brings New Life to the Barrio after High-Rise Developers and Highway Planners Nearly Tore It All Down." *Americana*, January–February 1979, 54–57.

Nequette, Anne M., and R. Brooks Jeffery. *A Guide to Tucson Architecture*. Tucson: University of Arizona Press, 2002.

Neufeld, Ronni. "Santa Cruz River Project May Be Last Chance to Preserve Tucson's Birthplace." *Changing Tucson*, October 1974. Arizona Historical Society/Tucson, MS 1134, Torres, Alva, box 2, file 15, Historic Preservation: Tucson, 1969–1980.

Nevins, Allan. *Frémont: Pathmarker of the West*. New York: Longmans, Green, 1955.

Newlon, Bonnie. *Pueblo Center Redevelopment Project, 1967–1969*. Tucson: City of Tucson, Department of Community Development, Urban Renewal Division, 1969.

Niblo, Steven R. *War, Democracy, and Development: United States–Mexican Relations, 1918–1945*. Wilmington, Del.: Scholarly Resources, 1995.

Nirenstein's National Realty Map Company. *Business Section, City of Tucson, Arizona*. Springfield, Mass., 1950?

Norris, Frank Blaine. "The Southern Arizona Guest Ranch as a Symbol of the West." Master's thesis, University of Arizona, 1976.

Officer, James E. *Hispanic Arizona, 1536–1856*. Tucson: University of Arizona Press, 1987.

———. "Power in the Old Pueblo: A Study of Decision Making in a Southwestern Community, 1961." Typescript photocopy, Special Collections, University of Arizona Main Library.

———. "Sodalities and Systemic Linkage: The Joining Habits of Urban Mexican Americans." Ph.D. diss., University of Arizona, 1964.

Officer, James E. "Yanqui Forty-Niners in Hispanic Arizona: Interethnic Relations on the Sonoran Frontier." *Journal of Arizona History* 28, no. 2 (Summer 1987): 101–134.

Omi, Michael, and Howard Winant. *Racial Formation in the United States: From the 1960s to the 1980s.* New York: Routledge and Kegan Paul, 1986.

O'Neil Lyons, Bettina. *Zeckendorfs and Steinfelds: Merchant Princes of the American Southwest.* Tucson: Arizona Historical Society, 2009.

Otero, Lydia R. "Refusing to Be Undocumented: Chicanas/os in Tucson during the Depression Years." In Katherine Morrissey and Kirsten Jensen, eds., *Picturing Arizona: The Photographic Record of the 1930s,* 42–59 Tucson: University of Arizona Press, 2005.

Padilla, Genaro M. *My History, Not Yours: The Formation of Mexican American Autobiography.* Madison: University of Wisconsin Press, 1993.

Pardo, Mary S. *Chicana/o Women Activists: Identity and Resistance in Two Los Angeles Communities.* Philadelphia: Temple University Press, 1998.

Pateman, Carole. "The Patriarchal State." In Amy Gutmann, ed., *Democracy and the Welfare State,* 231–260. Princeton, N.J.: Princeton University Press, 1988.

Paulison, C. M. K. *Arizona, The Wonderful Country: Tucson Its Metropolis; A Comprehensive Review of the Past Progress, Present Condition and Future Prospects of the Territory of Arizona, Showing the Advantages Possessed by Tucson as the Commercial Metropolis.* Tucson, Arizona Territory: *Arizona Star,* 1881.

Pérez, Emma. *The Decolonial Imaginary: Writing Chicanas into History* Bloomington: Indiana University Press, 1999.

Pope, Sarah Dillard. "Hispanic History in the National Register of Historic Places," at the National Registry Web site, http://crm.cr.nps.gov/archive/20-11/20-11-5.pdf/.

Pulido, Laura. *Black, Brown, Yellow, and Left: Radical Activism in Los Angeles.* Berkeley: University of California Press, 2006.

Raaf, Daniel W. "Downtown Tucson and the Woman Shopper." *Arizona Business and Economic Review* 7, no. 4 (April 1958): 1–3.

Radding, Cynthia. *Wandering Peoples: Colonialism, Ethnic Spaces, and Ecological Frontiers in Northwestern Mexico, 1700–1850.* Durham, N.C.: Duke University Press, 1997.

Regan, Margaret. "There Goes the Neighborhood: The Downfall of Downtown." *Tucson Weekly,* March 6–12, 1997, at http://www.tucsonweekly.com/tw/03-06-97/cover.htm/.

Reséndez, Andrés. *Changing National Identities at the Frontier: Texas and New Mexico, 1800–1850* (Cambridge: Cambridge University Press, 2005).

Richards, Donald Wayne. "Economic Development Efforts of the City Government: Tucson, Arizona—1963 to 1973." Master's thesis, University of Arizona, 1973.

Richardson, Harold C. "John C. Frémont: Territorial Governor." *Journal of Arizona History* 3 (Summer 1962): 41–46

Riling, John J., Jr., and Bertha O. Whitterson. Office of Urban Renewal, City of Tucson, "Workable Program for Urban Renewal, 1958–1959." *Arizona Architect*, May 1959, 8.

Robinson, Cecil. *With the Ears of Strangers: The Mexican in American Literature.* Tucson: University of Arizona Press, 1963.

Roediger, David. *Towards an Abolition of Whiteness.* New York: Verso Press, 1994.

———. *The Wages of Whiteness: Race and the Making of the American Working Class.* London: Verso Press, 1991.

Romo, Ricardo. *East Los Angeles: History of a Barrio.* Austin: University of Texas Press, 1983.

———. "The Urbanization of Southwestern Chicanos in the Early Twentieth Century." In Manuel G. Gonzales and Cynthia M. Gonzales, eds., *En Aquel Entonces: Readings in Mexican-American History,* 125–133. Bloomington: Indiana University Press, 2000.

Rosaldo, Renato. *Culture and Truth: The Remaking of Social Analysis.* Boston: Beacon Press, 1989.

Rosaldo, Renato, Robert A. Calvert, and Gustav L. Seligmann, eds. *Chicano: The Evolution of a People.* Minneapolis: Winston Press, 1973.

Rosales, Francisco A. *Chicano! The History of the Chicana/o Civil Rights Movement.* Houston: *Arte Público* Press, 1996.

Rothman, Hal K. *Devil's Bargains: Tourism in the Twentieth-Century American West.* Lawrence: University Press of Kansas, 1998.

Ruíz, Vicki L. *From Out of the Shadows: Mexican Women in Twentieth-Century America.* New York: Oxford University Press, 1998.

Salpointe, John Baptist. *Soldiers of the Cross: Notes on the Ecclesiastical History of New Mexico, Arizona, and Colorado.* Banning, Calif.: Saint Boniface's Industrial School, 1898.

Sánchez, George J. *Becoming Mexican American: Ethnicity, Culture, and Identity in Chicano Los Angeles, 1900–1945.* New York: Oxford University Press, 1993.

Sandoval, Chela. *Methodology of the Oppressed.* Minneapolis: University of Minnesota Press, 2000.

Saragoza, Alex. "The Selling of Mexico: Tourism and the State, 1929–1952." In Gilbert M. Joseph, Anne Rubenstein, and Eric Zolov, eds., *Fragments of a Golden Age: The Politics of Culture in Mexico since 1940,* 91–115. Durham, N.C.: Duke University, 2001.

Saunders, James Robert, and Renae Nadine Shackelford. *Urban Renewal and the End of Black Culture in Charlottesville, Virginia: An Oral History of Vinegar Hill.* Jefferson, N.C.: McFarland, 1998.

Saxton, Alexander. *The Rise and Fall of the White Republic: Class Politics and Mass Culture in Nineteenth-Century America.* London: Verso Press, 1990.

Schorr, S. L., and the Citizens' Advisory Redevelopment Committee. *Urban Renewal: A Teamwork of Private Enterprise and Government for Slum Clearance and Redevelopment of the Old Pueblo District, Tucson, Arizona.* Tucson: City of Tucson, 1961.

Scott, James C. *Domination and the Arts of Resistance: Hidden Transcripts.* New Haven, Conn.: Yale University Press, 1990.

Scribner, Christopher MacGregor. *Renewing Birmingham: Federal Funding and the Promise of Change, 1929–1979.* Athens: University of Georgia Press, 2002.

Segoe, Ladislas, and Associates. *The Rehabilitation of Blighted Areas: Conservation of Sound Neighborhoods.* Cincinnati, 1942.

Segoe, Ladislas, and C. W. Matthews. *Tentative Report on Survey of Low-Rent Housing Needs: Tucson, Arizona.* Tucson: Tucson Housing Authority, 1941.

Seibold, Doris K. "Cattle Raising and Spanish Speech in Southern Arizona." *Arizona Quarterly* 2, no. 2 (1946): 24–34.

Sheridan, Thomas E. *Arizona: A History.* Tucson: University of Arizona Press, 1995.

———. *Los Tucsonenses: The Mexican Community in Tucson, 1854–1941.* Tucson: University of Arizona Press, 1986.

Sietz, Don C. *The "Also Rans": Great Men Who Missed Making the Presidential Goal.* Freeport, N.Y.: Books for Libraries Press, 1968.

Smith, Michael Peter. "Postmodernity, Urban Ethnography, and the New Social Space of Ethnic Identity." *Theory and Society* 21, no. 4 (August 1992): 493–531.

Smythe, William E. *The Conquest of Arid America.* New York: Harper, 1900.

Soja, Edward W. *Postmodern Geographies: The Reassertion of Space in Critical Social Theory.* London: Verso Press, 1989.

———. *Thirdspace: Journeys to Los Angeles and Other Real-and-Imagined Places.* Cambridge, Mass.: Blackwell, 1996.

Sonnichsen, C. L. *Pioneer Heritage: The First Century of the Arizona Historical Society.* Tucson: Arizona Historical Society, 1984.

———. *Tucson: The Life and Times of an American City.* Norman: University of Oklahoma Press, 1987.

Spicer, Edward Holland. *Cycles of Conquest: The Impact of Spain, Mexico, and the United States on the Indians of the Southwest, 1533–1960.* Drawings by Hazel Fontana. Tucson: University of Arizona Press, 1962.

Stack, Carol B. *All Our Kin: Strategies for Survival in a Black Community.* New York: Harper and Row, 1974.

Starr, Kevin. *Golden Dreams: California in an Age of Abundance, 1950-1963.* New York: Oxford Press, 2009.

Sugrue, Thomas J. *The Origins of the Urban Crisis: Race and Inequality in Postwar Detroit.* Princeton, N.J.: Princeton University Press, 1996.

Thomas, June Manning, and Marsha Ritzdorf, eds. *Urban Planning and the African American Community: In the Shadows.* Thousand Oaks, Calif.: Sage, 1997.

Trouillot, Michel-Rolph. *Silencing the Past: Power and the Production of History.* Boston: Beacon Press, 1995.

Tucson and Tombstone General and Business Directory for 1883 and 1884. Tucson: Cobler and Company, 1983.

Tucson Chamber of Commerce. "Did You Know?" *Tucson Magazine.* May, 1938.

———. *Tucson: A City, an Opportunity, a Way of Life.* Tucson: Chamber of Commerce, 1958.

———. *Tucson: Arizona's Playground, Home of Health and Sunshine.* Tucson: 1906. Special Collections, University of Arizona Library.

———. *Welcome Visitor: Official Guide to Tucson.* Tucson: Tucson Chamber of Commerce, 1935–1936.

Tucson Department of Community Development. *Tucson's New Opportunity: Model Cities Program.* Tucson, 1970.

Tucson Sunshine-Climate Club and G. Curiel. *Tucson, Arizona: Man-Building in the Sunshine Climate.* Tucson, 1925? University of Arizona Library, Special Collections.

———. *Tucson, the World's Sunshine Center.* Tucson: Consolidated National Bank, 1925.

U.S. Department of Housing and Urban Development. *Annual Report.* Washington D.C., USGPO, 1965.

University of Arizona. *Twenty-First Arizona Town Hall on Arizona's Heritage— Today and Tomorrow: Research Report, Recommendations, and List of Participants, October 15–18, 1972.* Phoenix: Arizona Academy, 1972.

Valley National Bank, Research Department. "Spotlight on Tucson—New Community Center Opens." *Arizona Progress,* November 1971.

Van Slyck, Abigail A. "What the Bishop Learned: The Importance of Claiming Space at Tucson's Church Plaza." *Journal of Arizona History* 39 (Summer 1998): 127–128.

Vélez-Ibáñez, Carlos. *Border Visions: Mexican Cultures of the Southwest United States.* Tucson: University of Arizona Press, 1966.

Wagoner, J. J. *History of the Cattle Industry in Southern Arizona, 1540–1940.* University of Arizona Social Science Bulletin 23, no. 2. Tucson, University of Arizona, 1952.

Waugh, Robert E. "Percentage of Mexican-American Pedestrians in the Downtown Tucson Shopping Area." *Arizona Business and Economic Review* 5, no. 5 (May 1956): 1–2.

———. "What Does Your Vacationer *Really Want*—and How You Can Find Out." *Arizona Business and Economic Review* 7, no. 8 (August 1958): 2–5.

Weber, David J. *The Mexican Frontier, 1821–1846: The American Southwest under Mexico.* Albuquerque: University of New Mexico Press, 1982.

White, Richard. *"It's Your Misfortune and None of My Own": A History of the American West*. Norman: University of Oklahoma Press, 1991.

White, Richard, and John M. Findley, eds. *Power and Place in the North American West*. Seattle: Center for the Study of the Pacific Northwest in association with the University of Washington Press, 1999.

Wiebe, Robert H. *The Search for Order, 1877–1920*. New York: Hill and Wang, 1967.

Williams, Jack. "Tucson Was Dude Ranch Capital for Ranching Experience." *Nogales International*, July 22, 1987.

Williams, Raymond. *Keywords: A Vocabulary of Culture and Society*. London: Fontana, 1976.

Wilson, Chris. *The Myth of Santa Fe: Creating a Modern Regional Tradition*. Albuquerque: University of New Mexico Press, 1997.

Wolff, Janet. "The Real City, the Discursive City, the Disappearing City: Postmodernism and Urban Sociology." *Theory and Society* 21, no. 4 (August 1992): 553–560.

Works Progress Administration. *The WPA Guide to 1930s Arizona*. 1940. Reprint, Tucson: University of Arizona Press, 1989.

Wright, Harold Bell. *The Mine with the Iron Door: A Romance*. New York: D. Appleton, 1923.

Zukin, Sharon. *The Cultures of Cities*. Cambridge, Mass.: Blackwell, 1995.

Index

About the Author

Lydia R. Otero has a PhD in history and is an associate professor in the Department of Mexican American and Raza Studies at the University of Arizona. Her work on claiming place, historic preservation, and Mexican American resistance in the 1930s has appeared as contributions to various anthologies. Otero has family roots in Southern Arizona on both sides and for several generations.